PENGUIN BOOKS

LLAMAS & EMPANADAS

Eleanor Meecham mastered the art of cycling at the age of six, inspired by a fit of envy when her younger cousin pedalled past unaided by trainer wheels. Determined to keep up, she climbed into the saddle and has never looked back. She has since cycle-toured in ten different countries and owned nearly as many bicycles. To fund her addiction she has been living on and off in London, riding a rickshaw in the West End. She is currently of no fixed abode.

Eleanor Meecham

LLAMAS & EMPANADAS

5000 kilometres by bicycle through South America

PENGUIN BOOKS

PENGUIN BOOKS

Published by the Penguin Group

Penguin Group (NZ), 67 Apollo Drive, Rosedale,
North Shore 0632, New Zealand (a division of Pearson New Zealand Ltd)

Penguin Group (USA) Inc., 375 Hudson Street,
New York, New York 10014, USA

Penguin Group (Canada), 90 Eglinton Avenue East, Suite 700, Toronto,
Ontario, M4P 2Y3, Canada (a division of Pearson Penguin Canada Inc.)

Penguin Books Ltd, 80 Strand, London, WC2R 0RL, England

Penguin Ireland, 25 St Stephen's Green,
Dublin 2, Ireland (a division of Penguin Books Ltd)

Penguin Group (Australia), 250 Camberwell Road, Camberwell,
Victoria 3124, Australia (a division of Pearson Australia Group Pty Ltd)

Penguin Books India Pvt Ltd, 11, Community Centre,
Panchsheel Park, New Delhi – 110 017, India

Penguin Books (South Africa) (Pty) Ltd, 24 Sturdee Avenue,
Rosebank, Johannesburg 2196, South Africa

Penguin Books Ltd, Registered Offices: 80 Strand, London, WC2R 0RL, England

First published by Penguin Group (NZ), 2007

1 3 5 7 9 10 8 6 4 2

Copyright © Eleanor Meecham, 2007

The right of Eleanor Meecham to be identified as the author of this work in
terms of section 96 of the Copyright Act 1994 is hereby asserted.

Editorial services by Michael Gifkins & Associates
Designed by Vivianne Douglas
Typeset by Egan Reid Ltd
Printed in Australia by McPherson's Printing Group

ISBN 978 0 14 300640 4

A catalogue record for this book is available
from the National Library of New Zealand.

www.penguin.co.nz

for Daniel

Contents

The whole hotchpotch journey by bicycle, bus and plane. Approximately 5500 kilometres of pedalling took me through some of the highest, driest, windiest and most wondrous parts of South America.

PROLOGUE

Scared

Trundling along in my habitual daydream, having neither seen nor heard another vehicle for several hours, the abrupt appearance of a car full of men took me somewhat by surprise. It shot past from behind, braked hard and slewed to a stop in the roadside gravel. Two doors were flung open, two burly blokes leapt out and one of them fumbled with the fly of his jeans.

This was not how I wanted it to end. I thought of all the warnings I had ignored and the pleas for caution I had so blithely dismissed, and cursed my stupidity.

But the man with his trousers open had his back to me and from the deeply contented sighs he was making, and the steam that was rising, it was obvious that relieving his overfull bladder was his only immediate intention. His friend was still leering my way, however. I moved to the other side of the road and pedalled faster.

'Are you cycling around the whole world?' he called. I glared at him.

'Twice, actually.' His companions smirked from the backseat and I shot them a withering look as I passed.

The gravel crunched behind me and the engine revved. They drew alongside. One of them leant from the rear window with his arm outstretched. He was holding something long and black, and he was pointing it at me.

'Bloody hell!'

I swerved, and my heart danced a tarantella against my ribs, but my imagination was playing tricks. It was not a gun he was holding. It was a bar of chocolate.

He grinned, and the others grinned too.

'We're from Brazil,' he said. 'Aren't you scared cycling around alone?'

My brain buzzed with an angry reply but the words stuck in my throat. I shook my head and took the chocolate, and they roared off into the distance.

The lake district, where I crossed the Andes twice in a week to experience the distinctly different climates and cultures of Argentina and Chile.

1

Spare Tyre

If I had taken all the advice seriously, I would never have gone.

'No, no, no,' said my Argentine friends. 'It isn't possible.'

'But why not?' I countered stubbornly, unwilling to believe it.

'Because it's just too dangerous. The roads are terrible, the distances too far, and there are thieves and kidnappers and bad people of all kinds. Foreigners go missing all the time, you know. Please don't make this trip. Really, it's suicide.'

These were somewhat alarming words.

I began to wonder if expecting to travel around Argentina by bicycle was overly optimistic. The more the words of caution revolved in my head, the more I worried that I was being foolishly naïve.

Then again, I wasn't entirely convinced that *porteños* – people from the frenetic world of Buenos Aires – were reliable authorities on their own country. Undeniably, city living can be a dangerous business, but too many hours watching highly sensationalist television news programmes could persuade anyone that the entire country is jam-packed with gun-toting gangsters and ruthless murderers. Much as I wanted to return home alive, preferably still in possession of my bicycle and all my limbs, I was determined not to let the pessimistic predictions of paranoiac city dwellers stop me from fulfilling my objective. I would make the trip and find out about Argentina for myself.

Judging by the way I felt now, struggling to make headway on a flat and perfectly surfaced asphalt road, it seemed the greatest danger was of death by exhaustion. The day was windless, the air was warm, and under the glorious summer sky I should have been speeding along like a Tour de France competitor. Instead, my burdened bicycle felt alien and cumbersome, my heart was thumping wildly and my limbs had the quivery feeling of imminent collapse. I began to wonder how I was going to survive until the next campsite, let alone across the country.

In the midday heat the sun-bleached plains of central Argentina swam before me until my head throbbed. I half-closed my eyes against the intensity of the light and decided not to stop for lunch; imagining myself weak and helpless in the shade of a stunted bush, at the mercy of the wheeling birds of prey, I pushed on.

I was seriously beginning to regret the previous month of beer drinking, pizza eating and general idleness. I had been in Buenos Aires taking a language course, travelling on pollution-spewing buses, breathing the toxic air and trying to avoid death-by-homicidal-taxi-driver. It is not a city that inspires a desire to cycle, and for this reason my bike, Vagabunda, had spent the month languishing in a garden shed. My thigh muscles had shrivelled. Now, the physical effects of neglect were impossible to ignore, and the lack of sleep suffered on the overnight bus ride out of the capital was beginning to take its toll. It seemed as though the only thing between me and oblivion was my dignity; whatever would they say back home if I expired for want of a little training?

It was with great relief that I arrived at my destination on the shores of Lake Nahuel Huapi. I tumbled off my bike and fell instantly asleep in the heat of the long grass, oblivious to the typically rambunctious noises of an Argentine campground. It was only when I woke half an hour later, fuddle-headed but hungry, that my surroundings began to seem worth the effort. The perfect blue of the lake hinted at the depth of its waters and, above, the clarity of the cloudless sky was complete. Just audible above the shouts and laughter of my neighbours was the swish of waves on the pebbled shore. Insects chirred in the undergrowth, there was a scent of distilled summer, and I felt far from the possibility of danger.

The enormously round lady who ran the campsite further put my mind at rest. With arms worthy of a heavyweight champion, boxing-glove hands and breasts large enough to smother the most formidable opponent, she still managed to project an air of complete serenity. Her teeth stuck out at all angles, like evidence of years in the ring, but her smile was beatific. Under her motherly and protective gaze, I couldn't have felt less at risk.

I made a cup of tea, ate half a packet of biscuits – setting a dangerously gluttonous precedent for the months to follow – and perused my map. Ahead was the Route of the Seven Lakes, stretching some hundred kilometres through the heart of Argentina's lake district, famed for its beauty and popular with cyclists both pedal-powered and motorised. In fact, I was about to follow in the tyre tracks of Argentina's most enduring icon, Ernesto 'Che' Guevara. He and his friend Alberto Granado had also travelled this route on two wheels, those of *La Poderosa*, the motorbike on which they began their famous journey through Latin America. It was the trip that introduced the twenty-three-year-old Guevara to the injustices suffered by the poor and oppressed of his continent, the trip that sparked in him the passion to dedicate his life to the liberation of the proletariat. Their haphazard expedition had taken place more than fifty years before, but I imagined the route hadn't changed that much. The road remained unsealed, and my plan of attack was to take it slowly, stopping every cyclist I met and gathering information to plan the rest of my journey. This was necessary because, under-researched and unprepared, I knew fairly little about the country I was hoping to cycle through. Actually, it was something of a surprise to find myself there at all.

True, I had been dreaming of a trip to South America for a long time, ever since making Latino friends in London. Their gregarious natures appealed to me, their sense of fun and the sound of their Spanish, and I imagined myself visiting them in their homelands, cycling to meet them under hot desert skies. But I didn't really expect to find myself buying a ticket there quite so soon. Instead, my plans had been to go to Spain and learn the language, in order to sensibly prepare myself for the distant possibility of one day, maybe, going to South America.

And then I met Galo. I was working as a rickshaw rider at the time, in London's West End, and it was while I was waiting for passengers at Covent Garden Station that he approached me. He was from Buenos Aires, he told me; he liked my bike, and me. I took him for a spin around the block, tried out my few words of Spanish on him, and by the time we got back to where I had picked him up my heart was thumping with more than the exercise. He asked me to meet him for a date the following day.

We spent just one perfect afternoon together, picnicking in Hyde Park and feeding the squirrels, and all too soon we were saying goodbye at the bus station. He was going to the airport, to catch his flight to Argentina, and between farewell kisses he whispered, 'Come and visit me.'

Utterly enchanted, I promised that I would.

Impulsive? Yes. Reckless? Maybe. But there was something about the romance of the situation that compelled me onwards, and with a Shakespearean sense of the dramatic I convinced myself that it was perfectly justifiable to cross seas and continents in the name of love. My friends encouraged me, and when an Argentine workmate heard that I would be visiting his country he insisted that I stay with him and his family. He would even pick me up from the airport, he said. Everything was falling smoothly into place, as though fated to be, and in the excitement I remained blithely unconcerned about my lack of Spanish. I would learn it from my Latin lover.

I spent four heady weeks in Buenos Aires, meeting up with Galo after my morning language lessons and trying out my grammar on him as we sipped sweet coffee in dark cafés. We strolled arm in arm by the river, drank beer to the sound of the tango and ate gnocchi at his mum's house on Sundays. It was the perfect introduction to a new culture, and it made me hungry for more. To Galo's dismay, however, the prospect of exploring the rest of the country proved to be as strong a lure for me as the romance of our intercultural exchange; our love was sweet, but adventure was sweeter, and there was a lot more to see than the city. With tears this time, and hastily scrawled love notes, we hugged a tragic farewell at the coach stop. Then I left him behind for the alpine air of San Carlos de Bariloche, my bicycle travelling beneath me in the grumbling belly of the bus.

And now here I was, zombie-like at the end of the first cycling day, hoping that the next four and a half months wouldn't kill me. I was wearily eating my dinner when another cyclist showed up, a long-haired biologist from the United States who was travelling with a guitar in his backpack. He came over to introduce himself. He was no hippy, but his name sounded like it had been chosen by his parents while they were on acid.

'Hey dude. I'm Bojo,' he said.

'Bobo?'

'Bojo.'

'Bow show?'

'Yes, Bojo.'

'Oh, right. Bow-joe.' I tried to commit it to memory.

We shared my crackers and tomatoes, and I quizzed him about the road ahead. He had been backpacking and cycling around the north of the country for some weeks, he told me, and had never had any problems. Female friends of his, also backpacking, had been perfectly safe too.

'So you reckon I'll be all right then?' I asked hopefully. He grinned.

'Man, you're gonna have an *awesome* time.'

I sighed with relief and offered him my last tomato in gratitude. He considered it briefly and shook his head.

'Dude,' he said, 'I've been *cycling*.' He got to his feet. 'I need protein.' He waded through the long grass back to his tent, and within minutes the smell of frying steak wafted towards me on the evening air. I finished my biscuits, crawled into my sleeping bag and fell instantly into an impenetrable coma.

I was impressed to discover that, on their summer holidays, the people of Argentina like to pack their tents, leave the city and head into the countryside to make the most of the abundant fresh air and sunshine that their nation has to offer. It didn't take me long, however, to realise that 'camping' is a somewhat flexible concept. While I had always thought it was about getting away from neighbours, traffic, television and general urban chaos in search of beauty, purity, and peace and quiet, the Argentine definition seemed to be just about the exact opposite. Apparently, the thing to do is erect your double-garage-sized tent next to the family car, hang some pictures that you took from the walls of your lounge, plug in enough electrical appliances to drain the national power grid of neighbouring Paraguay and sit back and enjoy the ambience with the 3000 other families who had the same idea.

Getting back to nature it is not, but I couldn't help but admire the enthusiasm with which Argentines can apply themselves to having fun. They play raucous games of football, barbecue enough meat for four times the number of people actually eating, drink vast quantities of Quilmes beer and play their car stereos at full volume until dawn. Children scream, parents shout, dogs go mad and everyone has a wonderful time.

Although I was something of a misfit in these places – with a shamefully tiny tent and a tendency to fall asleep at nine o'clock in the evening – I felt obliged to use them anyway. In heavily visited tourist areas, or in national parks, it doesn't do to be seen flouting the rules by putting up your tent under the 'camping prohibido' signs. I was pleased to find, then, that despite the general family mayhem the campsites were pretty nice. They were affordable and well organised and I was always allowed to choose my own tent spot. They had plenty of grass and trees, and ground that was tent-peg friendly. Best of all, there was continuous hot water in the showers. I was impressed; campsites like this are not found the world over. Anyone who has ever had to pay a tear-inducing amount of money for a horrible patch of gravel in the shade of a smelly toilet block and then discovered that the shower only works on insertion of a pocketful of small coins will know exactly what I'm talking about.

On the second day of cycling, having managed only a pitiful thirty kilometres, I arrived at Villa la Angostura and checked into the woodsy campground. In my depleted state, the normally simple task of erecting the tent took on Herculean proportions and I struggled with swathes of ribbed green nylon as though with a feisty reptile. I had just managed to take the upper hand, and was lashing my opponent to the ground, when one of my tent-dwelling neighbours sauntered over. He looked delighted to have some company. I struggled to compose my face into a welcoming expression.

'*¿Andás solita?*' he asked, curiously – you're travelling alone?

'Um. Well. *Si*,' I admitted reluctantly. It was no good lying; the size of my tent clearly indicated my solitary status.

He grinned, and shook his head in astonishment.

'*¡Qué increíble!* I'm alone too! I'm Luis, from Córdoba. Would you like to come and have a beer with me?'

I thought about it for all of two seconds. Sitting in a stuffy campsite cafeteria, being chatted up by a balding, middle-aged man with a beer gut was about the least appealing thing I could think of. I didn't want to hurt his feelings though. Fobbing him off with claims of extreme tiredness, I made a vague promise of 'tomorrow . . .' The hopeful expression on his face as he walked away made my heart sink. I knew with certainty that there would be no avoiding that date.

The small distance I had cycled really didn't justify the extent of my hunger. I was starving. With the tent up, panniers stowed inside and Vagabunda locked to a tree, I walked into town for dinner. The main street thronged with tourists of every description. Wandering past the chocolate shops and pizzerias, I caught snippets of conversations in Spanish, English, French and German. From the open door of a camera shop came the sound of a loud and grating American accent.

'But I need ya to tell me the prices in *English*,' insisted a huge-arsed lady in an irritated tone. And I need rude gringos like I need a kidney removal, I heard the salesgirl thinking to herself, in Spanish.

In a busy restaurant I sat by the window and read the menu. Despite the fact that it was four pages long, there were only one or two things on it that I could order. Argentina's cuisine is comprised of meat, meat and more meat, with the plate-sized beefsteak playing the starring role, and I could see that as a vegetarian my options were going to be somewhat limited. *Matambre*, *lomito*, *chorizo*, *costillas*; the meat dishes were endless, but even my keen cyclist's hunger couldn't persuade me to change my habits. I looked around for inspiration. At a nearby table, a couple were tucking in to a plate of *empanadas* – small semicircular pies, stuffed with various fillings and deep-fried. My mouth watered. *Empanadas* were my new favourite food. I ordered four, and a beer.

It wasn't until I was chewing and slurping and licking my greasy fingers that the pain of the day came back to me. The spare tyre that I had grown in Buenos Aires had definitely not made life any easier. Maybe, I thought, if I spent less time eating fatty food and more time cycling, there would not be so much of me to haul up the hills. I could go faster, and further, for less effort. Yes. These unhealthy dinners had to stop.

The waiter appeared at my elbow.

'Anything else?' he asked.

'Umm . . . yes, please. Three more *empanadas*. And the dessert menu.'

Sod it. I had months to cycle it all off.

I woke, the next morning, to the sound of birdcall, and emerged from the tent to find the sun already up. Planning to stretch out my legs with a day of walking, I cycled over the hill to the entrance of Los Arrayanes National Park, which perches on a peninsula that pokes out into Lake Nahuel Huapi like a bulbous thumb. I tethered my bike to a fence using three hefty locks and went into the park office.

'*Buenos días,*' said the lady behind the desk.

'*Buenos días.*' I smiled, and hesitated, searching for words. My mind was a blank. I made a walking motion with two fingers and pointed in the general direction of the park entrance. 'Um . . . *quiero caminar,*' I said – I want to walk. She nodded politely and handed me a map. Then she cleared her throat, looked me in the eyes, and launched into a high-tempo monologue in Spanish. Oh dear. I strained to understand, blinking and nodding and making affirmative murmuring noises as though I had some idea of what she was talking about. In fact, the only words I caught clearly were the last two.

'*Doce pesos,*' she said, pointing to a price list on the wall. I mentally breathed a sigh of relief, handed over the twelve pesos in exchange for the entrance ticket and stepped outside before she could ask me any questions. Really, my language skills needed some serious work. I may have become competent at ordering pizza and beer, but that, it was now apparent, was going to be of somewhat limited use.

It was early. The track was empty of other walkers and the trees were alive with the scuffling and squawking of birds. Shafts of sunlight pierced the forest canopy, leaf litter lay thick underfoot, and I stepped among twisted tree roots as though through a storybook fairytale. It made me feel nostalgic. It made me feel melancholy. To my surprise, I burst into tears.

The sudden change of mood was unexpected, but the emotions were very real: a nasty mixture of self-doubt and homesickness, with an uncharacteristic twist of loneliness. I sat down on a tree stump and let the wave of negativity wash over me. What was I doing here, half a world away from everyone who cared about me? I had no career and no proper boyfriend. No fixed abode and no plans for the future. My incurably fickle nature kept me constantly seeking change, with my tolerance for staying in any location exhausted after a bare six months, and for this reason I had so far been unable to stick at any job or make a proper go of any relationship. My twenties had been a whirlwind of experiences, each as valuable as the last, but there were times when I wondered if I would ever be capable of building a life in one place, with one partner. Travelling alone was exciting, and very much what I enjoyed doing, but it was also indisputable evidence of my restlessness. My tears flowed, unabated; it was impossible to deny that, at the age of twenty-eight, I was still drifting without direction.

What are you snivelling about, Nelly? Why don't you stop feeling sorry for yourself and just get on with it?

I sniffed, and wiped my face with a sleeve. Those were my brother's words. I took a deep breath. It was the sort of thing he had said to me a lot. Tears had been my instant response to fear when I was a child, and a willingness to follow my big brother into all of his adventures had put me into endless nerve-wracking situations. It must have been a real drag having a small and weepy sister to deal with every time things got interesting, but Daniel had been infinitely patient with me. Little by little he had taught me to override my emotions and to trust my own capabilities. Giving up had never been an option.

I blew my nose. What a sissy I was. Dan had lived his whole life pushing his own physical and mental limits, and I had never once seen him be anything but confident about it. With an apparently nonchalant attitude to danger, he had dedicated himself to rock climbing and mountaineering as though risk and challenge were what made living worthwhile. While bravery didn't come so naturally to me, I had always wanted to prove to my brother that I could live like he did – that I could step fearlessly into the unknown, letting nothing and no one stop me. It was only after I discovered cycle-touring, and the intense pleasures of solitude and self-sufficiency, that I realised how much we had in common. Freedom of movement was what I craved, a lack of boundaries, and experiences that would challenge me and make me stronger. Like Dan, pursuing my personal goals had become far more important than having a career, or money in the bank.

So what was all this doubt and self-pity about? Was it really so indulgent to go on holiday for half a year? Did it matter that I didn't know what I would do next? It had taken a long time to find the courage to embark on a journey of this scale, and here I was spoiling it with melodrama.

I wiped away the last of the tears. It was time to get on with it.

It was dusk by the time I returned to my tent. My legs ached. I was sweaty and dusty, physically and emotionally drained. But Luis was waiting for me, recently showered and daubed with aftershave, the little hair that remained plastered to his scalp.

To make the occasion as informal as possible I invited him to share the picnic table that separated our tents. We drank wine from enamel camping mugs, cracked monkey nuts and talked for an hour or more. I was wary at first, unsure of his intentions, but he was easy company and the conversation flowed smoothly despite my faltering Spanish. He spoke slowly for my benefit, prompted me when I lacked vocabulary and was patient when I had trouble with my past tenses.

We spoke of our jobs and our countries and our reasons for being alone. Inevitably, the conversation turned to his recent relationship break-up. Alarm bells rang. Here I was, in the dark, with a lonely, single man. I needed to make my position clear. It wasn't that I lacked friends to travel with, I assured him, it was just preferable to be without them for a while. I liked the feeling of strength that came with independence, and the freedom to make my decisions without consulting anyone else. I had *chosen* to travel on my own, and was happy that way.

Whether my meaning got lost in translation, or whether Luis simply decided to ignore it, I'm not sure. Certainly, nothing I said distracted him from his increasingly intimate line of conversation. He wanted to know if I had a boyfriend.

'Why of course,' I joked lightly, 'one in every country.'

His eyes lit up.

'Then maybe you'd like to take a little walk beside the lake?' he asked. 'I know the names of all the stars. I can point them out to you.'

Without a doubt, it was time to say goodnight.

'Well, it's a nice offer,' I said, 'but I'm very tired and I have to get up early tomorrow so I think I'll go to bed now. Goodnight.' I held out my hand to be shaken.

Luis looked at it thoughtfully, and took it between both of his.

'No, no, *chica*,' he said gently, 'we don't do that here.' He pulled me towards him, and whispered in my ear. 'In Argentina, we do it like this,' and he leant even closer to deliver the traditional kiss on one cheek. It was something of a surprise, however, when he tried to plant it on the *inside*, with his tongue.

Good God, I thought, extracting myself with some difficulty, if that's how they treat strangers here, it's going to be very easy to make new friends.

2

Tea for Two

I stocked up with enough food for a week. Although the Route of the Seven Lakes was only just over 100 kilometres long, I didn't know how many days it would take me to complete it. I knew that the road wasn't paved, that it was hilly, dusty and soft in places, but also that it was exceptionally beautiful. It might be slow going, and it might be worth staying and camping for a couple of nights. I didn't expect to see any shops on the way and I didn't want to run out of things to eat. So I bought about twice my own body weight in biscuits, oats, bananas, dried figs and cake, and promptly ate half of it outside the supermarket. Then I stuffed the rest into my panniers and hit the road.

Turning north, away from the tarmac road that led towards Chile, I left civilisation behind for the rocky back-route. At first I was cautious on the unsealed surface, getting used to handling my heavily laden bike on the gravel. Although Vagabunda had been with me for almost twelve years – had been the one I learnt to ride off-road on – we hadn't been on rough terrain together for a long time. When, a couple of years previously, I had bought a new mountain bike more suited to the hills of Wellington, my hometown in New Zealand, my first love had been demoted. Now she was my street-cruiser-cum-touring bike, old-fashioned and heavy but completely reliable. Over the years her components had been replaced, many more than once, and now the only thing that remained of the original bike was the steel frame. The paintwork was chipped and she was a bit rusty in places, but elaborate use of electrical tape had brightened her persona. The colours of Spain, Italy and Argentina – all of which we had now visited together – gave her a zany character, and her forks were striped red and black, for that devil-may-care Dennis the Menace air. I had recently given her a new drive train, a set of hand-built wheels and two new tyres, making her sturdy enough to withstand the toughest of roads.

The rest of my gear was equally old and well loved. In four battered, non-waterproof panniers I carried a one-person Macpac Microlight tent and an MSR WhisperLite stove that had both provided me with years of diligent service, as had my soot-blackened billy, battery of bicycle tools and super-absorbent Therm-a-Rest packTOWL. My limited clothes ration was made up of a mismatched assortment of fraying T-shirts, shorts and polyprop tops, as well as cut-off striped socks for keeping my knees warm. My rain jacket almost kept the rain out, my gloves nearly always kept my hands warm (but not dry), and my ancient baseball cap kept most of my face out of the sun most of the time.

I was working on the principal of 'if it ain't broke, don't fix it' and this configuration of cycling paraphernalia had suited me well enough for the previous few years. It also occurred to me that the less new and shiny stuff I had with me, the less anyone would be inclined to try to steal it from me. The only newish items I had with me were my Fairydown Scorpion sleeping bag – which I had finally splashed out on after my brother's last hand-me-down had wore thin enough to see the stars through – a ten-litre Ortleib water bag and an increasingly grubby Spanish-English dictionary. After just two months in my hands, having gained a reinforcing covering of duct tape, greying dog-eared corners and a spattering of tea stains and biscuit crumbs, the dictionary was the only item that I thought might not be capable of surviving the rigours of the road.

My pride and joy, a Nikon SLR, lived in my handlebar bag, along with my compass, dictionary and Swiss Army knife, and everything else was stowed in my panniers. I had learnt, over the years, to keep the weight as low as possible to aid balance and for that reason tried to avoid carrying anything other than my foam sleeping mat on top of the rear rack. Anyway, it was good to have that space free for the times I really needed it; when, in a fit of over-exuberance in the supermarket, I bought way more food than could possibly be squeezed in on top of my other stuff, for example. Everything had its place, and was packed away methodically each morning so that in an emergency I always knew where to find what I needed.

The first downhill on the Seven Lakes route was a long section of washboard – a series of lateral ruts caused by too much traffic on a poorly maintained surface. Unlike rocky obstacles and potholes, which give a road character and test a cyclist's skills of balance, washboard is, literally, a pain in the bum. Going at the wrong pace over these ruts throws the bike into a horrendous bumpy rhythm, which, if you don't get out of the saddle, could damage you for life. I soon discovered that the trick to avoiding a most uncomfortable ride is as follows: approach with as much speed as you can muster, stand up on the pedals, relax all joints, steer straight and allow your wheels to skim across the tops of the ruts at consistent velocity. Hold on tight and don't touch the brakes. With any luck you'll survive with both bike and backside intact.

The cumulative weight of my panniers gave me an amazing sensation of stability, as well as a forward momentum that I was reluctant to tame. Clipped into my pedals, charging downhill at top speed, I began to feel properly at one with Vagabunda. Although we'd seen more than enough tarmac together on recent trips in Europe, not to mention our daily commute through London, it appeared that neither of us had forgotten our muddy beginnings.

The cyclist's law of physics dictates that what goes down must go up again. The opposite side of the valley was steep and sandy, and equally scarred with ruts. It was hard to maintain balance while climbing and I needed every ounce of my strength to keep the cranks turning. But although I was struggling, and puffing and wheezing like an asthmatic donkey, my muscles already felt stronger than a few days ago.

I sweated copiously, and the fine dust of the road coated my wet skin. My hair, thick with powder, stuck stiffly out from under my cap like straw. Smudged and grubby, I began to feel like a scarecrow come to life.

Later that afternoon I came across three cyclists resting in the shade of a roadside tree. From a distance, it looked like two Latin Americans and a gringo. I was right. I pulled up beside them to hear the tail end of the Canadian's effusive monologue.

'Man,' he drawled, 'I've bin havin', like, such a wild time on this trip. Yeah, man, this place is great, you know, I mean, even though I can't speak Spanish, it doesn't really matter because there's, like, always someone around who speaks English and . . . say, what sort o' bike you got there, dude?'

If enthusiasm was an Olympic sport he could have won gold on the width of his smile alone, but the Argentine lads were nevertheless regarding him with distaste, as though his freckles and red hair and verbal leakage were proof of some malignant disease. They were all headed in the same direction, and in the eyes of the two quiet Latinos was the fear of being stuck with this unceasing flow of words until the end of their journey. I tried to distract the redhead with a few questions, and he eagerly assured me that I would be going uphill all the way from here on in, and that the road would be sandy.

'But man, ya gonna love that campsite when ya reach it!'

I couldn't help but admire his spirit, but it was a relief to wave the three of them goodbye. His voice was audible from some way up the road.

'Wow, guys!' he said to the others, 'Didya *see* that? That was a *girl!*'

My strength was waning. My legs were beginning to flag and I was dying for a cup of tea. When the road passed beside an alpine meadow, invitingly grassy and drenched with afternoon sun, it seemed far too good a campsite to pass up.

Alas, what had appeared to be a gentle paddock turned out to be a minefield of prickly seed-bombs, poised for detonation at the tops of long stalks. Triggered by the slightest movement, they showered my lower legs with shrapnel – tiny brown kernels on Velcro-style hooks. Tenaciously, the seeds stuck to my shoes and my clothes until my shorts had grown beards and each foot resembled a russet-coloured hedgehog.

Then the horse flies spotted me. The size of marbles, they hurtled towards me as though propelled by slingshot, and no amount of frantic whirling around in circles would deter them. I tried swishing my hefty Spanish dictionary like a fly swat, but despite causing one or two of them to ricochet back into the stratosphere, it was of little effect against their ruthless bombardment. They bit wherever they landed, I was cruelly outnumbered, and there was no option but to retreat to the safety of the tent.

It was then I discovered that the seeds, which had seemed to cling so immovably to my clothing, had in fact managed to migrate to all sorts of unlikely and uncomfortable places: my hair, the insides of my socks, the depths of my pockets, even the intimate reaches of my knickers. And that was why, instead of watching the last of the sun's rays silhouetting the mountains and breathing the heady alpine air, I spent the evening zipped inside a fusty tent, picking prickles from my arse.

The following night's campsite was far less troublesome. It was situated on the shore of beautiful Lake Falkner, and for cyclists it was only one peso per night. Although I arrived there about lunchtime, full of energy and the enthusiasm to keep moving, it seemed wasteful not to stay in such a magical spot. Due to the nature of the road, and the available transport options, most tourists see the area from the dusty windows of buses that roar through in one day. This leaves the stunning views to be properly enjoyed by the hitchhikers, the pedal-powered, those on motorbikes and the handful of people who brave the potholes in their own cars. Choosing a secluded spot, I pitched my tent beside the lake and the bleached skeleton of a fallen tree. It lay half submerged, like the bones of a stranded whale, and long-legged birds fished between its ribs.

There is a stereotype, prevailing in much of Latin America, that draws the modern Argentine male as an insufferable egotist: arrogant, self-centred, and wholly aware of his own good looks and animal magnetism. There is even a joke that epitomises this view:

Q: How does an Argentine commit suicide?

A: He jumps off his own ego.

Personally, I found this to be true of very few of the men I met. However, as if to prove that all stereotypes do have some basis in reality, I was about to meet the perfect example in a young man who was as good as blinded by his own imagined brilliance.

I was returning from an afternoon stroll when a sinewy cyclist pulled up next to me.

'Do you know if there's a campsite around here?' he asked, in English.

'Yep. You're very close.' I pointed to the entrance some hundred metres ahead. 'And it only costs one peso per night for cyclists, so you're in luck.'

'Seriously?' He got off his bike and walked beside me.

José, from Mendoza, was two months into a trip from the southernmost city of Argentina to the northern border of Mexico. He was dressed in logo-splashed synthetic clothing and rode an expensive aluminium bike which, he lost no time in telling me, had been given to him by his sponsors. Even one peso per night was expensive, he said. Usually, he stayed for free in police stations, fire stations or family homes.

'The people of my country,' he said with pride, 'are amazingly generous. They've fed me almost every night of my journey.' He pointed to his rear rack, piled high with luggage. 'I'm still carrying some of the food I started with.'

I was curious.

'Do they just invite you in?' I asked. 'Or do you knock on their doors?'

'Well,' he replied with studied nonchalance, 'they've usually heard about me before I arrive. I'm becoming quite famous actually.' He dug into his handlebar bag and pulled out a business card. 'Check out my web site,' he said. 'You'll find loads of great photos of me.'

I laughed. I hadn't realised that cycling was such a serious pursuit.

He followed me to my campsite and expressed astonishment

that I had chosen to place myself away from the other campers. As though to teach me a lesson, he put his tent directly next to mine. Whether I wanted it or not, I had company. I went and bought a couple of beers from the campsite shop and we shared a meal as the stars filled the sky.

'So how are you funding your trip?' I asked through a mouthful of instant mashed potato. 'Are your sponsors paying for everything?'

'No, I have a business in Spain. It's been good to have a break from it too. My business partner fell in love with me and our relationship was getting difficult.' He looked thoughtful. 'Actually, that seems to happen to me a lot. The problem is that I just don't have time for a girlfriend when I'm cycling the Americas.'

I snorted impolitely with laughter. Both incredulous and fascinated by his unabashed self-importance, I was finding it difficult to keep a straight face at anything he said. There was no danger of offending him, however. He misconstrued these little outbursts as girlish appreciation of his masculine charms.

Despite my having grave doubts about our compatibility as travelling partners, it was inevitable that we would cycle together the following day; there was only one road north. Climbing steadily out of the valley, side by side on the virtually empty road and distracted by conversation, I found the increasing incline and the heat of the sun went almost unnoticed. We twisted through a puzzle of steep green hillsides and glimpsed, through gaps in the foliage, secret views of mirrored lakes. The final stretch into San Martín, which marked the end of the scenic Seven Lakes route, was an exhilarating downhill on a flawless stretch of asphalt. We freewheeled for kilometres, with a panoramic view over glittering Lake Lacar, and I bit my lip with joy. It was a great day to be a cyclist.

San Martín de los Andes is named after General José de San Martín, who led Argentina to independence from Spain in 1816. The main avenue and central plaza also bear his name, as in other towns I had passed through, and I noticed that lesser streets took the names of presidents, politicians, generals and explorers. It seemed to indicate the strength of the nation's patriotism; the enduring pride for Argentina's short history and for those who have made the country what it is today. What was also notable, however, was the absence of any reference to pre-colonial history. Among the myriad historical reminders, the names of the indigenous races, their territories and the chiefs of their tribes were barely to be found.

We cycled down Avenida San Martín, looking for a place to stock up on calories. It was siesta and the streets were quiet, but we found a little place selling cheap food and sat at an outside table, our bikes causing a pavement-blocking pedestrian hazard nearby. We ordered a gloriously unhealthy lunch of pizza and beer (I was never going to get fit at this rate) and the bulky restaurateur warned us that his pizzas were LARGE. It was obligatory, he said, to finish everything, and if not . . . he looked at us meaningfully and crossed his mammoth forearms like a striking dock worker at a picket line. He needn't worry, I assured him, even if his pizzas were the size of dustbin lids we wouldn't be having any problems. He beamed hugely, winked at me like a navvy and strode off into the kitchen.

I don't know what it is about cycling, but it seems to give males a bottomless appetite. I am not known for my reserve when it comes to enjoying a good meal, but even I couldn't match José when he finished his half of the pizza and ordered a second lunch. While I rubbed my distended stomach, closed my eyes and stretched my tired legs into the sun, he devoured, with the greatest of ease, a *lomito completo* – a gargantuan sandwich with steak, egg, cheese, salad and chips.

Later, cycling back down the main road in search of an ice-cream shop, I tried to regain control of my legs. They felt strangely detached, as though only they and not the rest of me had been drinking. It took the barest persuasion from José to call it a day.

'Wait here,' he instructed as we stopped outside a *gendarmería* – a station of the border police. He propped his bike against a wall and disappeared inside, returning several minutes later, strutting, with a self-satisfied smirk on his face. 'I've found us a place to stay for the night,' he said. 'Follow me.' Too lethargic to argue, I cycled after him around the corner. We pulled up outside a house with a grassy garden. 'This is the *quincho* of the *gendarmería*,' José explained. 'It's where they hang out and have barbecues when they're not working.'

We knocked, and a shy-looking man welcomed us in. Shaking hands, José launched into a long, well-practised monologue. How heart-warming it was, he said, that his countrymen constantly offered him such spontaneous hospitality. It was just the material he needed for the book he was going to write. I suppressed my giggles: I couldn't help but be reminded of Che Guevara and Alberto Granado, whose indefatigable enthusiasm and smooth talking had secured them free accommodation all over Latin America. While their appeals for lodging had been born from necessity, however, José's brazen requests seemed to be more about being remembered in each town. The caretaker, who also appeared to be hiding amusement behind politeness, showed us into a long room with a banquet table and indoor barbecue, pointed out where the toilets were and told us to make ourselves comfortable.

I had to admit, it was a novel way to spend the night, and as we had saved money by staying there it was a good excuse to celebrate. I dragged José back into town to inject some cash into the local economy. We returned, a mere couple of hours after lunch, to the same tiny restaurant. The proprietor laughed rumblingly as we came in, wobbling his three chins with mirth at our apparently endless capacity for food, even though, judging by the size of his belly, we were still a long way from matching his. We ate pasta, drank wine and cycled back to our banquet room with some difficulty on weaving bicycles.

And so it was that without having run over any old ladies or set fire to any national parks with my camping stove, I spent my first night in an Argentine police station.

The next morning, under a brooding sky, we rode northwards to Junín de los Andes, a small and dusty town whose quiet streets gave no hint of its origins in a turbulent and bloody period of Argentina's history. Junín began, my guidebook told me, as a military outpost in a brutal war known as the Conquest of the Desert, in which colonial forces stole vast tracts of land from the original indigenous inhabitants.

Ever since the arrival of the Spanish conquerors, or *conquistadores*, in 1516, the native peoples of the Argentine region stubbornly resisted imperial rule. In return for the loss of their ancestral lands, which the King of Spain granted to new settlers, the indigenes took livestock from the invaders' farms. Thefts and disputes escalated, becoming all the more violent, until the Argentine minister of war was appointed to 'clean' the territory of native inhabitants. General Julio Argentino Roca, compassionless and fervently patriotic, intended to wipe out the indigenes as though they were no more than noxious weeds.

And so, in 1878, the genocide began. The tribespeople, lacking the superior weaponry of the Spanish, didn't stand a chance. The ruthless assaults against them, continuing until the following year, were ultimately 'successful' and those who were not murdered were forced either to flee south towards

Patagonia or were captured by the military. Some 14,000 people were rounded up, sent to Buenos Aires or other provincial capitals and used as forced labour. Families were separated and women and children were distributed among the upper classes as domestic servants. The men were enlisted into the armed forces or put to work on cattle farms, on vineyards or breaking rocks to pave the streets of the capital. Untold numbers died of hunger, lack of hygiene, overcrowding or from diseases that the Europeans brought with them. Other tribes were gathered into communities under military rule and converted to Catholicism.

Despite the decimation and dispersion of the Mapuche people, a large indigenous population remains in Junín. We met some of them at the pub. The scenario when we walked in brought to mind a TV western: the outlaw pushes into the smoky bar, arrogant stance and ten-gallon cowboy hat backlit by the sun, the saloon doors swinging behind him. The pianist stops playing and the bar falls quiet as every eye in the house turns on the new arrival. As we stood there under the silent stares of the locals, I had the overwhelming urge to tip my hat, curl my top lip and greet them with 'Howdy, y'all'. Instead, we found ourselves a table in the corner and tried to blend in. I soon realised that any stares directed at us were not ones of suspicion, nor malevolence, but merely curiosity. In fact, the pervading atmosphere was one of generous affability, due to the fact that almost everyone was in a drunken befuddlement of good humour.

We ordered *empanadas de choclo* – with sweetcorn filling – and they were without a doubt the best I ate in the whole of Argentina: volcanically hot, crisp and oily, and erupting with a cheesy, corn-studded lava that had to be cooled with long draughts of Quilmes. We ate them in no time flat, ordered more and sat back to watch a small drama unfold as a local woman drank herself into a horizontal appreciation of the floorboards.

This caused a flurry of excitement as first her brother then the police and then the ambulance were enlisted to help her out of her condition. Various community members staggered unsteadily in and out of the bar, some looking for a solution to the problem while others sought another beer in solidarity with the fallen woman.

Many of the men were dressed in the traditional clothes of the gaucho, Argentina's equivalent of the cowboy. Tucked into their calf-length riding boots they wore the characteristic baggy trousers known as *bombachas*, billowing voluminously and fastened around the waist with colourful cummerbunds. With white shirts, waistcoats, red ponchos and wide-brimmed black hats, they looked all set to leap on their horses for a spot of cattle herding. However, at this time of day they were far more interested in rounds of beers than rounding up steers, and the dashing image they cut was marred slightly by their inability to retain control of their legs, focus and capacity for speech. Several of them weaved their way over to our table for some enthusiastic but more or less incoherent conversation and to wish us luck on our journey. I felt well on my way to joining them in degeneracy, but José, the voice of reason, pointed to the ever-darkening sky and suggested we find a place to stay before the inevitable rain.

Deeming the campground unnecessary, he led the way once again to the police station. The officer on duty told us we were more than welcome to sleep in the carport, which had a concrete floor and was enclosed on three sides. José was disappointed; he didn't like sleeping 'outside' if he didn't have to. I told him to be grateful for the hospitality and to stop being such a big girl's blouse. With hurt pride, he huffed off to have a shower while I made a cup of tea and watched the clouds grow blacker and more menacing by the minute.

Then, with a rush of humid air that sent the dust of the roads and the fallen leaves whirling dramatically into the sky, the storm broke. Like the dropping of the curtain at the end of a play the rain fell suddenly and solidly to earth, releasing the thunderous applause of a million wet drops on asphalt. There was a neon flash, the noise of a whip cracking, and another hot breath of electrically charged air blew the rain into my face. José ran sloshing back through the fast-forming puddles, towel over his head, bent low. He shook himself off like a dog and we sat together on my camping mat, watching forks of lightning split the thick air. And suddenly it was over, as abruptly as it had begun. The clouds backed off, clean-edged and light with relief, the asphalt shone silver and the guttering dripped a syncopated tattoo. The air was cool and fresh, and we made the most of the last light by walking down to the river for a picnic.

It was to be our last dinner together. The following morning we would be going in separate directions; José was headed north towards his hometown, Mendoza, and I had decided to go west towards Chile. On one hand, I couldn't wait to say goodbye – his overbearing egotism was beginning to annoy me – but I had to admit that there was a curious attraction there as well. I found myself alternating between loving and hating his company several times each day, and it seemed a good idea that we parted before my emotions swung too far in either direction.

3

Crossing the Cordillera

I knew even less about Chile than I did about Argentina. I didn't even have a map. But it lay tantalisingly close – just on the other side of the Andes – and I couldn't resist the desire to go there. Unfortunately, José seemed to think it was a good idea too. His plans had changed, he announced, as we fitted our panniers to our bikes. He was going to accompany me through the mountains to make sure I was okay.

'I'm in no rush,' he said gallantly. 'It won't be any inconvenience.'

No matter how tactfully I tried to assure him that I would be perfectly all right cycling on my own, and that perhaps it was a better idea that we continue our respective journeys alone, he was not to be dissuaded. He led the way, cycling west into the morning breeze with an eager and purposeful expression. I followed with gritted teeth.

The Andes, which stretch almost the length of South America on its western side and form a natural border between Argentina and Chile, become gradually smaller the further south they go. At many points, I discovered, Argentina's wide plains slope gently upwards towards the frontier, while in Chile the mountainside falls away steeply and the descent is almost to sea level. The mountains, acting as a barrier to the east-moving weather pattern, force most of the rain to fall in Chile while Argentina enjoys drier and relatively predictable weather, especially in the summer.

Tromen Pass, where we were to cross the national border, is found at the end of a long, gradually inclining road that passes westwards through a wide river valley of ochre grasses. On the horizon, distant volcanoes appear like piles of icing sugar. Despite the relative flatness of the terrain, it was tough going. The road was an unmaintained stretch of rocks and volcanic sand and, much to my dismay, traffic action had created washboard ruts along almost its entire length. To make matters worse, the prevailing wind was from the west, blowing into our faces and increasing in strength as the day went on.

Physically, I was up to the challenge – now capable of cycling without approaching self-combustion – but mentally, I struggled. The thing is that when I sling my leg over the crossbar and clip into my pedals, I like to feel as though I'm going somewhere. But when the wind and the road conditions conspire to slow even the strongest cyclist to a crawl, frustration overtakes me in no time. I seemed to be making virtually no progress at all. What with the ruts, which bumped me off balance, and the sand that kept stopping me dead in my tracks, it took most of my strength just to keep the bike going in a straight line. The wind, although by no means gale force, was relentless, chapping my lips and hands, and drying my throat.

Worst of all was that José seemed to be having no problems whatsoever, skimming across the top of the sand like Jesus on wheels until he was no more than a speck on the horizon. It was partly a relief to finally get some time without him, but I was also angry with myself. Not only had I been incapable of insisting on continuing my journey alone, he was now highlighting my feebleness with his superior strength. I wanted to match his pace, but couldn't, and before long he had entirely disappeared from view. Seething, I resorted to blaming him for my black mood. Before racing off ahead he had told me, in an irritatingly pompous tone, that I simply wasn't trying hard enough. If only I put in a bit more effort, he assured me, I could go faster. Although this was obviously his clumsy way of trying to encourage me, it had still managed to drive me to mutinous thoughts.

My brother was the one who had really known how to motivate me. The day I got stuck up a tree in the back garden, when I was eight years old and Daniel twelve, he gave me my first lesson in determination. Dan was a keen climber, and was setting up a rope in our favourite tree in order to abseil down. It was familiar territory, but we ventured higher than usual to maximise the drop to the ground. Everything was going well until, bridging a wide gap between two branches, I looked down. Suddenly, the danger of my position became horribly clear. I froze.

'Dan! I'm stuck!' My heart was racing.

'No you're not,' he replied calmly from the branch above.

'I am! I'm going to fall . . . help me!'

He looked at me evenly, close enough to offer his hand if he chose.

'You climbed up,' he said. 'You know how to get down.' His cool blue eyes were fixed on mine and he was smiling ever so slightly.

I was sure of my impending death. The ground was a long way below and my grip was slipping. I trembled, I howled and I cursed my brother with words that no eight-year-old should know. And then I climbed down.

'You see?' he said, from far above. 'I knew you could do it. Now, do you want to abseil this tree or not?'

Thinking of this, my anger dissolved. By the time I reached José, huddled against the wind on the lee side of a tree and patiently waiting, I had realised I was being unfair. He may not have been a good teacher, but it wasn't his fault that I was slow. And when a surprise trough of sand threw me dramatically from my bike and pitched me headfirst into the dirt, I could do nothing but lie there and laugh at myself.

From the Argentine side of the border, Lanín Volcano was a view worth getting out of the tent for. Like a child's impression of a mountain it was a perfect cone shape, wearing a simple cap of whitest snow and set against a clear blue sky. By the time we packed up and got on the road though, the sky was overcast and the head of the volcano was lost in swirling cloud. The closer we cycled, the more the mountain revealed its true nature: the deep blue hanging glaciers, the brown scree of the lower slopes and the dirty greys of old summer snow.

The wind increased and the road deteriorated and the sand seemed determined to suck me down. A gaucho in a thick woollen poncho passed us on his horse, his wagging dogs bowled ahead by the wind, fur ruffled the wrong way and noses thrust forward.

'There's rain at the pass,' he told us, pulling his hat down against the cold. 'Good luck, *adios*.'

The entrance to Lanín National Park was a pair of stout wooden posts, one on either side of the road, between which a welcome sign swung creaking in the breeze. Passing underneath, we left behind the stunted bushes of the plains for stands of the characteristic pehuén tree, stretching perky green fingers towards the sky. Around us, the forest grew thicker and the colours deeper, evidence of the wetter climate ahead.

We passed the Argentine border and, with passports stamped, cycled into the no-man's-land that separated us from Chile. It was the last day of February, and we chanced upon the tail end of an annual festival being held in a clearing. A mixture of Argentines and Chileans were gathering up children and belongings, saying their goodbyes and piling onto buses. Forgotten lumps of blackened chicken smoked on the barbecue, popcorn was trodden into the grass and cheap toys, newly bought and newly broken, lay abandoned in the dirt.

But in a corner of the field, fuelled by music and alcohol and showing no signs of tiring, a hard-core crowd of revellers continued the party. Gathered around a group of guitarists and a scuffed patch of earth that served as a dance floor, they clapped and cheered in time to the music, firing the footwork of an enthusiastic couple dancing Chile's traditional *cueca*. With white handkerchiefs held high above their heads, the dancers courted one another face to face, eyes locked and upper bodies held still, the stomping of their feet growing in speed and intensity until they were enveloped by a cloud of dust. Couple after couple took their turn, the men in the heeled riding boots and clothes of the Chilean cowboy, the women in skin-tight jeans whose contents wobbled with every step. The music was incredibly catchy and we stayed to the end, caught up in the mood of the people and enchanted by the amicability between two nations. José, buttering up some members of the Chilean police, managed to secure us the promise of a camp spot at the border control.

Clattering on down the steep and winding road, the load on my bike jumped and jolted and my joints complained as they took the strain. It seemed strange to be descending so steeply when we had hardly climbed at all, but suddenly it felt like we were in the mountains. The plunging valleys were full of lush rainforest, waterfalls gushed down vertical rock faces and ethereal mists hung in the air.

On the other side of the border the park ranger invited us

for dinner. Outside the little cottage where he lived with his family, at a table stacked with plates and home-made bread, we were given glasses of beer and invited to sit. Our mouths watered and our stomachs growled in anticipation as the ranger brought a massive cast-iron dish to the table. It was full to the brim with *estofado*, a stew of chicken, onions, carrots, potatoes and wine that had been cooking over an open fire for several hours. The sauce was thick and aromatic, perfect for dipping the bread into, and I was compelled to break my vegetarian diet for the first time in years. There are times, I had decided, when politeness is more important than habit, and my hunger helped me to overcome any doubts. José and I ate at least three times more than anyone else, but even when we had finished, bellies almost at bursting point, the dish was still a third full.

We camped in a damp picnic site behind the ranger's house, the roar of a nearby river testimony to the massive volume of water channelling through the valley. In the small hours of the morning the first fat raindrops burst on my tent. I lay awake, half delighted at being protected from the elements by my cosy nylon bubble and half dismayed at the thought of venturing out into the wet the next day. But I knew that from the inside of a tent, the rain always sounds worse than it is, and I was keen to make an early start in the morning.

My attempts to rouse José were fruitless. When all that emerged from his tent were plaintive cries of, 'But it's RAINING', I realised that at last I had found his weak spot. For the last two days he had stubbornly refused to entertain my frustrations, proclaiming the wind, the speed bumps and the sand as 'easy' if only I would have the right attitude. But now, like a spoilt Hollywood actor, he was refusing to appear for action until the conditions were favourable. He accepted a cup of tea in bed, shooed me out of his tent and zipped it up before my sodden jacket could drip on anything, and continued to stay holed up for the better part of the morning.

The ranger, dressed in waterproofs but seemingly unconcerned by the streams of water running down his face, sploshed down to see if we were all right. He suggested that we use his shed to have our breakfast in, made sure we had everything we needed and strolled unhurriedly back up the hill, humming to himself. For him, it appeared, it was just another day at work in the rainforest.

Finally, when I could stand the inaction no longer, I began to pack up, transferring my wet things to the shed and firing up my stove for porridge. Reluctantly, José followed, shaking himself at the door like a dog and peering dismally out at the grey drizzle as though it was nuclear fallout. Shivering, he began to systematically hang all his wet things over beams, using a piece of cardboard to flick leaves and bits of dirt off his groundsheet, and unpacked his panniers for a major reshuffle.

It seemed that he was planning to delay his departure until either the rain stopped or he was invited for lunch at the ranger's house. As it was apparent that neither of those things would happen for some time, I decided not to hang around. I left him oiling his chain and skittered on down the rocky road, rain in my face and tyres throwing up mud, elated by the speed of descent and the sudden sense of solitude.

It didn't last for long. Half an hour later he overtook me, complaining about the rain and expressing his dismay at not being invited to lunch. I put my hood up and cycled on in silence.

It was late afternoon when we rolled into Pucón, a little lakeside town that acts as a base for ascents of the surrounding volcanoes. Despite the fact that it was the end of the summer season the streets were heaving with Chilean, Argentine and

European tourists. They were bundled up in scarves and winter jackets, ruddy-faced and good-humoured, eating ice-creams in defiance of the chilly weather.

There was no campsite, and José was determined to find someone willing to offer us some hospitality. We stopped at the police station. As he delivered his well-rehearsed speech to a couple of impassive policemen, I wondered exactly what they were thinking. I was in two minds about José's approach. On the one hand, I liked the concept he was travelling with: searching for the goodness in his own people and opening himself to interactions with the locals in the places he passed through. On the other, I wasn't entirely sure that asking for free accommodation was really the best way to discover genuine hospitality. Once he had explained to the Chilean police how welcoming were their Argentine counterparts, they were left with little option but to offer us a place to stay. They were polite, but not necessarily delighted by the chance to house two wet and smelly cyclists.

We were on our way out for dinner when a chubby young officer stopped us, resplendent in immaculate green uniform and genuinely interested in our travels. We chatted, and José pointed out that we were, essentially, on separate journeys. The policeman looked at me thoughtfully and raised one eyebrow. Later, when were sitting in a restaurant waiting for pizza, José brought this up.

'You know what?' he asked, in a pensive tone. 'That policeman was impressed that you were travelling without me before.' He paused, and frowned. 'I thought *I* was supposed to be the hero here?'

It was an immense relief to go our separate ways the next morning. José had to keep travelling north, and although I had no particular plans it seemed a good opportunity to go in the opposite direction. We said goodbye at Villarica and it felt like the adventure was starting afresh; here I was, independent again, with no one to challenge my decisions or accuse me of not trying hard enough. I felt charged with enthusiasm and a light wind blew away the last shreds of frustration.

After the relative wilderness of the last few days, the landscape was cosy and bucolic. Tall hedgerows full of blackberries bordered the narrow road and from beyond came the contented sounds of cows huffing and ripping at grass. Farm vehicles roared past and from the fields came the rich smell of sun-warmed earth.

Evening found me still surrounded by fields. I didn't feel good about trespassing, but as there was no one around to ask for permission, there wasn't much option. In a gateless paddock, which was studded with clumps of thistle and cowpats, I slotted my tent discreetly into a corner. I cooked dinner by torchlight and practised an apology in Spanish in case the landowner should stumble across me. Surely, with a smile and a few well-chosen words, no one would take offence at a solitary cyclist? In the adjacent meadow cantankerous cattle bellowed. Their stomping footfalls sounded so close that I lay awake in fear of being squashed in the dark.

Back on the gravel the following day, negotiating the maze of dusty back roads, I gathered from the stares of the locals that the route I was taking was somewhat unconventional. Despite a large number of cyclists in this area, the bulk of them can be found on certain prescribed routes: short but beautiful off-road tracks (for those on week-long trips) and fast, smooth, asphalt arteries (for those cycling the whole of the Americas). Having an aversion to heavy traffic, I was trying to travel south without using the Pan-American Highway, which forms the most direct way down the length of Chile. Consequently, I was spending a disturbing amount of time wondering exactly where I was, stopping at un-signposted intersections and peering in confusion at the under-detailed map I had bought in Pucón.

I enlisted the help of various policemen and farmers to keep me on the straight and narrow, and on the whole the people were polite but distant. Apart from the enthusiastic babble of one shopkeeper, who filled my water bottles and tried to sell me his sausages, most people answered my questions without engaging in further conversation. There even seemed to be a hint of suspicion in the eyes of some, and I began to wonder if the closed faces and the reluctance to speak to strangers were small indications of the wider national psyche. In my tent each night I had been reading *My Invented Country*, a memoir by Chilean author Isabel Allende, in which she describes the characteristics of her countrymen with merciless honesty and insight. Maybe my perception was coloured by her words, but although it had been more than a decade since the end of the dictatorship I felt sure I could sense the shadow it had left on the people.

Chile spent seventeen dark years under oppressive military rule, an epoch that began on 11 September 1973 with a violent and bloody coup. Democratically elected President Salvador Allende, who was inside the House of Government when it was bombed by fighter jets, died during the raid and General Augusto Pinochet, the classic stereotype of a dictator in his military uniform and dark glasses, stepped immediately into power.

A cloud of fear descended on the people. Within the first three years of Pinochet's fascist dictatorship approximately 130,000 people were arrested, including union leaders, politicians, journalists, lawyers, doctors, intellectuals, artists and students: anyone who had, or was suspected of having, liberal leanings. Hundreds of thousands of people – including Isabel

Allende, whose father was the late president's cousin – fled the country to seek exile wherever they could.

Those who were arrested were often brutally tortured; some three thousand were murdered. The bodies were disposed of in mass, unmarked graves, destroyed with explosives or dropped from helicopters, drugged but alive, into the sea or onto the peaks of the Andes. The dead whose bodies have never been recovered are known as *Los Desaparecidos* – The Disappeared. More than a thousand people belong to the official list of victims who vanished without trace, taken from the street, or from their homes, and never heard of again.

What fascinated me the most about this horrendous period of history was the extreme polarisation of political opinion that led up to it. During the three years prior to his death, President Allende – the world's first democratically elected Marxist leader – led his country in a socialist experiment. Aiming to stifle the capitalist aspirations of Chile's bourgeoisie he reformed the health care and education systems and began to nationalise banks, businesses, industries and agriculture in an attempt to create social equality for the nation. The process soon caused chaos, however, and with production falling, inflation rates reaching world-record levels and the United States directly collaborating with Chile's right wing, the country plunged swiftly into economic decline. Something had to give, and Pinochet seized power with the support of many of the people.

His reign is over now, and democracy has long been restored, but Isabel Allende believes that fear continues to rule. After years of enforced silence, she writes, people are still scared to speak their opinions out loud. They avoid confrontation and treat each other with mistrust. She likens her country to an abused child: traumatised, and always waiting for the next smack.

Whether that was what I was experiencing now or not, it couldn't be denied that the people were far more reserved on this side of the Andes. Out of curiosity, I stopped to ask directions more than was necessary. One stony-faced old farmer seemed so disconcerted by my appearance that he refused even to look in my direction. He stared at the distant horizon with a perturbed expression, as though I was a manifestation of his own imagination, and tried to ignore me.

'Excuse me, but do you know where this road goes to?' I asked.

No response. He dug his hands deeper into his pockets.

'Does it go to Los Lagos?' I persisted.

He replied with a curt nod of the head and a shuffling of feet.

'And do you know of any campgrounds around here?'

He paused, looked at the ground, and grunted.

I sighed, thanked him with just a hint of irony, and left him standing alone and as motionless as an obelisk in the middle of his field.

Trespassing didn't seem like such a good idea after that, nor did asking people for a field to camp in, and I continued on to the small town of Los Lagos hoping there would be a campsite. There wasn't. It was early evening and I cycled around the main square in a quandary, wondering if the police station had a garden big enough for a tent. But it was not my style to ask, and I realised by my third turn of the plaza that I couldn't bring myself to adopt José's tactics. I left town to join the impersonal main road south, in search of a public rest stop.

The Pan-American Highway was not as manic as I had feared. Two, and in some places three, lanes wide, the road was accommodating enough for the cars and trucks to give me plenty of room. But it was not camper friendly. Across the road, past a tall median barrier, a concrete escarpment tilted upwards to an unreachable pine forest; on the near side the soft shoulder was immediately followed by a steep drop to impenetrable scrub.

It was unusual to cycle for so long without finding a place to put my tent. I didn't need much room, just somewhere out of sight of the road that wasn't too hard to get to. This was normally pretty easy to find, and past experience had taught me that a camp spot would always present itself before nightfall. Even in densely populated Europe I had been able to find forgotten corners, unnoticed by swiftly passing motorists, where I could hide myself away for the night with a sense of perfect security. People often asked me if I got scared camping alone, and it was never easy to convince them that I actually felt safer in some random spot beside the road than in an organised campground where anyone could watch my every move.

It wasn't until the air was cool and the twilight had begun to draw in that I finally found a place big enough for my tent. It wasn't ideal, being no more than two metres from the road and only partially hidden by a low wall of mud, but it would have to do. The ground was strewn with telltale strands of toilet paper in various stages of disintegration, and I cleared the space with a stick, checking for any recent deposits and practising my golf swing on anything suspect.

The possible health risk posed by my surroundings was soon forgotten once I got the stove cranked up and my evening cup of tea brewing. For me, there is nothing better at the end of a day's cycling than a hot cuppa, and the ritual of it serves as a small oasis of calm. Actually, it's kind of comforting to have some semblance of daily routine when travelling, and this is one of the reasons I have come to prefer camping over nights in hotels. No matter whether I'm in New Zealand, Nigeria or Nantucket, in my tent, I'm always at home.

Once I've found a campsite, my nightly schedule is more or less always the same. First of all I pitch the tent, unpack my panniers and stow everything not immediately needed into the vestibule, light the stove and get some water boiling. Then I sit and relax with a cup of tea or two, munch some biscuits and read a few pages of whichever book I'm carrying. In theory, my leg muscles also get stretched out at this point, but I get easily distracted and forget about it if the book is any good. Before it gets dark I make dinner, which tends to be different every night, then I clean my pots, make some more tea and lie down inside the tent to write in my diary. The idea is to stay awake long enough to describe the events of the day in a witty and insightful way that can later be transcribed into emails home, but in practice I tend to fall asleep over my notes, wake up with a start, rush outside to empty my bladder of several gallons of tea and return to my sleeping bag with just enough energy to finish my jottings in scrawl-hand before slipping into the oblivion of the critically knackered. To those who prefer fine dining, cultural events, twilight strolls or nightclubs, it may not seem the most scintillating way to pass an evening on holiday, but it suits me just fine.

I woke to an interesting collection of smells. During the previous evening I had been only vaguely aware of the odours of unwashed socks, raw garlic, cyclist's armpits and sunblock, but it now appeared that during the night they had joined forces to form a palpable smog. Trapped inside the tent with me, it was more than enough encouragement to get out into the cool air of the morning.

For another forty kilometres on the smooth Pan-American, Vagabunda needed virtually no propulsion, seeming to speed along of her own accord like a spirited steed. It was great to be covering so much ground with so little effort, but the main route was dull and noisy and I eventually turned off on to a minor gravel road to follow a river valley south. On my map, the road hugged the riverbank, and I anticipated a long lunch stop at a swimming hole, as the sun was now out and the day hot. I could have done with a wash. But the map was unreliable and the river, although undoubtedly in the valley with me some- where, was nowhere to be seen.

The impossibility of buying sufficiently detailed maps was proving to be the one great sorrow of the trip. I love maps. One of my favourite pastimes when travelling is to lie in my tent and plot the route ahead, considering all options and angles of attack as carefully as a military strategist. But on a map with a scale of 1:2,500,000 – the best I had been able to find – the decision-making process was a rather too simple affair. Take the red roads, as the yellow roads have too much traffic. The green roads don't have tarmac. It's about 100 kilometres between where you are now and where you hope to go next, but what's in between? You'll find out as you go! Hills? This is a two-dimensional map! How can we show hills on a two-dimensional map? It seemed that on this trip I would be guided more by intuition than by information.

However, unlike other parts of the world where lacking a good map means missing the most cyclist-friendly back roads and the most picturesque villages, the parts of South America I intended to visit were blessed with relatively few routes. I wasn't about to miss anything by sticking only to the main roads, but I still felt somehow robbed. Perhaps it was only a small and personal tragedy, but I lamented the loss of those potentially happy hours map-gazing: deciphering hieroglyph- ics, scrutinising contour lines for sign of impending uphills, working out the exact distance to the next place where I could buy chocolate biscuits. Important stuff like that.

I sighed and folded the dog-eared map. My unwashed fingers left black smudges on the cover.

4

A Rooster on my Table

Entre Lagos was so small that I would never have guessed it to have a campsite. In fact, it had over a dozen: small, homely, family-run businesses, all in a row and backing on to Lake Peyehue. The summer season had now ended, the bulk of Argentine and Chilean holidaymakers had returned to work and the sites looked deserted as I bumped down the potholed track and peered hopefully into each of them. There was only one with an open gate, the last in the row, and it had an inviting name. 'Vista Hermosa' – beautiful view – was empty of campers, but I spied a white-haired old lady busy with a trowel in the vegetable garden. I felt sure that she wouldn't turn me away.

She looked a little startled by my appearance

'How did you get here?' she asked, 'I didn't hear your car.' I pointed to my bike, which was resting stoutly against the house, and she chortled with delight.

'¿Andás solita?' she asked. She looked past me for possible companions.

'Well, yes, just me. Me and my bicycle.' She chuckled again and gave me an informal tour of the beans and lettuces, pointing out the finer specimens with earth-covered hands. There had been a bumper crop of tomatoes too, she explained proudly, but they were now all finished. She led me down to the grassy garden, studded with windfall apples.

'Camp on the east side,' she warned, 'to avoid being fruit-bombed in the night and come up to the house if you want some home-made bread.'

It was perfect. I chose a spot, with a table, next to the lake, from which blew a stiff and invigorating breeze, and introduced myself to the chickens.

The corrugated-iron toilet block was quaintly dilapidated, housing two electric showers with disintegrating plastic curtains and suspect wiring. The overhead light went dim when the shower was turned on, but the water was fantastically hot and as there were no other guests I made the most of it. I soaped and shampooed and scrubbed and rubbed, and discovered that what had appeared to be suntan – having developed over the last week to a rich and healthy bronze – was now disappearing down the drain.

Several shades cleaner, I sat in the door of my tent with a cup of tea while a hen and her seven chicks squabbled over the oats that I put out for them. The light faded, the moon rose over the lake and the breeze picked up, bringing with it the promise of rain. I said goodnight to the rooster, who was perched regally on my picnic table, and zipped myself in against the elements.

It was raining when I woke. The pattering on the flysheet made the inside of my tent irresistibly cosy, and it was enough to persuade me to have a day off. If it was not for the fact that there was no food left in my panniers, I could happily have stayed snuggled in the depths of my sleeping bag all morning. As it was, I pulled on my rain jacket and wandered into town in the drizzle, looking for a café where I could read my book and write in my diary and maybe find some cake to eat.

It was a Friday and there was a dismal crowd of people in the street, huddling under coats and umbrellas, hunched against the grey weather, trying to sell a most pathetic collection of cheap merchandise. There were second-hand clothes, out-of-fashion shoes, flimsy kitchen implements and assorted plastic toys. Laid out on blankets on the ground, the goods were either getting drenched or hiding under plastic tarpaulins. What surprised me was not that people were stoically trying to sell their goods in the increasingly heavy rain but that hordes of others were casually browsing, picking through piles of wet clothes and discussing the merits of vegetable peelers as though the rain was not falling in vast quantities from the sky and pouring directly down their necks.

There were fruits and vegetables from the back of farm vehicles; a young boy was selling heads of garlic from a long rope slung over his shoulder; and a man at a little table offered slabs of home-made butter. I bought tomatoes from some sodden men, who had the grace to smile weakly when I made an optimistic prediction about the weather, and disappeared guiltily into the nearest café. It was warm inside, the windows were fogged and locals and visitors alike sat with hands wrapped around steaming mugs.

The proprietor brought me my cake and coffee with an air of complete solemnity. Balanced delicately on one graceful hand was a battered tin tray bearing a slice of tart, a catering-sized tin of powdered Nescafé, a thermos of hot water and a jug of cold milk. With all the professionalism and flair of a Parisian waiter he placed a spoonful of instant coffee in the chipped tea cup and asked which I would like first: the water, or the milk? He poured the hot water deftly from a height, wielding the thermos as though it were an expensive bottle of wine, and finished by genteelly adding a dash of milk from the petite jug. It was an elegant performance, but the air of sophistication was spoilt by the fact that the milk was as thick and lumpy as cottage cheese. It splashed into the coffee like paint-factory effluent into a pond and I watched in dismay as the thick white chunks bobbed and settled. The café owner, unperturbed, swished silently back to the kitchen with his tray held high.

I tried a tentative sip. It was revolting. It was not so much the taste that put me off as the chunky texture. I pushed the cup to one side and tried the strawberry tart. That, thankfully, was delicious and I scoffed the lot in no time. But my cup was still full and I was in a moral dilemma. In my peripheral vision, the proprietor hovered. How, I wondered, could I explain the un-drunk coffee without damaging his professional pride? I took the coward's way out. I waited until he was busy with another customer, left some money on the table and made a quick get-away to the rain-swept street.

The weather hadn't improved at all by the following day, but I was ready to move on. I said my goodbyes to the fowl, thanked Señora Hermosa for the stay and filled my panniers with her home-made bread. Then I headed for the hills.

I had decided to return to Argentina. It was nothing to do with the bad coffee, or my continued lack of a decent map, it was simply due to the fact that I don't really like getting wet. If I continued south on the west side of the Andes I would have to resign myself to the rain, whereas crossing back to the east would see me cycling under clear blue skies. True, traversing South America's major mountain range twice in one week did seem a little masochistic, but if it saved me from a daily dousing I reckoned it was worth it.

The road was paved all the way from Entre Lagos, and the lush forest on each side was misty and beautiful. Ferns lined the roadside and the humid air was full of the rich smell of decomposing leaf litter. It felt familiar. It reminded me of home.

I don't know what it is about mountain scenery that stirs this feeling of recognition, but in the months to come I discovered that my experience was not unique. I met Germans who told me how much Chile reminded them of Germany, Canadians who were fondly reminded of Canada, Swiss who recalled the Alps and Spaniards who drew parallels between the Andes and the Pyrenees. No matter where we come from, or how far we go, we never seem to lose the habit of comparing every place we see with those landscapes that are closest to our hearts.

For me, the alpine atmosphere stirred memories of Fiordland, that wild and powerful land where my brother chose to spend so much of his time. Lured by the grandeur of glacial valleys, addicted to the challenge of sheer granite walls, he had unrolled his sleeping bag in a tramping hut and called the place home. I felt closer to him here, in the mountains, but the melancholy of separation was stronger too. I put my head down and pedalled steadily, lost in bittersweet thoughts of home.

All morning I climbed to passport control. After that, the road was pristine, newly laid and clearly marked with a numbered plastic post at each kilometre. I continued to climb. And climb. And climb. Occasionally the swirling mist would clear just enough to catch a glimpse of an immense swatch of green forest far below and I would feel sure that the top must be close. Then the cloud would shift, all colour would disappear, and I would pass another hour or so enveloped in a fog of memory.

The trucks were going almost as slowly as I was, and as one behemoth crawled past, the young man in the passenger seat leaned out of his window and indicated with enthusiasm that I should grab hold of the side for a tow up the hill. I looked at the chunky, cyclist-pulverising-sized tyres as they rolled past and imagined what they would do to me if I faltered. I declined the offer with a smile and a thumbs-up; I didn't fancy being turned into jam and spread along the road all the way to Argentina. The truck pulled ahead, its gears complaining almost as much as my knees at the steepness of the incline.

It was still raining when I finally spotted the twentieth kilometre marker and reached Cardenal Antonio Samore Pass. It was freezing. At 1308 metres, the pass was relatively low but I had long since left the humid valley climate behind for windswept, horizontal-rain territory. To celebrate my arrival, I went for a short run up to a statue of the Virgin Mary who, with hands clasped in prayer and ecstatic expression aimed gratefully at the sky, seemed to be giving thanks for the deluge we were both receiving. I didn't entirely share her view, but had to concede that there was a certain grim beauty to the desolate hilltop, a wild and moody atmosphere that made me feel wholly alive.

I leapt back on my bike and threw her into top gear for the fast and furious descent, my wheels parting puddles like Moses with the Red Sea and my hands becoming so numb with the cold that braking was virtually impossible. Although they remained hidden from view by cloud, I could sense the steepness of the peaks and cliffs above me as I aquaplaned down the narrow valley. The road snaked steeply in sinuous curves, bringing me, at last, to Argentina.

Dripping like a wet dog – and no doubt smelling like one too – I squelched into the border control office, forming little puddles at each step. I was shivering with cold. As I approached the desk to have my passport stamped an immaculately groomed lady with big hair and seriously misjudged perfume pushed agitatedly past me to the front of the queue. Pointing her finger accusingly at a startled official, she commenced a long and convoluted tale about why she didn't have her documents with her and what she thought *he* should do about it. I sighed, I waited, my passport grew soggy and the last vestiges of warmth left my bones. Another officer took pity on me and beckoned me over. He inspected my visas carefully before stamping a new one, and looked me up and down as he handed the documents back.

'*¿Andás solita?*' he asked, one eyebrow raised. I nodded, releasing a shower of droplets onto his desk. He raised the other eyebrow and smiled at me warmly. 'Welcome back to Argentina,' he said.

Somehow it felt like coming home.

My legs were beginning to seize up in the cold but eventually, at dusk, I arrived at Lake Espejo campsite. It was still raining. Two hardy-looking men welcomed me in, shook my hand, offered their congratulations for a hard day's cycling and eyed Vagabunda with interest. Their enthusiasm for being outdoors didn't seem to be dampened one bit by the pelting rain, although I couldn't say the same for myself. Everything was wet, and getting wetter. I battled with the tent, crawled shivering into my sleeping bag, made half a litre of porridge to warm me up from the inside out, gulped it down at top speed and fell immediately into profound slumber.

At nine o'clock the next morning, while I was peacefully drinking tea and contemplating the mist rising from the lake, my campsite neighbours were breaking open beers for breakfast. This would have been perfectly all right with me had they not also seen it necessary to play bad rock music at maximum volume, but their slurred and raucous sing-along to the car stereo was enough to put anyone off their cornflakes. To everyone's relief they soon got ready to leave, but their car was old and ailing, and half an hour passed before they got it running smoothly. Constant revving of the disgruntled engine caused clouds of black smoke to issue forth from its rear.

Eventually, when no one was left sleeping, they managed to get rolling. The noise, as they blatted off up the hill in their patchwork wagon – apparently held together with bits of string and Sellotape – was like a sumo wrestler's fart after a hard night on the *sake*. They passed out of sight around the bend, but for the next ten minutes I could hear them making their laborious way up the steep and potholed incline with a series of comical noises: high-pitched whines from the engine, rattles and clunks and alarmed shouts, even the sounds of branches snapping. I half expected to hear the car disintegrate altogether – spilling its innards with a sudden 'SPROING!' in the manner of a dismantled wristwatch – and to see parts come flying back down the hill, wheels bouncing dramatically over the tent and splashing into the lake. But at last they crested the hill and drove out of earshot and I went back to my breakfast in the remarkable silence that followed.

5

The Chalk and the Cheese

To celebrate my return to Argentina, I spent most of the day in the pub. I was back in Villa la Angostura – coming back over the Andes had brought me in a big circle – and I was determined to make the most of the tourist facilities. I sat in a window seat, as before, eating a pile of *empanadas* and drinking a well-deserved pint.

I took stock of the first leg of the journey. It had been okay so far, I thought. In the two-and-a-bit weeks since I began no one had shot at me or tried to run me over or stolen my bicycle. I hadn't injured myself or had any major tantrums or lacked enthusiasm. In fact, my desire to cycle was getting stronger by the day. I felt fit and healthy, and determined to keep it that way.

I ordered another beer.

When, after lunch, I returned to Vagabunda, slung a leg over the crossbar and climbed into the saddle, she seemed strangely reluctant to go in a straight line. We weaved for a few wobbly moments along the pavement, dropped off the kerb onto the road, veered momentarily into the oncoming traffic and came to a somewhat ungainly stop in the gutter just centimetres from a parked car. Through the windscreen, a startled family stared at me as though I had just fallen from the sky. I gave them a little wave, a chummy wink and leant forward to pat their bonnet fondly before cycling off. Beer certainly makes me act in strange ways.

Needless to say, I didn't make it much further that day. By the top of the first hill out of town my heart was racing and my head was spinning. My legs were shaky, I still couldn't steer straight and for the safety of myself and the other road users I stopped at the nearest campsite. Lying spread-eagled under the pine trees, my companion beside me, I conceded that we would both benefit from an afternoon off.

The sun was out again by the next morning. I was pedalling dreamily alongside Lake Nauhel Huapi, enjoying the warmth and watching the light on the water, when I spied some bicycles and a group of people in tight shorts. It was an organised tour. The cyclists were leaning against their support van, refuelling with hot drinks and snacks. I was curious to know where they had come from, but too shy to intrude. I cycled past and waved. The reaction from them was one of unanimous enthusiasm; whistles and shouts of encouragement followed me down the road.

Some minutes later the van overtook me and pulled onto the soft shoulder ahead. The driver leant from his window.

'Do you want something to eat?' he asked.

I have never been known to pass up an offer like that. I slammed on the brakes and pulled up beside him. He got out of the van, rummaged in the back, handed me a cup and poured tea from a thermos.

Mariano was the owner of the tour company. He was lean and muscular, and as we talked I began to realise that he was a complete cycle nut. He dragged a crumpled map of Argentina from the dashboard and we scrutinised it together, his finger tracing the paths of his many cycle trips. He asked me where I was planning to go. I had to admit, somewhat shamefully, that my plans were still vague (non-existent, in fact) and that any advice would be welcome.

'Well,' he began, 'you could head on south down Ruta Cuarenta, through Patagonia to Tierra del Fuego, and then . . .'

I looked at him in horror. Ruta Cuarenta – Route Forty. I had heard terrible stories about this road, stories of the endless, rocky, bike-breaking surface, the massive distances between habitations, the lack of water and places to find food. Not least, I had read frightening accounts of the relentlessness and ferocity of the wind. I told him I thought it might all be a bit much for me. He looked disappointed.

'Well,' he said, 'why don't you have a think about it? I'm sure you're capable.' He gave me his business card, a brochure and a muesli bar, before driving off to check the progress of his cyclists.

Thoughtfully, I watched the van disappear, ate the muesli bar and had a look at the leaflet. I was awed by what I read. With his bicycle, unsupported, Mariano had been twice around the world, twice around Argentina, once the length of the Americas and once to the top of Aconcagua in the Andes, the highest mountain outside of the Himalayas at nearly 7000 metres. I wouldn't have imagined it was actually possible to do all of that in one lifetime, let alone by one's mid-thirties. Reading further, I discovered how he had managed it.

His trip down the American continent, some 22,000 kilometres from Alaska to Tierra del Fuego, took him an unbelievably brief five months: an average of 147 kilometres per day, not accounting for rest days. If we assume that he took one day off a week (for surely it isn't possible to cycle for five months without a break?) the average goes up to

175 kilometres per day. Certainly, many people would find it possible to cycle as far as that in a day, but to continue to do so, constantly, for five months, whilst also having to deal with such banalities as shopping, eating, camping and sleeping, is a feat beyond imagination. I couldn't decide whether he was a real-life superman or just plain mad.

I met the group again shortly afterwards, drinking yet more tea and enjoying the view. I stopped to express my admiration. How, I asked Mariano, was it physically possible to do what he had done? He shrugged.

'It's definitely possible to do it faster,' he said. I shook my head in amazement and looked him in the eye. He showed no hint of pride at having his achievements praised and I sensed that he was a harsh self-critic.

I joined the group on the final leg back to Bariloche and we swapped cycling stories. They quizzed me with typical *porteño* warmth, and a depth of curiosity that I was starting to be familiar with. In bus stations, campgrounds and supermarket car parks, I was frequently corralled for questioning by Argentines on holiday.

'*¿Andás solita?*' they would ask.

'Yes, I'm travelling alone.'

'Aren't you scared?'

'No. Why should I be?'

'Because of the bad people! The robbers!'

'But all the people I've met have been just as nice as you.'

'No, no, no. You must be careful! Where do you sleep?'

'In my tent.'

'Alone?'

'Of course.'

'But what about the animals?'

'What animals?'

'Umm, pumas?'

'Haven't seen any.'

By this stage my interrogators would be biting their bottom lips and shaking their heads: a typical gesture of astonishment. Often one of the women in the group would put her hands to her face and say dramatically: '*¡No puedo creerlo!*' – I can't believe it!

Their reaction was way over the top, but I loved their enthusiasm; it seemed to say a lot about them as a nation. What amused me most about these meetings was that there was always one excited lady who would call out to her friends to stop whatever they were doing, *right now*, to come and see this. No matter whether they were already engaged in conversation, buying souvenirs, eating, reading or looking for a toilet, her friends would come. Then, when they had exhausted the limits of my Spanish and told me off on behalf of my parents, they would send me on my way with cries of 'Good luck!' and 'Take care!' and I would ride off wondering just when all the kidnappers and bicycle thieves were going to appear.

The cyclists were a little less dramatic in their questioning, but they still wanted to know everything I was prepared to tell them. It was only as we passed a small shrine by the side of the road, where bright red flags flapped boisterously in the wind, that I managed to divert their attention. I asked one of my cycling companions to tell me about it.

The shrine, Diego told me, was for Antonio Gil, otherwise known as the 'Gauchito' – the little cowboy. Gauchito Gil, who lived in the nineteenth century, was a deserter from the army who spent several years on the run, sheltered by the people of the province of Corrientes in north-east Argentina. According to popular belief, he was something of a Robin Hood figure, becoming legendary by looking after the needs of the poor until he was eventually captured and hanged. This raised his status to that of a martyr and secured his place as an idol of devotion among the Argentine people. To this day, with a surprisingly Catholic fervour, people worship their hero in the same way they might worship Jesus or the Virgin Mary. They place offerings in small shrines, ask for favours and blessings, and give thanks for miracles received. I would see these shrines all over Argentina, their distinctive red flags a reference to the red poncho that the Gauchito once wore.

I had been planning to cycle straight through Bariloche, having already spent time there, but as we entered town Diego invited me to join him and the group for a late lunch. Naturally this was not to be refused. I followed them back to their hostel and installed myself at the long wooden table, accepting glasses of beer and plates of food as they came my way. Mariano was sitting across the table from me. Buzzing around in my head were a thousand questions that I wanted to ask him, although my Spanish was still at the rudimentary stage and I was shy. He sensed my interest. After lunch he brought his photo album from the van and we sat together to look at it.

His photographs were excellent. Not only did he have images of his own bike in incredible landscapes all over the world, he also had a collection of candid shots of bicycles at work, carting all manner of unlikely loads. Having long been convinced of the capabilities of the humble bicycle, I was nevertheless astounded by the feats of balance and strength I saw in that album: furniture, stacks of bricks, assorted animals and families of six clung precariously to rickety rickshaws, clapped-out two-wheelers and treacherous-looking trailers. I dug into my handlebar bag and extracted a photo. It was a flattering shot of the rickshaw that I rode in London, on which I had earned the money to get to Argentina.

It was becoming obvious that Mariano and I had a few interests in common and I cursed the language barrier that made our conversation so stilted. But with the help of a dictionary and a good deal of mime, I managed to describe my job for him: the hectic hustle of a Saturday night in Soho, the endless diversity of my passengers, the fun, the freedom, the tips and the tales. Each night was an adventure in itself, comprised of random and unexpected events, and apart from the bellicose black-cabbies – who seemed to have a special hatred for us – our presence on the streets was well received. We provided more than a taxi service; I had given endless directions, rescued countless lost people from dodgy backstreets, called ambulances for injuries and delivered people safely to their doors when they were too drunk to get home alone. There was satisfaction in that, a sense of money well earned – and it was the first job that had really seemed to fit me.

But I didn't want to speak about myself. I wanted to know more about Mariano and the logistics of his mammoth voyages. He showed me pictures of his kit and pages from his logbooks, and admitted that at times he didn't sleep very much when he had his mind set on getting somewhere. Often, he told me, he got up at three in the morning and cycled until after dark. He was by far the toughest, most focused man I had ever met but what impressed me most was that, despite all his achievements, he was not the slightest bit boastful or proud. In fact, he came across as unduly modest, as though he truly considered his personal best to be not good enough. The contrast between his attitude and that of José, my previous cycling partner, was so marked as to be laughable. I looked at the iron-man sitting across the table from me, quietly denying his considerable abilities, and I thought of José's arrogant belief in his own heroism. I giggled to myself quietly and said nothing. It was beyond my ability to explain it in Spanish.

By a stroke of luck, Mariano was due to give a slideshow at the hostel the following evening. It wasn't too difficult to decide to stay another day in the convivial atmosphere of 'Aventura'. It felt more like a home than a hostel and Anna, the Dutch owner, ran it as though all the guests were members of her own family. It was so relaxed that I spent most of the next day sitting at the polished wood table, talking to the other guests and saying goodbye to the cyclists, who were headed back to Buenos Aires.

In fact, sitting still seemed like quite a good idea as my right knee, which had never given me problems before, had become painful. The whole day I managed to venture only as far as the edge of the lake, immersing my legs in the icy water to lessen any swelling and hoping it was nothing serious. Previously my body had seemed infinitely robust, but now, with pain shooting up my thigh, I began to feel fragile and vulnerable. It was a bit worrying. This whole journey counted on my physical well-being; if my body failed me I would be stuck at Anna's table for who-knew-how-long, living vicariously on the stories of other cyclists and growing fatter on their titbits. It wasn't the worst fate imaginable, but I didn't think it would suit me for long.

When I returned to the hostel, friends and relatives of Mariano and Anna had already begun to arrive for the party. Many of them knew each other and as the wine began to flow the cosy kitchen filled with laughter. I was drawn into the circle of conversation as though I had always lived there. In Argentina, this form of positive energy is known as 'buena onda' – good vibe – and it grew until the party was fairly buzzing with it. We ate homemade pizza, poured apparently endless wine and eventually sprawled on the floor to see the slides.

Mariano is a man of few words, but his photos speak volumes. For half an hour of kaleidoscopic colour we entered his world, sharing briefly his love of adventure, glimpsing his determination and sensing the satisfaction that comes with solitude. Through infinitely varied landscapes and cultures we travelled with him around the globe, and for the first time I saw pictures of deepest Patagonia, that vast and little-populated wilderness that stretches south towards Antarctica like an arrow pointing to the South Pole. Perhaps it was something to do with the wine, but I found that my heart was thumping loudly with excitement. Suddenly, I wanted to go there too.

And so it was that with dreams of intrepid, world-encircling bicycle journeys filling my head, I cycled south the next day, so full of enthusiasm and inspiration that climbing the hill out of town seemed entirely effortless. I felt euphoric; meeting Mariano had confirmed that I was perfectly on track. I was not, by going on holiday for six months, escaping reality, but seeking it, testing my own abilities and limits through the mirror of the world, exactly as my brother had tried to teach me.

All through my teen years Dan had encouraged me to look for new experiences. 'Leave home. Move cities. Go travelling. Do *something*,' he had said. 'There's so much out there for you.' He had been right, of course, but I wasn't ready then. Now, there was no space left for doubts. I knew where I was going and why I was going there; I no longer needed to justify it to myself.

With the *buena onda* propelling me forth, assisted by a brisk tailwind, I flew along the road with the minimum of effort. Around me, the landscape opened up into a giant basin of golden grasses and gnarled trees. The surrounding peaks looked geologically young and pale rivers of scree poured down the sides of the mountains as though some interior force had recently been on the move. Above me, the sky was bright, but the wind was moving clouds at a dramatic pace. Dark, ever-shifting shadows flickered across the land, and sudden spotlights of afternoon sun were like the work of a lighting director gone mad.

The wild atmosphere of the landscape and the weather fitted perfectly with my mood, but my knee, unfortunately, was not collaborating. It hurt, damn it. I was wearing stretchy bandages for support and warmth, and stopped periodically to massage around the kneecap, but after only fifty kilometres I was beginning to wonder how much more I could take. Temporary relief came in the form of a mammoth descent that wound slowly down to a river valley far below. I slung my right leg over a front pannier and freewheeled all the way.

At the bottom, seemingly in the middle of nowhere, was a checkpoint. A portly policeman was standing in the middle of the road, enjoying the sun with his eyes half closed. He was middle-aged, impeccably dressed and he shook himself to attention as I rolled into sight. He waved me to a stop on the hard shoulder and walked over with a swagger. His boots scrunched on the gravel and he smoothed his greasy 1950s hairstyle with his palms. He looked past me up the road and I knew what he was going to say.

'¿Andás solita?' he asked. I grinned, nodding. He took off his dark glasses like a movie-star gangster, and looked me in the eyes. 'Why señorita,' he said in a flirtatious voice, 'what a beautiful smile you have.' He matched it with a mischievous one of his own, revealing a single gold tooth in a row of nicotine-stained stumps.

I hadn't anticipated that. I handed him my passport and giggled nervously; this seemed like highly irregular behaviour for a policeman. He glanced fleetingly at my details and fixed me with another penetrating stare. 'Where will you be staying the night?' he wanted to know.

'Oh, El Bolson for certain,' I lied. Actually, I had been hoping to camp next to the river, but it appeared that the police hut stood on the only patch of riverbank accessible from the road.

'That's a long way,' he said. 'You must be very strong.' He leered meaningfully at my thighs.

'Yes,' I said, taking my passport back, 'I am. Goodbye.' And with a show of strength that belied the stabbing pain in my knee, I started the long climb out of the valley. At the first corner I looked back. He was watching me go, still smiling, the sun glinting off his one gold tooth.

I didn't make it anywhere near El Bolson that day. Instead, I camped next to a tiny stream and numbed my sore knee in the icy water. It was soothing, but made no real improvement. The way onwards the next morning was immediately uphill and the joint in question was soon throbbing under the strain. I began to intersperse bouts of cycling with stiff-legged walking. I even considered hitchhiking but it was such a lovely day that it seemed a shame to whiz past the fantastic landscape in the cab of a truck. When the road flattened out again I made some experiments in one-legged pedalling.

The logistics of this took my mind off the discomfort for a while. The main problem was where to put my bad leg to keep it out of the way of the revolving empty pedal. Tucking it up behind me and hooking it over my rear pannier strained the joint, while balancing it on the front pannier made steering difficult. I tried resting my foot in front of me on my handlebar bag but that seemed needlessly dangerous, given that I was already wobbling all over the road with my one-sided exertions. In the end, after narrowly escaping plummeting off the edge of the road to considerable injury, I resigned myself to the sensible but more uncomfortable method of holding the offending limb out to one side, adding to my list of pains with cramp of the buttocks.

I arrived at the outskirts of El Bolson in the early afternoon and stopped at a pharmacy to buy some painkillers. Leaving the shop, I was greeted by three old men who were relaxing with their shirts off in the shadow of a tree. Two of them were overweight in the way that many Argentine men are, not flabby but big all over with turgid stomachs and firm brown skin. In contrast, the third bloke was as pale and skinny as a crack addict. They were drinking *mate*, a delicious South American tea, and with typical Argentine generosity they invited me to drink with them.

They smiled up at me as I took the cup. After one blisteringly hot mouthful from the silver straw I understood why they were all missing teeth; just a single sip of the highly sweetened brew would have been enough to send any diabetic into an instant coma. But it was very refreshing and I drank it down as fast as my burning lips would let me. Then I handed the cup back with a grateful '*Gracias*' and returned to the blinding sun, leaving them and their tombstone grins in the little pocket of shade.

I had never thought that I would encounter a national drink more ubiquitous than the British cup of tea. But the people of Argentina, it seems, drink more *mate* per day than the English can drink tea in a year. On street corners, on front-door stoops, in parks and in millions of homes, *mate* is slurped mouthful by scalding mouthful – all day, every day. Old guys playing dominoes sit and sip together. Families on long train journeys pass *mate* endlessly. Couples picnicking in parks, lonesome truckers behind the wheel, policemen in their cop cars and street sweepers on their lunch break: all can be seen with a thermos of hot water, a bag of *yerba* (tea), a *mate* (cup) and a *bombilla* (a slim silver straw). Even the delinquent youth, who hang out in scowling packs, partake of this truly Argentine phenomenon. The passing of *mate* between family members is a ritual of bonding, forming a tight, apparently closed circle.

Handed to a stranger, however, *mate* becomes a gesture of welcome, a token of friendship, a social leveller.

It comes as no surprise that it tastes so good.

Cycling into the centre of El Bolson was like going back in time. Everywhere I looked there were hippies of every description: ageing grey-haired flower-children from the seventies; thirty-something, child-toting, new-age traveller types; dark-eyed, new-generation vagabonds, covered in tattoos and piercings. Never before had I seen so many bead-wearing, bracelet-jangling, sari-clad, dreadlocked, bearded, or sandalled people gathered together in one place. Spirited music was belting forth from a live band in the middle of shady Plaza Pagano and people were lying dreamily on the grass, staring up at the sky or playing with their barefooted children. It was like a miniature South American Woodstock.

Surrounding the plaza, the thrice-weekly artisan fair was in full swing. Locals and travellers alike had set up their stalls and rolled out their blankets to display and sell an enormous and diverse array of goods, anything a rumbling tum or a magpie eye could desire. There were gourds for drinking *mate*, carved wooden animals, silver necklaces, leather bracelets and handmade gnomes – the characters said to inhabit the forests of Patagonia. There was no shortage of hippy paraphernalia either: pipes for smoking weed, rainbow-coloured headbands, strings of beads, dream-catchers and naff tie-dyed T-shirts. Multicoloured jars of jams and pickles were made with local fruit and delicious smells wafted from the numerous stalls selling vegetarian food. I tethered my bike and wandered through the crowd, feeling strangely modern and urban with my baggy shorts and cycle shoes. Beautiful youths caught my eye as I passed, but my mind was on other things. I ate half a dozen *empanadas*, had another couple for good measure and went in search of dinner.

I was wary of cycling anywhere while drugs masked the pain of my injured knee. Instead, I installed myself in a campsite on the edge of town and stayed for two nights. I felt frustrated at not being able to apply my enthusiasm to some sort of physical action and spent most of the time tentatively bending the offending joint to see if the pain had gone away. It hadn't. I wondered what it meant for the future of the trip. Would I be stuck for ever in El Bolson? Would I end up wearing a sari and spawning dark-eyed children with some dreadlocked hippy? It was a worrying thought and I tried to divert myself with the laborious task of sampling every flavour of ice-cream available at the shop on the plaza. It certainly took my mind off the pain, but despite my best efforts the endless choices eventually defeated me. Sore knee or not, for fear of an impending heart attack I was forced to leave town.

6

In Praise of Cakes and Duct Tape

Travelling ever further south, on a virtually traffic-less gravel road, I began to get a hint of the sort of solitude glimpsed in Mariano's photos. The really empty parts of Patagonia were still a long way off, but even here, with the tourist season over, I seemed to have the landscape and sun almost all to myself. The peaks visible to the west were snow-covered and majestic, the plains around me huge below the magnificent spread of the sky. Energised by being on the move again, I forgot about my ailing joint, and the euphoria of motion acted as a natural painkiller.

I arrived at Los Alerces National Park at dusk. At the park office, despite the swiftly fading light, the enthusiastic ranger gave me a twenty-minute introductory speech. She spoke slowly and clearly, determined that I should get the full benefit of her expertise. The park, she told me, is named after the *alerce*, the species of Patagonian cypress that it protects. Some of these giants are estimated to be around 4000 years old and measure up to four metres in diameter. The water in the lakes and rivers is 100 per cent pure, she continued, perfectly safe to drink, and visitors must avoid contaminating it with soaps and detergents. I was impressed. I would be more than careful,

I promised; employing complete avoidance tactics, I would simply not wash.

I handed over the twelve pesos it cost to enter the park, rolled down the track to the edge of a lake and set about the onerous task of trying to insert tent pegs into mercilessly rocky ground. It was completely dark and the batteries in my torch were low. It was cold. I was knackered. The bloody pegs would not go in. I took off one shoe to use as a mallet, but it wasn't heavy enough. Went to find a suitable rock. Tripped over a suitable rock. Rubbed my sore knee, which had taken the weight of the fall, cursed, and picked up the tripper-upper. It was curiously light for its size. I brought it closer to my face, into the weakening yellow beam of torchlight.

It was not a rock. It was a cowpat.

Fortunately, being the only camper there allowed me the freedom to vent my frustration in a manner that could have been deemed antisocial had there been any small children present. I will not repeat the words that were hurled after the cowpat as I biffed it into the bushes, nor will I go into detail about how the tent pegs finally found themselves embedded up to the neck in apparently solid rock. Suffice it to say that there are times when anger can be a surprisingly productive force.

A good night's sleep improved my mood tenfold. The campsite, when I finally saw it by the light of day, was wonderful. My tent was perched above a tiny rocky beach and the lake was silver in the slanting morning sun. I clambered out of the tent, blew clouds into the chill air and looked for the toilet. There wasn't one. That, I thought, was a bit strange. It's true that the campsite was free – the park entrance fee entitled me to the use of several such spots – but I hadn't expected there to be no facilities whatsoever.

Now don't get me wrong, it's not that I have a problem with relieving myself in the open. On the contrary, I quite enjoy it. After many years of practice, being discreet with my offerings and taking my toilet paper with me is no hardship. But this is not the case for everyone, and I tried to imagine the campsite at the height of summer, with fifty or so people pooing in the scant bushes a mere twenty metres from the lake and leaving toilet paper to blow all over the park. It was not a happy thought. I wondered how the rangers expected the water to remain pristine when there was no system for keeping human waste out of it. The potential for spreading disease seemed significant and I thought that in the face of the possible health risk, the digging of a long-drop would be a small but worthwhile investment. As it was, I made my way as far from the lake as possible to execute my morning evacuations.

It took a whole day to travel the fifty kilometres from one end of the park to the other. The road, rollercoastering steeply beside the lake, was of rocks the size of apples. They threw me off balance while riding, bruised my ankles while pushing and impeded progress greatly as I hauled Vagabunda up the hills. My sore knee was complaining again and I felt horribly weak as I struggled to make headway.

The sensation of feebleness took me back to my first proper mountain-bike ride. I had ridden bicycles since the age of six, but it wasn't until I was about eighteen that the thrill-factor and adventure potential of off-road tracks had begun to appeal. I had only a $200-bike at the time, with limited braking power and a small sticker on the frame warning against serious off-road action, but I planned to get a purpose-built machine just as soon as I had the money. Until then, Dan told me, he could show me a couple of tracks around Wellington that he had cycled with his mates. Nothing too serious, of course – we'd start with an easy afternoon circuit to Red Rocks beach.

I should have known better. I should have known that my brother's interpretation of 'beginner's track' would bear no resemblance to mine, but with blind faith, and a devotion practised since birth, I followed him out of the driveway on my suspension-less boneshaker, oblivious to the terrors ahead.

We began with an ascent of Brooklyn hill. It was all on the tarmac, but steep enough for a beginner's thighs and by the time we reached the wind turbine at the top I was ready to call it a day. But we'd only just begun, according to Dan, and he pointed out a considerably higher peak, several kilometres further on.

'Don't worry,' he reassured me, 'it's all downhill from there.'

And downhill it was. *Straight* downhill, at a gradient that I had previously experienced only on waterslides and toboggans steered by my father. Now *I* was supposed to be in control, but the hunk of steel beneath me was bucking like a bronco and I had no idea how to take command. I skittered, skidded and stumbled down that damn hill, assisted rather too readily by the force of gravity, and conjured every evil curse I could think of to hurl at my sibling. Wisely, he was already far ahead and well out of earshot. I was a wreck by the time we reached the beach, quaking with fear and exhaustion, tongue-tied with fury and almost ready to throw my bike into the sea. I followed Dan back around the coast in steely silence.

Five or six weary and teary hours after we had started we finally creaked back into the driveway. I lay on the concrete, totally spent, and told Dan exactly what I thought of his 'beginner's track'. He listened impassively to my complaints, let me finish and nodded as though he completely agreed.

'I bet you're pretty pleased with yourself that you did it though, eh?'

I was pretty pleased with myself when I reached the end of Los Alerces National Park and pulled into a deserted campsite. The wind was roaring towards me off the choppy lake. High above, the grey clouds bustled impatiently south like irritable commuters. Around the water, wooded hills rose like stadium seats, turning the small beach on which I stood into a stage. I sang a few bars of a favourite song, but the words were whipped away on a gust of air. So I stood in silence, buffeted by the bullying winds, upstaged by nature performing her daily drama.

The wind was still blowing its best the following morning, but it was in my favour as I continued south. After the rocky park road, the asphalt felt frictionless. There was no other traffic and I bowled along past boggy fields of lush grasses with the greatest of ease. A road sign that had once said '*fin de camino sinuoso*' – end of winding road – had been changed by some wag to say '*fin de camino sin osos*' – end of road without bears. It was a lame gag, but I laughed out loud. As my first joke in Spanish it seemed oddly profound.

I spotted my first-ever armadillo. Hunched defensively beneath armour plating, twitching a triangular snout, he crossed the road ahead of me. He was hairier than expected, but just as comical. Startled by my presence, he scuttled off into the undergrowth and the waving tops of the grasses described his rustling path. Then he reappeared briefly, took a last look my way and plunged out of view over a small hillock. I also saw a Patagonian skunk on the road that morning, but as it was dead as a dodo and squashed as a sauvignon grape it hardly counted as a wildlife sighting.

It was not just the wind and my good mood that were driving me onwards. The thought of tea and hot scones in the small Welsh town of Trevelin spurred my legs to whirr round at uncharacteristic speed. I knew I was getting close when, zooming recklessly down a hill, virtually able to smell the hot waft of baking ahead, I spied a hard-at-work Gaelic gaucho on his horse. Red-haired, freckled and considerably sunburnt, he nevertheless looked entirely at home against the backdrop of stony fields and dazzling blue sky.

It was more than the sheep-farming potential that brought the Welsh to Argentina in the mid-nineteenth century. With their traditions endangered by the encroachment of English culture, a small group of Welsh nationalists chose to leave the lush green paddocks of their homeland in search of a place where their lifestyle would be respected. In order to keep their language alive they suffered endless adversity – insufficient food and water, lack of irrigation, bad harvests and floods – but the first tiny coastal community survived, flourished and spread. Retaining their cultural identity until today, little pockets of Welsh can now be found all over southern Argentina.

I arrived in Trevelin's deserted main street at noon, passed the Spanish-Welsh bilingual school, and headed straight to 'Nain Maggie', a teashop I had read about that promised an unforgettable afternoon-tea experience. But when I got there, the cupboard was bare; at least, Maggie's was closed, to my bitter disappointment. A note on the door said that it opened at five o'clock each evening and a passing local told me I would have to wait until 'teatime'. But, I thought, *any time* is teatime. Especially about midday after cycling all morning. I peered in through the window at the upside-down chairs on the tables and sighed.

My knee ached from such enthusiastic exertions. Actually, it didn't just ache. It bloody well hurt. Cakes or no cakes, it was definitely time for a lunch stop. There were still a few crumpled consumables in my panniers that had been bouncing about since El Bolson, and the town plaza was invitingly shady. I cycled over to a park bench.

It was as I was dismounting that I heard the ominous cracking noise. Then my seat went all wonky. Oh dear. I looked underneath. One of the rails had snapped. Dear oh dear. Without a functioning seat on my bicycle it would be very difficult to go anywhere. I cursed and kicked the bench.

'Aaaaaarrrrgggghhhh! Sod it!' Maybe it wasn't such a good idea to use my bad leg for vigorous displays of temper. I collapsed onto the bench and rubbed my throbbing knee. I was angry. My Specialized bike seat was only two months old and it had cost a serious amount of cash. It claimed to have titanium rails, which ought to have been virtually bombproof, and I failed to see how I could have broken the seat just by sitting on it. I hadn't eaten that much ice-cream.

The day seemed to be conspiring against me. I ate lunch furiously, wondering where to find a bike shop that would sell me a replacement seat. Despite the now apparent fault, the seat was of excellent design, with a cut-away centre to reduce pressure on one's delicate parts. It was doubtful that I would find anything to match it outside of a big city. I finished my last banana, made some temporary repairs with duct tape and cycled on in a lopsided sort of way to Esquel. What with my sore knee, my broken seat and a dire lack of cake, the short twenty-five-kilometre ride took a horribly long and painful time.

Esquel cheered me up. As towns go, it wasn't particularly pretty, but it had an atmosphere that some of the towns I had visited so far had lost: it felt *real*. Unlike Bariloche, with its perfect Swiss-style wooden buildings and hundreds of tourist-luring souvenir and chocolate shops, or El Bolson, with its transient, gotta-be-alternative-to-fit-in crowd, Esquel was full of locals.

They were going about their daily business as though the tourist trade didn't exist.

On every corner, large groups of teenagers were hanging out together, utterly preoccupied with themselves in that endearing way that teenagers have. The girls, dressed in jeans so tight they could have been born with them, were flicking their long black hair. The boys were standing with studied nonchalance, trying to catch glimpses of themselves and their perfectly gelled hair in shop windows. Dozens of them were buzzing up and down on motor scooters, and a large number of them were standing astride gleaming bicycles. Cycling actually seemed to be the preferred way of getting around in Esquel, and that made it even more appealing.

At Home of the Backpacker, which was a comfy little back garden in a residential street, I put my tent in a shady spot. Then I walked the two blocks back into the centre, determined to find cake. In fact, finding cake in Argentina is not normally a difficult task. Although the thought of a real scone with jam and cream had made my mouth water in Trevelin, I would have to say that Argentina's traditional bakery goods rival anything from the British Isles. Known as *facturas*, these little two-bite pastries come in endless shapes and flavours. The most basic of these is the *media luna* – half moon – which is like a small croissant but a bit sweeter, and not so much flaky as doughy. The same recipe is used to make hundreds of variations on the theme. Some contain fruit, some quince jam and many are stuffed full of Argentina's deadliest dessert: *dulce de leche*.

Dulce de leche is so addictive it should come with a health warning. This tantalising taste-bud teaser is good for the soul but not for the arteries, being made of nothing more than milk and sugar boiled together until they form a thick and irresistible brown gloop. It can be eaten with virtually anything: on toast at breakfast, on ice-cream, on fruit salad, in *facturas* and on cheese sandwiches (my own invention). It's delicious any which way but especially, an Argentine friend once told me, licked from a finger dipped illicitly into the tub in the middle of the night when everyone else is asleep.

Wandering the pubescent-packed streets of Esquel, I soon located a bakery and followed my nose inside to the mind-bending array of edible treats. *Facturas* are so small and so delicious that it is impossible to stop at just one. I was capable of managing six at a time and, for economy's sake, I usually bought a dozen.

Happy again, mouth stuffed full of sweet dough, I bumbled about the town centre, pleasingly invisible to the gathered youth. As a member of the 'older generation', I drew no attention, which made it that much easier to observe the behaviour of the common teenage Argentine in its natural habitat.

Like many people, one of the main reasons I travel is to see and learn about other cultures, not through the distorting filter of television or books or stereotypical hearsay, but through actual experience and interaction. Past experience as a back-packer, however, has taught me that it is all too easy to end up on the well-beaten tourist trail, sleeping in accommodation with other tourists, eating in tourist restaurants, taking tourist excursions and shopping in tourist shops. This can be very nice if all you desire is a week-long, stress-relieving break from work, but if you're looking for something a little less super-ficial, holidaying in the places where everyone else holidays can be quite frustrating. On the teeming streets of tourist towns, I had always found it impossible to see a culture as it really is.

For me, one of the most compelling motives for travelling by bicycle is that with map in hand and the freedom to go anywhere I like, I often end up in places where the locals don't deal with tourists on a large scale. This leads to all sorts of curious and unexpected exchanges with people for whom a visitor can still be something of a novelty. Of course, the flip-side of this is to find myself in a place so remote or unfrequented by strangers that I end up being the day's entertainment, treated with far too much interest, like a visiting royal. And this leads me to wonder whether I should be there at all; whether, by exhibiting my independence and economic freedom, I am inadvertently having an impact on how other people view their own lives. It's an ongoing dilemma.

So Esquel was perfect. Like many Argentine towns, it was quite western in atmosphere, and as I didn't stand out as being too different from the locals it wasn't difficult to blend in with the crowd. There were virtually no other tourists, making it possible to observe unadulterated Argentine street-life from close quarters.

Teens flirted, elderly folk doddered along in last century's fashions, mums pushed prams full of shopping while their kids trailed behind, and middle-aged men with beer bellies argued about football. The shops were full of the ordinary necessities of a not particularly rich town: cheap food, cheap clothes, cheap shoes, tools, kitchenware, washing machines and books. Hmm . . . books. I pushed open the door of the *librería* and went in.

Inside the small and cosy space, dozens of people of all ages were browsing and reading. It was jam-packed in there. For a working-class town, the enthusiasm for all things wordy was hearteningly alive and well. I browsed the shelves for a while, but after translating the blurbs of several books it was obvious that my Spanish needed a bit more work before I committed to any purchases. I returned empty-handed to the street and contented myself by reading the readily understood graffiti that were painted all over town.

Bold slogans of 'No to the Mine' and 'No is No' and 'Life is Worth More Than Gold' aroused my curiosity, and when I got back to the campsite an old leaflet that was pinned to the wall in the kitchen explained everything. Produced by a residents' association the previous year, the flyer called for locals to band together and oppose the Canadian mining company that planned to extract gold from the surrounding countryside. Meridian Gold Corp, said the leaflet, was attempting to sway the locals in favour of the mining by offering 300 jobs to the residents of Esquel (where there was considerable unemployment) and by promising to lay asphalt in those streets that were still unpaved (about half of them).

The residents' association was not convinced. The benefits of the project, they argued, would not outweigh the negatives. Not only would their considerably beautiful countryside be destroyed by the mining, and the contamination of their water supply and nearby Los Alerces National Park become a strong possibility, but the profits of the project would then be whisked out of the country and into the pockets of rich and greedy foreigners. By way of reactionary public meetings, united opposition and blunt refusal to work in the mine, the people of Esquel could save their town from exploitation and destruction.

And that is exactly what they did. In March of 2003, in a classic case of David versus Goliath, eighty per cent of Esquel's population voted a resounding 'NO!' to the proposed project, causing the mining to be indefinitely suspended. Until Meridian can assure Esquel's 30,000 residents that environmental catastrophe can be avoided, the project is at a standstill.

The kitchen of Home of the Backpacker was not particularly homely, but it did provide me with electric light long after dark. I sat at the table with tea and *facturas*, and tackled the problem of my broken seat. With the help of some thick wire, a pair of pliers and a roll of duct tape, I intended to make a sturdy replacement for the snapped rail.

Armed with a reel of super strong, stick-an-elephant-to-the-ceiling indestructible duct tape, I think I could probably fix just about anything. It has helped me out of difficulties so many times over the years that I have developed a deep admiration and respect for it; an affection so profound that it verges on idolatry. I have used it to splint snapped pannier-racks; mend tears in tyres; patch holes in clothes, shoes, tents and sleeping bags; repair disintegrating maps; hold dressings to wounds; attach lights to handlebars; protect precious packages against the wear and tear of the postal system; save ball-bearings from getting lost while dismantling hubs; re-cover overused phrase books and hold sore kneecaps in place when in need of support. The more I use it, the more uses I find for it and my fixation with the stuff has reached the point where I rarely leave the house without it – if not a whole hefty roll then at least a handy revolution or two wrapped around a short length of nylon cord. Cycling or walking, working or travelling, equipped with a spool of this invaluable sticky-stuff, I feel invincible.

By the time I had finished my task at the kitchen table, my bicycle seat was stronger than when it was new. I was having another cup of tea to celebrate, and admiring my handiwork, when a young backpacker from Spain came in. He seemed friendly enough and keen to talk, but unfortunately I couldn't understand a single word he said. I had thought I was making some sort of progress with my Spanish – if not with speaking it then at least in deciphering what people said to me – but trying to understand the mumbled consonants of this Andalucian was like trying to decode a language from another galaxy. The characteristically accented and clearly enunciated Spanish of

Argentina is so learner-friendly that 'real' Spanish, especially from the south of Spain, sounded to my beginner's ear like gobbledegook. I nodded and smiled and made lots of politely affirmative noises as he, presumably, described his travels to me, but it was something of a relief when he finally got tired of the sound of his own voice and went to bed.

I had a chance to develop my language skills the next day when two other cyclists turned up, both about my age and on holiday from Buenos Aires. Antonio and Ulices had both recently quit their jobs (life-saving and building, respectively). Having embarked upon their cycle trip while they decided what to do next, they were taking the relaxed approach to it. Their daily maximum was about thirty kilometres and they had just rolled in from Trevelin, where they had stayed for two days. I asked them if they had eaten scones there, but they hadn't; I soon discovered they were Argentine to the core and as such were far more partial to *mate* and *facturas*.

A moment after they arrived they had the kettle on the stove and within a few minutes we were companionably passing a sweet brew around and chin-wagging about the various places we had cycled through. As with so many *porteños*, they put me entirely at ease, and when they laughed at my grammatical mistakes it was in an affectionate, big-brotherly sort of way. They kindly displayed for me their own proficiency with English (limited) and assured me that I was doing okay.

We discussed our plans. They already liked Esquel, they told me, and as they had no particular destination and no real time-frame for their trip, they were thinking of staying for a while. Maybe even to look for work. I could understand the appeal of that, and with my knee still painful it was almost tempting to stay with them. But Mariano's photos were vivid in my mind; I was thinking about ending the first leg of my journey, taking a bus to Patagonia's wildest and windiest lower reaches, and cycling to the end of the continent. Antonio and Ulices were all for it.

'Go,' they said. 'It's beautiful down there. Do it now while the weather's still in your favour.' It was exactly the advice my brother would have given, and no further encouragement was necessary. Within half an hour I was back from the bus station, ticket to El Calafate in hand, ready for a celebratory round of *mate* and *facturas*.

There was a smell of snow in the air the following morning. As I poked my nose outside to assess the state of the weather, which was cold and damp, my attention was diverted by something much more calamitous than dropping temperatures: the zipper on my trusty Macpac tent wouldn't move. I wrestled with it. It didn't budge one bit. After years of use, and with far too much sand and grit grinding away at it every time it was zipped up, it had become harder and harder to close over the last weeks. Now it had given up altogether. It seemed like a bad omen. I was leaving that very night on the thousand-kilometre bus journey to southern Argentina, and the one thing I would need most of all in that distant land of unpredictable weather was a functioning tent.

After some worried deliberation about the best course of action, and a consultation with Antonio and Ulices, I decided that Velcro was the answer. I bought a long length of it at a local department store and spent the day sitting at the kitchen table, tent spread across lap, needle and thread in hand and tongue sticking from side of mouth in acute concentration as I sewed. Luckily for me, both the boys had repairs to make to their panniers as well, so we passed the hours together inside, sharing histories and advice, drinking *mate* and eating cake. In fact, we developed such a friendship over those few short hours that when I suddenly transformed into a damsel in distress at the possibility of missing my bus, they leapt on their bikes and escorted me to the station at a galloping pace like gallant knights on silver steeds.

The sun was going down as we cycled helter-skelter down the main street, the oblique angle of the light illuminating the town in a stunning manner. Golden rays slanted beneath moody black clouds. Wet roofs shone. At the northern end of town steep hills rose, painted with the reds, ochres and greys of mineral-rich earth. It was not difficult to believe that there was gold to be found in Esquel.

We were just in time. With the help of some cardboard boxes from the supermarket, and a few more metres of duct tape, we hastily wrapped up the delicate back end of my bike so that it wouldn't be destroyed in transit. I took off the pedals and turned the handlebars to make it as slim-line as possible, and looked expectantly at the baggage handlers. They were stressed out, and sweaty.

To my dismay, the portly porter in charge took one look at my crudely covered rear end, shook his head in disgust and turned away. His carton-stacking counterpart, who looked like he might be one cake short of a tea break, took his lead from the boss. After a theatrical show of shoulder shrugging, head shaking and palm raising in a 'what-can-we-do?' sort of way, he went back to loading the bags.

'Um, the man in the ticket office told me there would be no problems,' I said to the boss. 'And I've paid extra for the bike. Isn't there a little space for it somewhere?' He shrugged, made a face that clearly indicated his disdain and continued to ignore me.

I felt ready to cry. Although the prospect of being stuck in Esquel with my two cycling companions was not so bad, the possibility of not reaching deepest Patagonia just because some bus porter had got out of bed on the wrong side made me most upset. I stood with my lower lip trembling while Antonio put his arm around my shoulders and told me to be patient. He chatted with the porters in a relaxed way, commiserating with them about the difficulty of their job and telling them how his own bike had once travelled upstairs in the bus with three seats all to itself. As he spoke, their attitudes softened a little and I wondered what I would have done without him to lend his *porteño* charm.

Eventually, when everyone else was on the bus, their bags stored safely in the hold and their relatives waving to them from the platform, the baggage handlers turned to me. Yes, they conceded reluctantly, perhaps there was just enough space for the bike. They jammed it in with some ominous graunching noises and an unnecessary amount of brute force, but I was so relieved that I tipped them anyway. The less intelligent one turned suddenly friendly. He flashed me his best smile, gave me a double thumbs-up and made exaggerated brow-mopping gestures of relief, as if together we had just survived some arduous ordeal. But I forgave him; I was going to the Far South, and Vagabunda was going with me.

I bid a heartfelt farewell to my two faithful friends, skipped onto the bus with a gargantuan grin and waved gratefully to them from the top-deck window as we pulled out of the station and on to the darkened road east. With my legs tucked up under me, I watched the landscape zipping past outside and mused on Antonio's parting words.

'It was a pleasure to meet you,' he had said gently, as he hugged me goodbye. 'You have such a *buena onda*.'

The night sky was full of stars and I could swear that they were winking at me.

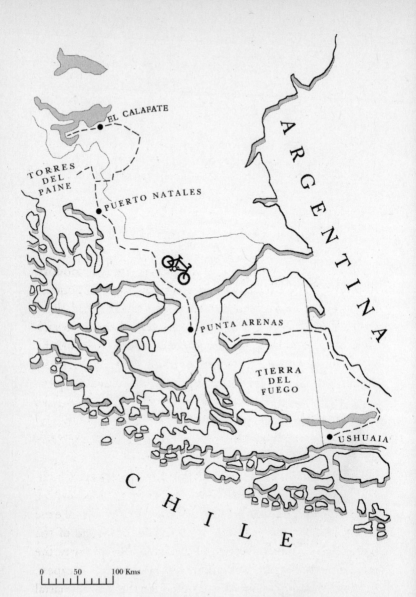

Argentine and Chilean Patagonia, that far-flung, little populated land where the incessant wind can be a cyclist's best friend or worst enemy.

7

Pancakes in the Rain

I awoke at dawn as the bus was pulling into Comodoro Rivadavia, a small and charmless oil-drilling town that cowers on the wind-lashed Atlantic coast. Far from the bustling holiday trade of Argentina's lake district, Comodoro displays no such poise or polish. In fact, presumably in an attempt to avoid the forced jollity of the tourist towns, the residents have cleverly disguised their own – by decorating it liberally with dirty plastic bags and broken glass – as a supermarket parking lot. I noticed as I cycled around the grubby streets that the disguise seemed to be doing a fine job of deterring visitors; the only foreigners in evidence were those who had got off the bus with me and were drearily waiting in the cafés for the next connection out.

I had no intention of lingering. That evening I was catching another bus, the second in a series of three that would take me the long and circuitous route to El Calafate. Because of the rocky, bus-unfriendly surface of the fabled Route Forty, the most direct way south was not the quickest, nor the cheapest. In the name of economy I had opted for the longer coastal road, which involved a day's layover in Comodoro. I left my bags in the office of the bus company and headed into town on my bike in search of a stiff cup of tea.

I had been led to believe, by the wide-eyed youth who sat beside me on the bus, that Comodoro was a manic metropolis: much bigger and brasher, dirtier and more dangerous than peaceful Esquel. He was studying, he told me, on the coast, but would be heading back to the hills just as soon as he had graduated. The bright lights and crowded streets of the big city were not for him. It was something of a surprise, therefore, after imagining Buenos Aires-like urban sprawl, to find myself at the beach mere minutes after leaving the bus station. I had already cycled the entire one-kilometre length of the tiny town centre.

The sun was rising from the sea in a glorious orange extravaganza, but the effect was marred slightly by the intimidating razor-wire fence of the local naval authority, the terse 'No Entry' signs, the out-of-service public toilet on the beach, and the stench of stale pee. I climbed over a barbed wire barrier to the only patch of grass in town, cleared a space among the cigarette butts, broken glass and dog turds, and sat down to watch the day break.

By the time the sun had finished hauling itself above the horizon the air was already hot. Around me the assorted smells were becoming unbearable as they simmered in the sunshine, and I was prickling with sweat. I felt acutely mucky. For some reason, sitting still for long hours in the unnaturally rarefied air of a bus or plane always makes me feel far more in need of a shower than cycling 100 hot and dusty kilometres does. I found a café and doused myself as well as I could in the pristine bathroom, guiltily leaving a collection of indelible greasy smudges on the previously gleaming marble.

I lingered as long as possible over my four cups of tea and five slices of toast, but it was still only nine o'clock in the morning when the waitress cleared the table. The remaining hours stretched emptily ahead. The only thing to do, I decided, was to make the most of Vagabunda while she was unencumbered by the weight of my camping kit. I unshackled her from the lamppost, clipped into my pedals, shifted into top gear and accelerated down Avenue San Martín as though propelled by a cannon.

Like a child's castle tipped from a bucket, the massively steep and sandy Cerro Chenque rises precariously above Comodoro on its northern side. Sun-bathed and warmly welcoming, the distant summit beckoned to me as I started off up the winding, heat-softened asphalt road towards it.

Halfway up, a squad of disintegrating automobiles lay twisted and mangled on a wide and sun-bleached plateau of wasteland. Far from being an eyesore, these rusting wrecks were winsomely attractive, their faded pastel paintwork blending perfectly with the delicate colours of the surrounding scrub. I stopped to take some photos and wandered among the decomposing carcasses, investigating their gutted innards and ancient bullet holes. Around the puncture wounds, the metal was crusted with oxidation like dried blood. In death, these abandoned beasts were beautiful in a way that functioning vehicles are not. Neglected and unwanted, they were free to return to where they came from, slowly becoming dust under the harsh glare of the sun.

I cycled and scrambled the precipitous path to the top of Cerro Chenque, wading my way through the debris of shred-ded plastic shopping bags that clung tenaciously to the coastal grasses. Then, freewheeling down the hill, I took the seaside road to the southern edge of town, wondering if it was possible to find any stretch of beach that was clean enough to sit on.

My naïve bus companion may have painted an erroneous and exaggerated picture of Comodoro for me, but he was understating wildly when he told me that coastal swimming was 'not recommendable'. The beach, strewn with plastic, Styrofoam and glass, not only looked like a rubbish dump but smelt like one too, and an effluent pipe was discharging black, bubbling sludge directly into the sea. An emaciated dog gnawed pathetically at the weather-beaten remains of a fellow canine. The atmosphere of neglect was just as strong on the other side of the road. Dilapidated houses squatted forlornly, their peeling paint testimony to the scouring strength of the salty east wind.

At the end of the road I came upon the saddest, most soul-less church I have ever had the misfortune to see, its metre-high barrier of rolled barbed wire lending it the air of a military bunker in wartime. Caught on the thousands of rusty spikes yet more shredded plastic flew, rustling and crackling in the wind like static from a shortwave radio. I couldn't decide whether the fence was there to keep Satan out, to stop the locals from finding God (in case, in joyous enlightenment, they realised what a dump they lived in), or to deter would-be vandals from spraying graffiti on the pristine concrete breeze-blocks that the church was built from.

Quite frankly, I thought to myself, it would be a good thing if someone were to discover gold under Comodoro. The mining company could shift its project from prettily situated Esquel to the coast, move the residents to somewhere nicer and dig up the entire town. At least there would be no shortage of broken glass and old plastic bags to fill the hole back in again when they finished.

Despite my conviction that this sad and dreary place was past the point of no return, it was partially redeemed by something that happened in the bus station that evening. I had just managed to get all of my luggage, including Vagabunda, stowed on the bus, and was garbling my relief and gratitude to the baggage handlers when two young men approached me. They were locals, on their way south to work on fishing boats that would eventually bring them home. I answered their questions about where I was going, where I was from and what I thought of their town (I had to lie), wished them luck on their trip and went inside the terminal to wait for my bus.

A few minutes later someone sat down next to me. I looked up. It was the cuter of the two lads and he was grinning at me with a cheeky expression. He was several years younger than me, casually dressed, and wearing a baseball cap with a ragged peak on top of his fashionably unruly blond hair. His eyes were piercingly blue. I offered him a pear and he looked me in the eyes as he bit into it. The juice ran down his chin, he chewed and swallowed.

'D'you like travelling by yourself?' he asked.

'Actually,' I replied, 'I love it.'

'But don't you get lonely?'

'Not much.'

He looked at me from under his eyebrows and took another bite of pear.

'It's a shame,' he said, 'that such a beautiful woman should be on her own.' I laughed, and blushed. I couldn't remember ever being chatted up in quite such a direct and appealing manner by someone so good-looking and charismatic. It was the legendary Latin Lover at work, and he was on top form; despite his youth, he had the true self-confidence of an experienced wooer of women.

I was dirty, my hair was greasy, I had turned bright red and we had only five minutes together before our buses left, but somehow none of that mattered. He would never see me again, but he was determined to leave an impression that I would remember. He loved to travel too, he told me. He had hitchhiked all over the country and wanted to buy a boat to sail the world when he had saved enough money. The only problem was finding a woman with whom to share his dream. He looked at me meaningfully. All the girls he met just wanted to settle down in Comodoro and have babies.

'And what happens,' he asked, 'if your bike breaks in the middle of Patagonia and you're all alone?'

I thought about it.

'Well, I'll either fix it or, if it's really bad, I'll hitchhike.'

He grinned and pointed to himself.

'It'll be me driving the truck,' he assured me. And with that he stood up, kissed me on the cheek with knee-tremblingly soft lips and whispered in my ear, *'Otra mujer tan linda no hay'* – no other woman is as beautiful – and walked out of my life for ever.

Two hours later, I was still smiling.

Long-distance buses in Argentina are some of the best I have ever travelled on. Because of the enormous distances they traverse, and the huge number of hours that passengers are required to spend on them, they are fitted with seats that recline to an almost bed-like angle, far more capacious and comfortable than those on an aeroplane. They have toilets onboard, play music and videos, provide coffee from a constantly hot machine and, if you're lucky, sometimes a man comes around and serves you an almost palatable meal. It is first-world, first-class service and, apart from the Arctic-level temperatures of the air-conditioning that I was forced to endure, I was very impressed.

Once I had climbed into my feather sleeping bag to counter the sub-zero, icicle-on-the-end-of-the-nose-forming draught that was whooshing my way from an overhead vent, I slept deeply on the overnight journey down the eastern seaboard to Río Gallegos. Then there was just enough time to yawn and stretch and wipe the crusty bits from my eyes before I was boarding yet another bus to commence the final leg of the journey to El Calafate.

While the other passengers remained glued to the fate of Arnold Schwarzenegger as he wrestled with a radioactive alien in the Amazon jungle, I was transfixed by the equally surreal scenario shooting past my window. Never in my life had I seen so much space with so little sign of humanity, nor such a massive amount of tree-less, hill-less, featureless landscape. Kilometre after kilometre we passed through the pale yellow steppe known as pampa, flat as a pancake and dry as a rusk under the grass-frazzling sun. It was hugely, utterly beautiful and it scared the hell out of me; this was what I was going to be cycling through for the next several weeks.

In El Calafate I stayed in the municipal campsite. It was late March and the evening air had a distinctly autumnal chill to it, but that was not enough to stop an enthusiastic couple from doing what Argentines on holiday do best: cooking up a storm on the barbecue. Dressed in unwisely short shorts and too-tight T-shirts, the two tubbies were preparing a lavish dinner that could possibly have fed most of the people in the campsite. Mrs Tubby, sitting in a splayed-legged plastic chair that looked on the point of collapse under her prodigious weight, was industriously carving an entire loaf of bread. Hubby Tubby was stationed at the barbecue, carefully tending to two whole chickens as they sizzled over the coals; one each, I surmised.

I put my tent in a far corner, had a cup of tea and went for a grime-stripping hot shower in the less-than-hygienic toilet block. At the sinks, beneath a large and commanding sign that said 'No washing of clothes in these sinks!', a girl was scrubbing stains from a mountainous pile of panties. I joined her beneath the sign with my own pile of sweat-sullied clothes that had been festering for weeks in the far reaches of my panniers.

As I emerged from the ladies', steaming and dripping with armfuls of wet washing, I was accosted by Christoph from Germany. He had dye-pink hair and sun-pink face, and was also travelling by bike. The following day, he told me, he was off to see the Perito Moreno Glacier. That was my plan too, and once I had made certain that he wasn't too nutty or boring or mad-keen on speed we decided to go there together.

Despite my friend Mariano's confidence-boosting encouragement, I was still apprehensive about the infamous Patagonian wind. I had read numerous stories of people who had come halfway around the world to these fabled lands for break-from-the-urban-grind cycling holidays, only to spend the entire time pushing their laden bikes into hurricane-style headwinds, losing tents and sleeping bags to the greedily grabbing gales, sheltering miserably in farm sheds and wondering why they had ever left home. To try and avoid such moments, I had chosen to cycle in a southerly direction towards the tip of the continent. With the prevailing wind from the north-west, I hoped that it would be mostly in my favour.

I think it is pertinent to point out that the wind and I have something of a dynamic relationship. Despite the fact that my hometown is an uncommonly blowy place – fondly, and understatedly, known as 'Windy' Wellington – I have never been able to resign myself to the inevitability of the weather. From blustery breezes to tyrannical tempests, the wind has always made me feel unreasonably pissed off and persecuted, and in my years as both a cyclist and a postwoman I came to suspect that the gods had a personal vendetta against me. This is not a good way to be. I knew this while yelling expletives at my omnipotent enemy after a handful of mail was ripped from my grip and scattered irretrievably out over Cook Strait, and I knew it when working up a rage after being knocked off my bike and pelted by wind-borne sheets of grit on Red Rocks beach, but until now I had been unable to temper my attitude. Patagonia, I hoped, would be the place to confront the wind and my anger head-on, and work through the issues to reach Zen-like equilibrium.

It was almost a disappointment then, to find no more than a brisk little breeze blowing the next morning. It *was* a head-wind, and it *was* continuous and increasing in strength as the day progressed, but it had none of the aggressiveness that I had expected. Under the enormous sky we pedalled westwards, moving slowly through the wide-open grasslands like two ponderous beetles traversing a vast yellow carpet. On our right was the glittering grey-blue of Lake Argentino, the largest body of fresh water in the country, and ahead, the snaggly spine of the Andes, from which the chill wind brought the scent of snow. We slipstreamed each other on the asphalt, taking turns to roll with frictionless ease behind the leader, while tourist-packed buses raced past us with buffeting blasts of air. My bandaged knee was not complaining too much and my duct-tape-doctored seat was holding up nicely. The conditions were all favourable, and I felt optimistic about the journey ahead.

At the entrance to Los Glaciares National Park I was pleased to see that the most was being made of the steady flow of foreigners; the entrance fee was a hearty twenty pesos. Currently, the money appeared to be helping to pave the road all the way to the glacier and we pushed our bikes through a morass of loose earth where the wheezing, grumbling bull-dozers were preparing the next stretch. The road workers grinned as we passed and one, leaning on his spade and bowing regally, waved us through as though he had laid the road especially for our visit.

We rattled the final few kilometres along the rocky track to the campsite at Bahía Escondida – Hidden Bay. There were few other campers. In summer, no doubt, the site is full of glacier-gazing sightseers of all descriptions. But now, with the cold drawing in and the holidays over, most tourists were of the bus-riding variety, zooming in and out from Calafate in one day. We set our tents on a spongy mattress of ground in a little clearing in the beech forest. Above us, the bird population chattered and gossiped like old ladies at a coffee morning. Through the trees rose a whimsical column of blue smoke from a campfire, and I followed the smell of autumn down to the lakeshore.

From there I caught my first glimpse of the spectacular Moreno Glacier. Its fourteen-kilometre length lay in a crook of the mountains and the late-afternoon sun picked out the peaks and troughs of its serrated back in intricate detail. The imposing, startlingly white front wall rose vertically from the milky-blue lake. It looked monumental and eternal, and it was difficult to imagine that such an enormous entity was constantly on the move. I filled our water bottles with finger-numbing lake water and hurried back up the hill with my breath making steamy clouds. We cooked dinner by torchlight, drank warming *mate* and crawled into our respective tents wearing multiple layers of clothing, hats, socks and gloves as buffers against the penetrating cold. Even from the depths of my sleeping bag I could hear, like distant thunder, the rumbling and crashing of iceblocks tumbling from the face of the glacier and splashing dramatically into the lake.

Although there were only a few other people camping nearby, our little tent site was far from peaceful. Just as I was drifting into sleep, a circus of mice arrived. They located the unwashed cooking pot for an energy-boosting feast before commencing a multimedia performance of impressive improvisation. While a couple of them ice-skated on my enamel plate, accompanied by clickety-clackety folk music made with my fork and spoon, a whole band of acrobats scaled the giddy heights in the space between the tent and the flysheet and tumbled down again with reckless abandon and squeaks of glee. When I peered tentatively outside the next morning, I found that they had also been chewing on my plastic water bottles and rubber jandals, leaving some interesting pieces of contemporary rodent art.

It was still freezing. The clouds had crowded in thick and grey, and a light rain was falling. Chris came over to my tent in his waterproofs and sat on the soggy grass to eat porridge with me – there wasn't room inside for both of us – before shaking himself off like a wet dog and going back to bed. I summoned all the enthusiasm I could and cycled the final muddy kilometres to see what I had come to see.

Perito Moreno is the largest advancing glacier in the world. Although it is growing faster than it is melting, its front face is nevertheless in a constant state of deconstruction. I was descending the slippery wooden staircase towards the viewing platform when there was a gunshot crack, followed by a collective gasp from the camera-toting tourists. I looked up to see a tower of ice as tall as a house break away from the body of the glacier and topple, with a slow-motion belly flop, into the lake. It plunged beneath the surface with the sound of a minor nuclear explosion and a gargantuan wave washed towards the beach beneath us. A couple of seconds later the block reappeared, rising up grandly through the surrounding debris and setting the frozen bergs clinking like ice-cubes in lemonade.

The sixty-metre-high wall of ice was a spectacular sight, veined with blue and topped with ornate, melt-sculpted pinnacles and fancy flutings, as though iced by an enthusiastic chef with a penchant for the piping bag. Its face was alive with falling chunks of ice; they plummeted like lemmings from the precipitous heights and made unbelievably noisy noises on impact. In fact, it was the constant snap, crackle and plop that told the true story of the mammoth glacial forces at work. Closing my eyes to listen, it was possible to imagine a battle in progress: a small skirmish here, a bombardment there, grenades detonating, machine-guns rattling and the occasional cacophony of a munitions factory collapsing.

The glacier is so active, and so unpredictable, that the once usual tourist practice of descending to the beach to view the ice wall from ground level has long been prohibited in the interests of public safety. I read the multilingual signs that told me of the various visitors who had been killed by projectiles of falling ice, and I peered over the parapet to the beach below, which was a minefield of massive white blocks sunk deep into the sand. This was the remaining rubble from the recent rupture of the glacier, an event that occurs once every few decades. As the glacier advances, pushing unstoppably towards the promontory from which it can be viewed, it slowly closes the channel between two arms of Lake Argentino to form a dam. Eventually, after decades, the water on its eastern side rises to such a height that the immense pressure causes the barrier to burst in a breathtaking spectacle of destruction. Unfortunately I was a mere week too late to witness this cataclysmic collapse, which had last happened in 1988, but I continued to hear all about it for weeks to come from people who had watched the whole thing live on television.

At the end of an unforgettable hour of icy antics, countering the noises of attack with the rapid fire of my trusty Nikon, I was frozen practically solid. Stiffly, I cycled the shivery kilometres back to the campsite where Chris instructed me to shed my wet jacket and shoes and get into his tent for a hot cup of tea. I sat huddled under his sleeping bag, my fingers thawing around a steaming mug, and watched in admiration as he whipped up a batch of pancakes on his camping stove.

At home in Germany, Christoph is a baker. For him, cooking

pancakes inside his tent was not such a difficult procedure, nor an unusual occurrence. For myself, however, whose larder consisted of the bare basics of oats, tea, biscuits and figs, it was nothing short of miraculous. I took the position of baker's apprentice, watching the batter-mixing process carefully, making note of the type of frying pan needed and, most importantly, taking responsibility for topping each perfectly cooked creation with a generous helping of *dulce de leche*. We sat together cosily, eating and chatting, licking our fingers and plates, and I thought to myself that there was no better place in the world to be than in a tent, in the rain, somewhere in the depths of Argentina, with a cycling German baker.

We drank more tea, and Chris kept me amused with travel stories from New Zealand, where he had been hitchhiking a couple of years before. He had a good appreciation for eccentric characters and an unintentionally comic deadpan delivery that made his anecdotes doubly mirth-making.

'This car full of Mongrel Mob members picked me up once,' he said, 'black leather, patches, tattoos and everything. They said they'd stopped because God had told them to help me.'

'Really?' That blew my own stereotype of the Mongrel Mob right out the window.

'Yeah. It was surreal. I told them that God must have heard my prayers, because I'd just been asking Him to make someone stop and pick me up.'

'And had you, really?'

'No, of course not. But it sure made their day to think so.'

I laughed.

'So have you ever hitched around Germany?'

'Well, it's not so easy, you know? We don't really have a culture of it there, and the people can be a bit paranoid. They don't understand why you would choose to stand in the rain with your thumb out rather than get your own car.'

'You know what? You Germans puzzle me. Almost all of the German people I've met while travelling have been lovely, and yet so many of you seem to have a poor opinion of your own people. Some Germans have even advised me not to visit Germany.'

'Hmm, well, I wouldn't say that to you. Germany is wonderful and you should definitely visit if you get the chance. I'm glad to be German, but I think many people are still careful about being too proud of our country. Because of our history, you know? And we *can* be seen as pessimistic and humourless sometimes. In their hearts though, deep down, I think people feel their nationality quite strongly. But you know what? In the end it doesn't matter where you come from. German, Kiwi, English, who cares? You can find something in common with everyone you meet.'

The sun came out by mid-afternoon, as Christoph had predicted, and I joined him on another trip to the glacier. Sparkling brilliantly in the sunshine, the ice had a completely different character from under the grey sky of the morning. Its peaks looked perkier and its crevasses looked deeper and the melting face was disintegrating at an incredible rate. Chris sat down to wait patiently with his camera for the perfect action photo and I sat a short distance away, admiring the shocking pink of his hair against the perfect azure backdrop of the sky.

We returned to El Calafate the following day, noticing as we cycled that all the tourists in the buses coming back from the glacier were sound asleep. It was a strange phenomenon, as though the ice had some mystical soporific effect, and it seemed a shame that the once-in-a-lifetime chance to see this magical place, such a long way from anywhere else, should be squandered by sleeping through it.

We rolled back into town in the early evening and put our

tents in a quiet corner of a privately owned campground. Although the dirty and dusty municipal site next door was still full of barbecuing, beer-swilling holidaymakers and boisterous boy scouts, our only neighbour, staring at us vacantly and munching on the lush grass, was a rotund and woolly sheep.

Planning a lavish, mission-accomplished post-glacier feast, we bumbled around in the supermarket together, gathering ingredients, looking for bargains and discussing the merits of various types of chocolate biscuits. Back at the tents, by torchlight, I chopped salad ingredients while Chris taught me his recipe for oat burgers over the sizzling sound of hot oil. We were just getting to the critical burger-assembling, tomato-sauce-squeezing stage of the operation when we were interrupted by the campsite owner. He came out of the darkness to watch us eat.

Like a strange android character from a science fiction novel, his outwardly normal appearance and wide grin were belied by his complete lack of basic etiquette. He refused an offer to join us for dinner but stood there unblinkingly as the food grew cold and we grew uncomfortable. I tried to ease the situation by attempting to make small talk but he was monosyllabic, apparently unable to judge that staring at us as we fidgeted and willed him to leave did not constitute fulfilling social exchange. I admired Christoph's tactic, which was to completely ignore him and begin eating in silence, challenging the weirdness with his characteristic reserve. Eventually, when the uneasiness had become almost overwhelming, the owner left us to it, bidding us goodnight and disappearing into the dark as silently as he had come. We burst into relieved giggles and I decided that, for once, it was very nice not to be alone.

As though we had been weeks without food, rather than a mere two days out of range of bakeries, we spent the following day lounging in the sun and stuffing ourselves with the edibles of El Calafate. Most importantly, we ate ice-cream containing the blue berries of the Calafate bush, which, according to local belief, ensured that one day we would return.

Chris wandered off to the bike shop in the afternoon and I stayed behind to tinker with my own bike in the sun. I was just getting down and dirty with my smallest sprockets when a shadow fell across me. My heart sank as I looked up. Grinning at me in an unconvincing imitation of normality was the campsite owner, and in one hand he was carrying a large, unfriendly-looking garden implement with a sharp blade. My heart began to race.

'What are you doing with that?' I asked.

'Just tidying up a bit,' he replied, swinging his menacing tool and beheading a few dandelions in demonstration. I moved nervously to the other side of Vagabunda and feigned concentration.

'I found your knickers in the shower,' he said.

'Oh, umm, right. I must have left them there this morning.' My face turned red. 'I'll pick them up later.' I turned back to the task at hand, but no matter how hard I focused, it was impossible to avoid the mental image of him sniffing my underpants.

I was relieved when Christoph came back. The man with the machete had long since grown bored – he was now on the other side of the campground wreaking carnage on some weeds – but I felt better now that we had been joined by a third. I made Chris a cup of tea and he told me some interesting news. He had been in the local bike shop, checking out the goods, when he had bumped into the guitar-toting American biologist with the funny name (Bo bo? Bing bong? Bed bug?) whom I had met on the first day of my trip, some 1500 kilometres away. He had given Chris the address of his hostel and invited us over.

So that evening, after a meal in an *empanada* restaurant, we scrunched our way through the dark and gravelly back streets to go visiting. We had shared a bottle of red wine and everything seemed hilarious. We both tried to remember the name of the guy we were about to meet but managed to only come up with ever more ridiculous possibilities: Bo jangle, Big bramble, No sandal, Pump handle. We were in fits of giggles, and when we peered through the window of the hostel kitchen to the brightly lit scene within, where people were either eating or earnestly talking, we realised we would have to compose ourselves. We took deep breaths and went in. Bojo – for that was, I finally recalled, his name – greeted us with a grin.

'What the hell are *you* doing here?' he asked. Good question. I had told him, more than a month ago, that there was no way on earth I was going to Patagonia.

'Umm, I sort of changed my mind.'

We sat down and he introduced us to his cycling partner, a small and wiry Swiss guy whose sun-wrinkled, deeply brown skin seemed to indicate that he had been on the road for years. Patricio was an odd character. He looked strong and full of energy, but in a hyperactive, nervously twitchy sort of way as though he had drunk far too much coffee. Either that, or he had taken far too many drugs over a long period of time. He spoke English with a strong German accent, spattering it with Spanish and stuttering his words out with a reluctant tongue. He was constantly fidgeting, as though itching to get back on the road, and I wondered what he would be like to travel with.

He and Bojo spoke to each other in an incomprehensible form of Spanish; what with Patricio's verbal tics, and the accents they spoke with, they seemed to have developed their own private language. They told us of their exploits travelling through Chile and part of the way down Route Forty, and about the ever-present wind that had constantly tried to throw them off their bikes. They spoke of other cyclists they had met, some of whom were headed north towards Bolivia and Peru, and others south towards Tierra del Fuego. It was becoming apparent that there was a strong bikers' network functioning in the Americas: an ever-flowing north–south highway that carried news of other cyclists, tips about places to stay and valuable information about road and weather conditions.

They would be leaving for the south in the morning, as I also planned to do, and they said they would see me on the road. It was a polite gesture. I knew and they knew that I would never be able to keep up. The way Patricio was jiggling restlessly in his seat, it seemed he would be waiting for nobody.

When Chris and I got back to the tents, still a bit drunk and swaying in the dark, I found a piece of cloth wrapped around one of my guy ropes. I couldn't remember putting it there, but it seemed to have been tied on securely. I untangled it and stumbled inside to investigate by torchlight.

It was my knickers, those that I had left in the shower, and they were still slightly damp.

8

Where the Wind Blows

The wind was more like its legendary self as we cycled east out of El Calafate. It was blowing from behind us, and after the leg-deadening effects of the previous evening's wine I appreciated the assistance. We covered the thirty kilometres to the Route Forty turnoff with ease and stopped to say goodbye. Apart from the short diversion to see the glacier, we were travelling in opposite directions; Christoph was now on his way north to rendezvous with a ferry that would take him on an unconventional border crossing to Chile. I was sorry that we hadn't shared a bit more time together. We hugged a reluctant farewell while the wind snatched at our clothing like a jealous lover.

And then I was alone again. Shooting across the golden landscape like a bullet, I shifted into top gear and accelerated until the wind and I were equal. It was a strange sensation. Apart from the hum of tyres on asphalt, there was no noise at all, and with no trees to indicate the wind speed the day appeared to be perfectly calm. Only by the gear I was cranking could I judge the immense strength that was bowling me along. Then I stopped to take off my jacket and the noise and force of the wind returned with the suddenness of a passing freight train. It roared in my ears and nearly knocked me over.

The road turned to the south-east. I was on a plateau, and with not a tree to be seen the wind was hurtling across the plain towards my starboard side with nothing to stop it. Pitching and rolling like a ship in a storm, I navigated a weaving course across an ocean of steppe. All there was to see, to each horizon, were undulating waves of grass. The sky was cloudless, the sun was bright, but I was forced to don my heavy-weather clothing. I reefed the sheets and continued on into the gale.

It was very exciting. The anxiety I had felt on the bus on my way to El Calafate had long since been blown away and replaced with the euphoria of adventure. There was virtually no traffic, and although the perfectly surfaced road was a dead giveaway, I felt light years from civilisation. I was a minute speck in the landscape, insignificant beneath the immense spread of the sky.

I felt confident about the road ahead. There would be a few long stretches to traverse between towns, meaning that I would have to carry plenty of food and water, but I was equipped with excellent information about my route all the way to Ushuaia, the southernmost city in the world. Mariano, who regularly took cycle tours through this area, had given me a list detailing the exact locations of towns, farms, rivers and wind-sheltered camping spots. My only problem would be judging how far I had gone, or had to go, in between each point of reference. Lacking a cycle computer, and with the wind and road conditions affecting my rate of progress, I would have no way of calculating my speed.

By mid-afternoon I reached the junction that would take me away from the sealed road and turn me towards the wind. On the corner was a little roadworkers' hut. I stopped to get water. The man who opened the door shook me by the hand and stood aside to let me in.

'Look what we have here,' he called over my head. There were several other guys inside, sitting around the table, drinking *mate*. They stood up in welcome. One of them took my bottles and filled them with filtered water, another offered a welcome slurp of tea. They teased me mercilessly, lamented the strength of the wind and invited me to stay the night. It was a charming offer and I almost said yes, but the pull of solitude was too strong. I thanked them sincerely, pulled my balaclava back on and headed for the middle of nowhere.

What with the strength of the crosswind, the cold and the bumpiness of the road, my knee was feeling the strain. Just a few kilometres further on from the hut, I pushed my bike into the pampa, pitched the tent and sat in the doorway, massaging my sore joint and replenishing my water levels with cups of hot chocolate. The sun was going down and in the low light the grasses were iridescent yellow. The whistling wind, which was still increasing in strength, was making my little tent billow and bulge, and the open flysheet was flapping like a loose sail. But I didn't want to close myself off from the view to the horizon. It was hard to believe that I was finally here, in Patagonia, and the only sign of humanity was the road that I had arrived on.

It was an amazing sensation to be so totally alone. I've always loved solitude, loved having space for my thoughts and the freedom to focus on my surroundings with no human distractions. But true isolation can be hard to find in the modern world, especially now that virtually everyone has a mobile phone and friends are expected to be instantly contactable at all times. I had railed against that for ages, irked by the changing rules of social etiquette that allowed the interruption of bike rides, meals or intimate conversation for the answering of unnecessary phone calls. But the tide was against me and I had eventually conceded defeat, accepting permanent reachability and the incessant jangling of ringtones as an unavoidable fact of life.

Here in Patagonia, I doubted if a mobile would work even if I had one. Sitting in my tent, in the middle of the pampa, I was completely uncontactable. Not one single person knew exactly where I was. It was a thrilling idea, one that made me feel entirely responsible for my every move. There was no one to help me if I set my tent on fire, spilt scalding water on myself or tripped over a guy rope and knocked myself out. I was in charge now; my life was in *my* hands.

The sun dropped below the horizon and the sky grew immensely black. Above me, appearing like a guardian angel to offer comfort and direction, hung the constellation of the Southern Cross.

In the morning there was complete calm. I was soon to realise that the wind had a daily cycle, beginning at around nine or ten o'clock in the morning, gathering strength all through the day and falling more or less silent again after dark. For this reason, getting up early would have been a good idea, but what with breakfast to make and panniers to pack, it was never easy to get going before nine.

I set off into the beginnings of a breeze and a light patter of rain, and within an hour I was crawling along in my granny gear – the smallest, easiest one to spin, supposedly named because even old ladies can manage some sort of forward motion when using it. Usually this gear is engaged only for tackling extreme uphills, and to be using it on a dead-flat road means either you're just recovering from having your hips replaced or the headwind is more than a little bit strong. I slogged on steadily into the increasing gale, prepared for a long, slow day.

Sometime after lunch, when I was wondering if I had gone

five kilometres or fifty, an expedition-style four-wheel drive appeared from the horizon. It slowed to a stop beside me and the elderly driver wound his window down.

'Doin' okay?' he asked in a strong American drawl.

'Yep. Bit windy,' I replied from the muffled depths of my balaclava.

'Oh, is it?' He sounded surprised, and turned to his seventy-something wife who was riding shotgun. 'Did you hear that, Sally? She says it's a bit windy.'

They peered at me from the cab.

'D'ya know how far it is to the paved road?' they asked.

'Well, it's taken me about five hours, but I really couldn't say in kilometres. Any idea how far it is to Tapi Aike?'

'Oh, it's not very far,' piped up the female half of the pair. 'How far is it, Jack?'

'Ooh, let me see now, very close, about twenty-five kilometres?'

I absorbed the information as the wind delivered a hefty broadside blow.

'In that case,' I said, regaining balance, 'I should be there in about two days' time.'

They laughed and wished me luck.

'Now that we're retired, we like to do things the easy way,' said septuagenarian Sally. 'My knees are too bad to do what you're doing.'

They waved goodbye and I watched them drive off. I flexed my sore joint. The pain hadn't gone anywhere.

In the end, I reached Tapi Aike that afternoon. It consisted of a petrol station and another roadworkers' hut, and apart from the local dog who raced excitedly to welcome me there were few signs of life. I had been going solidly for seven hours but had covered only fifty kilometres. It had been hard work, but not as hard as expected. In a perverse way I was sort of disappointed.

For 200 kilometres or so I was following an easy section of the 4700-kilometre Route Forty; those parts that weren't asphalted were being constantly upgraded to facilitate the ever-growing tourism of the south. The really isolated, badly surfaced, drive-a-cyclist-to-insanity stretches were to the north of me, traversing the sparsely populated steppe for hundreds of virtually identical kilometres. The road was infamous for its difficulty, and almost as legendary as North America's Route 66, attracting those seeking adventure and a taste of the real Argentina.

Mariano had tried to persuade me to do it, to head south from Bariloche and keep going till I reached the end of the Americas, but I had been sceptical. Going under-prepared into such barren territory had seemed like asking for trouble, and I had imagined myself desperate with frustration by the roadside, wilting with exhaustion, running out of water and hopelessly unable to calculate where I was.

Now though, as I pushed onwards with a stoicism that surprised me, I wondered if perhaps I had underestimated myself. Maybe I *could* have found the stamina to get all the way here under my own steam? Other people had done it. Why not me? Had it been cowardly to take the bus some of the way? Had I allowed my fear to dilute my belief in myself? Perhaps I should have trusted Mariano as I trusted my brother, and believed him when he assured me of my capabilities. There was no point regretting my decision now, but it would give me something to think about the next time I had doubts.

There was no reason to linger in Tapi Aike. I filled up with water at the petrol station, let the dog lick the snot from my nose, and returned to battle with the warrior wind.

In the eerie stillness of the next morning I hurried through my chores as quickly as possible. The tent was covered in a fine layer of ice and as I forced it, with freezing fingers, into a pannier, it crackled like cellophane. I set out with intent, my breath making clouds in the crisp air and my knees creaking with the cold.

At ten o'clock, someone switched the wind on. Within the space of a few minutes it went from non-existent to impressively zealous and it slowed my purposeful pace to a crawl. With head down, I thought calming thoughts and spun the pedals as steadily as possible. I was still alone, and the horizon was as distant as ever, but around me the sprawling plains were corralled by fences. Flaking wooden signs and old cartwheels marked the entrances to properties, and long gravel roads led off to distant farm buildings. I was in sheep country.

Dotted around one of the most sparsely populated places on earth, *estancias* – sheep ranches – are like oases in the vast, semi-arid wastes of southern Patagonia. On the list that Mariano had given me were the names of several farms I would be passing. He had assured me that help could be found there if needed; it was part of the culture of the south, he said. Traditionally, travellers have been safe in the knowledge that no matter how far it is to the next farmhouse they will be welcome to a night's refuge and a hot meal when they arrive. It was a comforting thought, and I had no doubt that in the case of a cyclist in distress it would hold true. But I had noticed, while browsing the leaflets in tourist offices, that things were changing, that the innate culture of hospitality that characterises the *estancia* was inevitably being turned into a saleable commodity.

The golden days of the late 1930s, when Patagonia was second only to Australia in wool production, are long gone, with various factors contributing to the decline of the industry. Overgrazing has damaged the delicate grasslands to such an extent that they are rapidly turning to desert. Wool prices have fallen dramatically due to the rise of synthetic fibres, and many farmers are no longer able to sell their product at a price sufficient to keep them in business. Hundreds of properties have been abandoned. To supplement their income, many of the remaining ranch owners are now looking to tourism. Glossy brochures invite guests to come and experience a slice of traditional Patagonian life: to watch the gauchos, to partake in the working of the farm and to sample the cuisine of the countryside – the outdoor barbecue, or *asado*. There is no doubt that some of the more accessible *estancias* are profiting well from a constant flow of European and North American tourists.

For the farmers who can't make their ranches pay, however, the other option is to sell. Overseas buyers, attracted by the rock-bottom prices, have purchased vast tracts of once profitable land. Perhaps the most notable of these is the Italian-owned clothing giant Benetton, which now owns an astonishing nine per cent of Patagonia – some 900,000 hectares.

By lunchtime I was on the country border at Cancha Carrera. I had decided to leave Argentina once more after backpackers in El Calafate had recommended a visit to Torres del Paine National Park, Chilean Patagonia's claim to fame. It was splendid, they told me, and it would be foolish to miss it. Although it would require a sizeable detour, and meant that I would have to retrace some of my tracks afterwards, I reckoned it would be well worth it.

Border control was a small hut by the side of the road, lashed to the ground with steel cables, and after getting my passport stamped I pushed on past into the no man's land beyond, up what was no more than a badly rutted four-wheel-drive track. From the deep puddles that filled the potholes blew a fine spray; like tiny seas, each was alive with waves. The wind was truly fierce and it was becoming impossible to steer in a straight line. My knee was painful again, and with the force required to turn the pedals and the constant blasts that knocked me off course, it was safer to walk.

At least there were no mountains to traverse. This far south the Andes had all but tailed out, and although I could still see some snowy peaks on the horizon the crossing into Chile was through rolling farmland. For the final five kilometres to passport control, pushing Vagabunda past wide meadows, I was humbled by the strength of the wind and the breadth and beauty of the landscape.

In the tiny Chilean border village of Cerro Castillo, I replenished my energy in a snug café. There were no other customers and the counter-girl, who had been watching television, served me distractedly before returning to her flickering corner. I warmed up by the potbelly stove and glugged a mug of coffee. The building rattled and shook and the wind moaned like a pantomime ghost. I ate biscuits and stared out of the window, gathering strength and summoning willpower before stepping back outside, calling out a thank you to the waitress as I went. Engrossed in her soap opera, she didn't look up.

The ferocious force of the wind was oddly satisfying. I flung a leg determinedly over my crossbar, but before I could manage a single revolution of the pedals an angry gust threw me to the ground. I climbed out of the roadside ditch where I had landed and extracted a small quarry's-worth of gravel from the fleshier parts of my hands. Cycling was obviously not an option. With grim delight in the seeming impossibility of it all I hefted my cumbersome bike upright, leant over the handlebars and plodded on with glacial slowness.

For some reason, the wind had yet to make me lose my temper. Perhaps it was because I had been expecting it – had even braced myself for something worse – or maybe it was because I really was coming to terms with it. Nature would do what it chose, that went without saying, and I could now see that getting upset about it would only waste valuable energy. In conditions this extreme, a tantrum on my part would render me incapable of forward motion. I needed every ounce of strength just to remain upright.

An hour later, having achieved some five kilometres or so, I decided that enough was enough. I pulled off the road and attempted to put up my tent without losing any parts of it to the thieving wind, weighing it down with panniers, fumbling with poles and pegs and guy ropes, and finally managing to wrestle it into shape. I imagined where it would end up if I lost hold of it. With the current wind speed and direction, it could well have made it to South Africa. But once it was tied down securely and cutting the wind with its aerodynamic fin-shape, my little Macpac house was sturdier than a barn. Even my haphazard sewing job seemed to be holding up well as I Velcroed myself in to a perfect bubble of calm.

The next day, unbelievably, there was no wind at all. The sun was hot, the sky was blue, and I hummed along towards Torres del Paine National Park without a care in the world. Apart from the pain of my knee, that is, which seemed to be getting worse. Cycling with one leg, which I was becoming quite good at, required a sort of trotting-on-a-horse motion. It must have looked quite ridiculous, and as there were park-bound minivans full of backpackers roaring past every ten minutes or so I felt a bit self-conscious. So I developed another technique, which involved using both feet on the pedals but pushing down on the offending kneecap with one hand as I straightened my leg. With a combination of the two methods, the occasional bout of walking and the added incentive of a chocolate biscuit every couple of kilometres, I made slow but steady progress.

Every now and again I would be raced by ñandú – pretty, ostrich-like birds with long legs and eyelashes – who would appear as if from nowhere and run along beside me through the scrub. They were always in pairs and eventually, when they realised I was no competition at all, they would turn back towards the steppe and speed off together at manic pace, like cartoon characters on fast-forward.

Los Torres del Paine, the three awe-inspiring granite towers that form the centrepiece of the national park, stood like proud sentinels on the skyline to my left, wearing tall helmets of snow. It was no wonder that I was only one of many who were on their way to see these imposing pillars up close. Climbers come to scale the heights, and trampers arrive in their thousands each year to walk the track that circles the base of the towers. It's not just the magnificent scenery that attracts visitors; the landscape is also teeming with wildlife. Since 1978 the park has been part of the UNESCO biosphere scheme, a project that allows species and ecosystems to flourish. Once devastated by ranchers, who overgrazed and burnt forests to create pastureland, the park is now on its way to recovery and home to many conservation successes. Hidden in the thick beech forest live around fifty of the world's rarest deer, the huemul, whose numbers have increased five-fold since their introduction to the park twenty years ago. The most notably thriving species is the endangered guanaco, the winsome, biscuit-coloured cousin of the llama. With their survival once challenged by over-hunting and the competition for pastureland due to farming, guanaco populations declined dramatically after the arrival of the colonists. Today, with the protection of the law, the only significant predator of these graceful, long-necked creatures is the puma.

The old and shrivelled park ranger, who welcomed me with a trembling handshake, took down my details in a ledger.

'Car registration?' he asked.

'None,' I said. 'I came on my bike.'

He peered short-sightedly past me through the doorway to where Vagabunda was propped against a tree.

'Ahh . . . a bicycle,' he said thoughtfully, as if it were a recent invention. 'And you're sure you don't have a registration number?' I looked at him and laughed. Now that you mention it, I wanted to say, I do. It's U R A PRAT.

Amazingly, although this park is so popular that it is necessary to book ahead for most campsites and huts, I managed to pass three nights there entirely alone. Alone with the rats, that is. Far from the crowds, in an old and dilapidated *refugio* where the grime in the corners told a story of neglect, I cooked my dinner in the company of two portly rodents. They appeared unconcerned by my presence, foraging under the table for bits that I dropped, investigating my bicycle, which was propped in a corner, and basically treating the place like home. As I sat with them in companionable silence, eating mashed potatoes while they nibbled biscuit crumbs mere centimetres from my feet, I realised that, in fact, they *were* at home. It was I who was the guest in their space, not the other way around.

And then we were joined by a fourth. I returned from washing the dishes outside to find a cute black and white Patagonian skunk bumbling around, snuffling at my bags, waving his fluffy tail and looking most disinclined to go back into the cold. I chased him out with the broom. Much as I was enjoying the company, I didn't fancy accidentally stepping on someone who was equipped with the ability to turn our little house into a gas chamber.

I slept in a wobbly top bunk, hauling all my panniers and anything edible up there with me and hoping the rats were too fat to climb. In the pitch dark I listened to them treading the boards like a couple of thespians. What with the energetic scrabbling of feet and the swishing of long tails, they might have been rehearsing a sword-fight scene from a Shakespearean tragedy.

Torres del Paine National Park was a scenic detour. Now, almost at the end of the sixty-kilometre dead-end park road, there were two choices. I could retrace my tracks for 100 kilometres to Cerro Castillo, or I could try my luck at joining a road that was enticingly marked on my map as 'private'. One park ranger had told me that it was not for public use as there was no bridge across the river to it. Others said that the bridge was under construction and that cyclists had passed through there only months before. Ask the construction crew nicely, they told me, maintain a *buena onda* and they will surely let you across. So it was in an optimistic frame of mind that I pulled up at the river, left my bike against a pile of rubble, and went in search of the foreman.

The concrete bridge looked, if not near to completion, at least sturdy enough to support a bicycle and a few lightweight panniers (my food supplies were dwindling by the hour). It didn't take long to locate the man in charge. He was having a tea break in the sun with a workmate and they grinned at me over their cups. This seemed promising. I shook them both by the hand and explained my predicament in flawed Spanish. My knees were sore. My grub was running out. The wind had exhausted me. And I knew that just on the other side of that river lay a road that would take me directly to a little town where I could rest and eat *facturas*. I looked at the boss expectantly.

'You can't cross the river,' he said. 'There's no bridge.'

I looked at the bridge. I looked at the boss.

'What's that then?' I asked.

He looked at the bridge and avoided my eyes. He sighed. 'It's not safe.'

I argued the point, politely. There were at least ten workers up there and none of them looked in grave danger of falling off. But stating the obvious did no good, my *buena onda* was getting bad reception, and even putting on my little-girl-lost-and-about-to-cry face had no effect on a heart as hard as concrete. He put his sunglasses on and went back to work.

But all was not lost. His workmate, who had been listening to our conversation, was compassionate. He was on his way to pick up another load of fill from the park quarry, he said, and would enjoy some company. He called over two burly lads and between them they hauled Vagabunda into the back of an empty tip-truck. I swung myself into the passenger seat, Jorge climbed behind the wheel and off we roared, back along the lumpy road through the park. It wasn't usual to accept a lift, but in this instance it felt perfectly justifiable. I had already cycled this road, and an impromptu hour with a Chilean truck driver was far more inviting than several hours with sore knees.

And what a comical hour it was. Above the growl of the motor and the worryingly clonky sound of my bike rattling round in the back, Jorge told me a string of increasingly dirty jokes. He was missing a few teeth – on account of too much sweet *mate* no doubt – but his smile was the genuine article. His throaty laugh, in which could be heard a long history of tobacco abuse, was that of a true lover of life.

The view from his cab, far above the road, was spectacular. It was another calm and sunny day and I asked him where the wind was. It came in cycles, he explained. First there would be a light breeze; the next day, a boisterous wind; the day after, a full-on gale; and finally, wind of the sort where roofs get blown off buildings. Then there would be a day of perfect stillness, and the cycle would start all over again. Thinking back, I realised that this was exactly how it had been.

'But you've been lucky,' he added. 'There's barely been any wind at all this year.'

We passed herds of dreamily chewing guanacos. Untroubled by the thudding noises the truck was making as it sped across the washboard surface of the road, they looked at us coolly and continued grazing. 'They're used to traffic,' Jorge told me. 'What really gets them sweating is the big cats.'

'See that one guanaco on the skyline?' he asked, pointing. 'That's the watcher. He's working for the good of the herd, to sound the alarm if he spots a puma.' All of a sudden we were slewing to a halt in the gravel and Jorge was flinging himself from the cab. 'Come on, Eleanora,' he said, 'there's something here you might want to see.'

A short way into a grassy meadow, which was scattered with small round poo pellets, we found a bloody carcass. Two days ago, Jorge explained, a puma had fancied this guanaco for its breakfast. The body was an empty shell and vestiges of drying skin clung to the hollowed-out ribcage. The once elegant neck was a long length of bloody vertebrae, the slightly gnawed head was thrown back, and the one visible eye stared blindly at the sky.

'That is what pumas can do,' warned Jorge as we climbed back into the truck. 'You're not camping alone, are you?' I looked at him and nodded. He shook his head in disapproval, pulled away with a graunch of gears and proceeded to relate gruesome tales of fishermen and trampers who had met gory fates. The stories and bloody evidence of death were all good warnings, but they didn't really worry me. I knew that pumas were relatively shy of humans, tended to hide out in the forest and were notoriously hard to spot even for those who wanted to. Obviously they *could* prey on cyclists if they chose – although the stringy muscles and cleated cycle shoes would make for a fairly unappetising meal – but like all dangers the risk was small enough to put to the back of my mind.

Some fifty kilometres from where we had started, Jorge dropped me off. Despite his big personality he was somewhat lacking in stature and I wondered how we were going to get my bike out of the back of the truck. He had it all worked out.

'We'll catch her as she falls,' he said, reaching into the cab to engage the hydraulic lift. I watched in disbelief as the massive container began to lift up at the front, as though about to tip a load of earth, and the tailgate swung open to reveal Vagabunda sliding swiftly towards us. Jorge caught my expression.

'*Sin miedo*, Eleanora,' he yelled over the noise of the motor, '¡*SIN MIEDO!*' – without fear. And with that he turned and deftly caught my bicycle, as easily as if it was a chocolate bar dropping from a vending machine.

Without fear, I thought, as he drove off. I should get that embroidered on my knickers so as to remember it every day of my life.

Puerto Natales felt like somewhere I had been before. Perched on the shore of Seno Ultima Esperanza – Last Hope Sound – the tiny town was suffused with the salty smell of the sea. The light was low as I freewheeled downhill to the coast and gulls flashed white like scraps of blown paper. The sea shone silver, and on the beach fishing boats formed a muted rainbow of weather-beaten pastels.

It was cold and beginning to drizzle. On the main plaza was a hostel with bicycles outside. They were lined up in a bike rack and not one of them was locked; it was that sort of town. I checked in. In the kitchen, a cast-iron gas stove was kicking out waves of welcome heat. A girl from Italy offered me a cup of tea and a guy from Santiago started to tell me jokes. There was such a homely atmosphere to the place that I felt like I could stay for days. So I did.

For four fantastically lazy mornings I sat in the kitchen of Patagonia Aventura, drinking tea and talking with the ever-changing crew of backpackers. In the afternoons I stirred myself only as far as the local café, or the cake shop, and in the evenings there was always someone with whom to share wine and tall stories over dinner. I hadn't been lonely out there in the pampa, but the company was a welcome contrast to my solitude. I soon began to wonder if I would be able to drag myself away from the enticing lure of convivial conversation.

The decision was made even harder when, on my last night there, I fell into heart-thumping infatuation with José, a young Chilean who was helping to run the place. We talked effortlessly for hours and he impressed me with his quick mind and gentle manner. He was attentive, curious and interested in my opinions, but he was most definitely not flirting. And that made him even more appealing.

But the journey had to go on, and with reluctance I loaded up the bike under an oppressive morning sky. José came out to see me off and hugged me goodbye.

'Don't take unnecessary risks,' he said, 'and be careful out there. If only for me.'

I fought back tears and cycled off into the rain.

9

Mr Bo-jangles, and Me

Despite the extended rest, my knee still hurt. My restocked bicycle felt heavy and slow, and the rain was particularly cold and wetting. The road was marked with plastic kilometre posts, and each one seemed to take me further into solitude.

Not surprisingly then, the sight of another loaded bicycle, propped against a bus shelter, was spirit-lifting. I rolled to a stop and peered inside. Sitting on the bench, wearing a hobo's collection of grubby clothes and boots, cradling a steaming tin mug between gloved hands, was Bojo.

He wasn't surprised to see me.

'You want some coffee? Get yourself a cup.'

We shared sandwiches and bananas and I asked him where Patricio had got to.

'Ach, he's probably in Ushuaia by now. I wanted to go to Torres del Paine, but he was too impatient. He went his way and I went mine.'

'You were in Torres del Paine?'

'Yeah man, three blissful days. And I came down this great road at the end . . .'

'Not the road with no bridge to it?'

'Yeah, that one. There's a footbridge further upriver that

one of the construction workers told me about. It's a bit of a hellish track on the other side, but it's so worth it.'

I drank my coffee and fumed.

But then we were moving again, racing through the wet landscape with the wind behind us, and my melancholy and regret were dispersed by our laughter. We picked up speed and enthusiasm as we went and very soon my ailing joint and the weight of my bicycle were forgotten.

The road, well frequented by tourist vehicles, was immaculate. The traffic itself – four-wheel drives and tour buses mainly – was uncommonly respectful, giving us plenty of room. The drivers, far from being annoyed by two wind-tossed obstacles on the otherwise perfect strip of asphalt, grinned and waved and gave enthusiastic thumbs-up signs as they passed. It was as though everyone agreed that just to be here, in this far-flung, gale-battered part of the world, was a unifying experience.

'We're here!' they seemed to say with each cheerful pip of the horn. 'And look: you're here too!'

This attitude also seemed to extend to the greater Patagonian population. As we had both experienced in Puerto Natales, the people were open and friendly, eager to give advice and curious about our journeys. It was a very different atmosphere from my first visit to Chile, more than a thousand kilometres to the north, and it wasn't difficult to understand why. Patagonia is tourist central, where the cost of a cappuccino is equivalent to that of one in central London, and the regular flow of Europeans and North Americans are happy to spend big money on sightseeing excursions, track and hut fees, equipment hire and accommodation. Tourism, it seems, is the livelihood of much of the resident population, and visitors are valuable. But unlike holiday hot spots I had been to in other parts of the world, where tourist fatigue can compel the locals to treat their guests with outright contempt, it was pleasing to find that the hospitality of Patagonia felt entirely genuine.

Bojo and I were so immersed in conversation that the hundred kilometres to Morro Chico were almost effortless. It was still afternoon when we pulled up beside the river, we both had plenty of energy, and we debated using the wind and our good humour to make extra distance. But there was a big empty barn by the side of the road, perfect for sheltered camping, and we decided to make the most of that instead. We asked permission at the police station – one of just three buildings for as far as we could see – and they told us to make ourselves at home.

I had never really considered looking for shelter when I camped. Positioning my tent with the door away from the wind usually provided enough of a calm spot to light my stove with ease, and at the end of the day I was happy to retreat to the comfort of my sturdy nylon hideaway. But Bojo's habit was to light a fire each night and to sit beside it with his guitar, and for that he needed a suitable location. There was a rough fireplace inside the barn, left by others who had been there before us, and we collected wood to light a blaze. I brought water from the river and Bojo cooked us his favourite camping dinner of spaghetti, fried onions and tomatoes with grated cheese. Night fell as we ate, visibility shrank to our snug circle of firelight, and the crackling of the flames played counterpoint to the steady roar of the wind. When our appetites were sated, Bojo pulled out his guitar and invited me to sing along, but the warmth of the fire made me drowsy and before long I was curled up in my sleeping bag beside it, falling asleep to Idaho-accented songs from Cuba.

Driven by tailwinds and intermittently spattered with rain, we rode two more days south-east. We set a cracking pace to

Vagabunda in Chile. The sign says, 'Road in bad state for the next 25 kms'. It doesn't mention that it's also all uphill.

Towards the end of the world through the windswept wastes of Southern Patagonia, Argentina.

Argentina's Perito Moreno, the world's largest advancing glacier. Its constant motion is spectacularly audible and visible.

Camping out with Bojo, my camp-fire-constructing, guitar-strumming, storytelling cycling companion. Ushuaia National Park, Argentina.

At a shrine for La Difunta Correa – a modern-day Argentine saint – the faithful leave bottles of water to quench her thirst. These also come in handy for parched cyclists.

'Bless my path', reads the painted tyre. Argentines stop to pray at roadside shrines, asking for favours and miracles from Gauchito (little cowboy) Gil.

Sore knees and Andes. Even in the heat of the desert I had to wear stripy socks to keep my ailing joints warm.

Adobe abodes, slowly turning to dust under the harsh sun of the Argentine altiplano.

My Macpac tent with a distant view of Aconcagua, the highest mountain in the Andes. Its summit is nearly 4000 metres higher than my campsite.

Spiky giants. In the dry landscape of Northern Argentina the comical *cardón* cacti tower metres high.

Six-wheeled foursome on the world's largest salt desert, Salar de Uyuni, Bolivia. From left: Philippe, Hugh, Gwen and Miriam.

Shadows on the salt. Camping at 3653 metres above sea level.

My brother Dan. At dusk on top of Mount Crosscut, Darran Mountains, New Zealand, 1995

beat the cold, but at each lunch break or chocolate stop our sweat froze and body temperatures plummeted. Bojo, who kept his stove easily accessible at all times, saved us several times from shivering misery by brewing billys-ful of hot sweet coffee. We spoke as we cycled, of our families and childhoods, our jobs and our journeys, and I discovered that he found the idea of a nine-to-five working life quite as unappealing as I did. His vagabond history had been a hotchpotch of volunteer positions and contract work to help endangered bird species, and had taken him all over the Americas. He spoke Spanish with a passion.

'So why do you have such an affection for Latin America?' I asked him.

'Well,' he said, thinking about it, 'I guess it's because I'm able to be somebody else here. It's not like I've entirely forgotten who I am, but being in an impoverished part of the world brings me closer to the Philippines, where I was born. My mother's Filipina, and I always wanted to be good at a second language because I never learnt her native tongue, Tagalog. And another thing: life is more vivacious here. It's like, Argentina is on the cusp of modern society, but it's still vibrantly linked to its historical roots and its traditions and arts. Whereas culture in the United States has been saturated by commercialisation almost entirely.'

'Does it bother you, your own culture?'

'Hell, yeah. It's impossible to ignore the disgusting reality of America. And not only that, but the west's "solutions" to other peoples' problems: the exploitation of other countries' natural resources, for example. It's an abomination. Human society has totally detached itself from sustainable existence by allowing the natural world to be valued as a commodity.'

'I guess you see that right up close as a biologist. It must be pretty hard to live in the States if you feel like that.'

'It's not easy. I've had to disengage myself from the conventional American lifestyle. But I'm a fighter, you know? I've been working in the natural sciences, gaining some knowledge to leave a legacy, and I still hope that young people will somehow overpower the mainstream.' With his wild beard and determined frown, his eyes full of inspiration as he gazed off to the horizon, he was every bit the modern-day Guevara.

We arrived, on a Sunday, at the coastal town of Punta Arenas. Tierra del Fuego, which lay just on the other side of the choppy Strait of Magellan, was almost in reach. But although we were itching to get there, drawn like magnets towards our destination, we would have to endure the anticipation; it was two days before the ferry sailed again.

We went in search of a boarding house. It was a cold, grey day, the streets were deserted and it took us an hour of leaning on doorbells before we managed to rouse anyone from their Sunday-afternoon stupor. The enormous lady who finally answered our pleas surfaced only as long as was necessary. She ushered us in out of the rain, showed us up to our room, steered us inside and closed the door on us.

'Breakfast between seven and nine!' she called boomingly from the hallway. Our floorboards shook to a series of resounding thuds as she hefted her considerable bulk back down the stairs.

We dumped our bags on the floor of the tiny room. It had two single beds and a TV. Bojo was ecstatic. While I went to investigate the vagaries of the plumbing system, he lay on the bed with his boots on to watch the news. When I returned, half an hour later, he hadn't moved an inch.

That flickering box on top of the wardrobe was hard to ignore.

Just five minutes, I thought, lying down among the scattered entrails of my disembowelled panniers, and then we can go and explore. It was a brave assertion, but not one that was to bear any relation to reality. It was only when night had fallen, my joints had locked, and the river of drool that had been making its way down the side of my face had reached the back of my neck that I finally managed to break my gaze away from the hypnotising grip of the television. I looked over to where Bojo lay, inert and silent on the other bedspread, like a corpse.

'Are you hungry?' I asked.

'Mumf,' came the enthused reply. He was alive. He sat up with a wide-eyed stare, as though rising from his coffin, and groaned like a Hollywood mummy as he tried to bend his knees. They were stiff with rigor mortis.

We went out for dinner. Punta Arenas seemed deserted, and a rain-laden wind was blowing discarded plastic and empty beer cans noisily down the wet streets. A warm yellow light signalled an open pub, and in the window handwritten notices announced the chef's specials. Inside, the bar was decorated in an ambitiously eclectic manner. The effect, as each style jostled for attention, was surreal. Above the pleated shades of the country-cottage lamps, which hung on vomit-coloured walls, a 1950s-American-fast-food-diner strip of garish pink neon ran the circumference of the room. Oriental wooden tables were placed incongruously beneath French Impressionist prints, and Japanese rice-paper screens – the most tasteful items in the place – were made absurd next to etchings of Victorian chimney sweeps. Above the door to the bathrooms, like the entrance to a cheap Paris brothel, a red neon sign flickered erratically, 'Toilette'.

But the food was great. The simple sandwich I ordered turned out to be a carbohydrate extravaganza; a challenge to even my voracious appetite. The loaf-sized bun, stuffed with tomato, cheese and avocado, was almost entirely invisible under a giant mound of crispy chips. Bojo's steak, centimetres thick and topped with three quivering fried eggs, was so big it was hanging off the plate and touching the table. He ate it all, and ordered another. We drank beer and talked rubbish and relaxed almost to the point of making acquaintance with the blue paisley carpet. But the swirling pattern was enough to make even a sober person sick, and before I could add to the décor with an involuntary imitation of a Jackson Pollock splatter painting, Bojo hauled me to my feet and propelled me back into the fresh air. We stumbled back to our hostel and slipped into deep, television-induced slumber.

The name of the boarding house was Patagonia Sweet, no doubt on account of the landlady's fondness for all things cakey. When we made it downstairs the next morning the table was already laid with enough doughy offerings to stop up the bowels of a dysentery-infected army. We sat down and surveyed the spread before us: white bread rolls with jam, coconut cake, fruit loaf, iced cupcakes, ham, cheese, cornflakes and tea. Our hostess squeezed herself into a chair at the head of the table, lit a cigarette and rested her chin on one fist to watch us eat.

And eat we did. The plates emptied one by one, and I think even Bojo was surprised when we emptied the jam jar and polished off the last slice of cake. We sat back, stuffed, and gave our heartfelt compliments to the cook. She shrugged, and blew a cloud of smoke into the air.

'I like to bake,' she said.

We waddled back into town to see what Punta Arenas had to offer in the way of diversion. What we found was a bar. Bojo's company, and that of a few beers, was more than enough entertainment for a wet afternoon. He was a tireless storyteller and his comic timing was so perfect that, with tears running down my face and abdominal muscles burning with overuse,

I had to lay my head on the table between bouts of hilarity, to recoup my energy. In all honesty, he is the only man to date who has actually made me pee my pants laughing.

But it wasn't just his ability to tell a joke that made his company so appealing; he also reminded me of Daniel. While his long curls, square glasses, part-Filipino features and Idaho accent were about as unlike my blond-haired, blue-eyed sibling as it was possible to get, there was something about the way he told a tale that was uncannily similar. While he related his Latin American travels, in an increasingly funny set of anecdotes, his facial expressions and infectious chuckle reminded me of the way my brother described his own adventures. With an eye for the humour in everyday life, and a soft spot for the quirks in people's characters, Dan could make even the most banal of situations sound hilarious. Some of his characterisations were so effective that I had a whole raft of people I had never met imprinted for ever on my memory. Occasionally one of them would pop into my head for no reason, inducing involuntary snorts of laughter and tears of mirth in all sorts of inappropriate public places.

After the exertion of listening to Bojo, I had to have a little lie-down in the afternoon. Accompanied by a bottle of red wine and a bag of doughnuts we lay prone on our beds, as though stricken with quadriplegia, and watched a rerun of *The Blair Witch Project*. Although Bojo assured me that it was one of the scariest movies ever made, it was difficult, in that cosy little room with floral wallpaper, to allow fear to reign. I laughed when I should have trembled, and even when the ill-fated characters met their gruesome demise I couldn't understand why Bojo was cowering under the covers with the pillow over his eyes. Little did I know that in days to come, as the wind howled like a torture victim outside my tent, the psychological force of the movie would haunt me and sleep would be a distant dream.

Tierra del Fuego – Land of Fire – is the archipelago that forms the pointed tip of the southernmost part of the American continent. In my mind, the two-dimensional map-outline was clear: a curved, organic shape (apparently sculpted by the sheer force of the wind), not unlike an upside-down shark's fin slicing towards the South Pacific. But that was all I knew about it. The landscape ahead was unknown.

I pictured us, in a jumbled daydream composed of all the adventure stories I had ever read, like two hardy nineteenth-century explorers: hauling our bikes along narrow trails through virtually impenetrable forest; crossing raging rivers with our supplies of ship's biscuit and salted pork held high above our heads; contracting malaria, and scurvy; falling into treacherously squelchy bogs and burning the leeches off our limbs each night as we huddled, shivering, under leaky canvas. I even imagined us wearing pith helmets.

That was why, from the deck of the ferry, the first sight of Tierra del Fuego was something of a disappointment. True, the weathered wood and corrugated-iron houses of Porvenir were unutterably charming, and the autumn sunshine was lighting up the fishing-boat-busy bay like something from a *National Geographic* photo spread. But there was no forest, and in contrast to the images in my head, the rolling green pastureland looked bland and domesticated. Gulls cried, power lines whined with the wind and the atmosphere was bleak as we rolled off the boat and headed east. The gravel road led past desolate, fenced-off fields, and the sheep – the few that we spotted – were motionless, like bleached boulders. But the roaring tailwind urged us along with inspired fury, as if to emphasise that the weather, unlike the land, would never be tamed.

We camped where a hotel had once stood. All that remained was the dilapidated signpost, a clump of pine trees and a small concrete shed in which an unfortunate sheep was decomposing. It was a bit creepy.

'Maybe this is where the Blair Witch hangs out,' I suggested. Bojo blanched.

'Don't even *joke* about it,' he warned. 'It's just not funny.' He stomped off to collect fallen branches for a campfire.

As the wind was still going at full blast, with little sign of abating, keeping a bunch of twigs together in one place for long enough to light them was no small feat. But it was Bojo's nightly ritual, as important as my evening cup of tea, and he managed the task with apparent ease. We huddled to cook in the minimal shelter of a tree, alternately scorched and frozen as the capricious wind swirled and eddied and blew the fire in every direction. It was not the most relaxing ambience in which to enjoy dinner, and when a particularly ferocious dragon's-breath of flame leapt up and singed both my eyebrows, I made my apologies and retreated to the safety of my tent. Bojo stuck it out. From the comfort of my bed, where I was writing my diary, I could hear him playing his guitar.

And then I heard another noise, close by but barely audible above the clamouring wind. It sounded like someone carefully moving rocks about. There was a scrape of stone, a thud, and a clonk. And then the same again.

And it was happening directly outside my tent.

I felt sick; it was the Blair Witch, for sure. We were both going to die. Bojo stopped playing. I froze and held my breath, straining to hear the sounds of his last moments, but the roar of the wind covered everything. Then, with perfect horror film timing, my torch bulb blew out and plunged me into darkness. The paralysis that had been locking my vocal chords broke and I let out a long wail of fear.

'Bojooooooooooo!'

'What? What's wrong?' he called, from his fireside seat.

Praise be, he was still there. My heart slowed in relief. I was sweating.

'Nothing,' I replied. 'Play us another tune?'

Like a pair of knackered old racehorses we laboured onwards the next day, creaking at the knees but never losing the enthusiasm to reach our destination. We crossed to the eastern side of the island, to Argentina, and turned right, cycling beside the leaden sea as we followed the coast south. It was cold and raining, and it was only the constant exercise that stopped us from freezing. But some flapping red pennants on the roadside flagged us down; we couldn't pass by a shrine to the Gauchito.

It was the largest memorial to Antonio Gil so far. The walk-in shed, painted red and complete with bench-seats, was full of offerings. The ceiling was festooned with swathes of red cloth. Dozens of red candles burnt, recently lit, and on a low table was a chaotic collection of red wine, red flowers, smouldering cigarettes, coins, toys and tiny statuettes of Gaucho Gil wearing his poncho. In hardbacked notebooks, people had left their prayers. The strength of belief was surprising.

'Gauchito,' someone had written, 'I thank you for all the favours you have done for me and I ask that you forgive me for being so distant from you. I thank you for the family I have and ask you to look after them. I leave everything in your hands. You know what my promise is, I'm going to do it, and I know that you will help me. I love you, and believe in you.' I put the book back and tiptoed out, securing the door carefully behind me as we left.

In a classic case of the sublime to the ridiculous, we had left the unmarked steppes behind for a veritable forest of signposts. Not only was each kilometre marked with a large, reflective, white-on-green marker, but for every five of those was a huge billboard stating our exact distance from every point between us and Ushuaia. We had 239 kilometres to go to our destination, I read. That was good. I liked to know. But just fifteen minutes later, as we approached 'Ushuaia – 234 km', I wondered if this final countdown was going to drive me nuts. The signs were useful, but overdone, and an unwelcome distraction from my nineteenth-century dreams.

I was thinking about the colonials. Trying to imagine the strength of character required to leave behind the familiarity of one's homeland, travel to one of the most remote parts of the earth and start a new life entirely from scratch. It wasn't as simple as a mere change of scenery; the possibility of starvation must have been horribly real. I knew I couldn't have done it. I was thrown into a panic when my stocks of chocolate biscuits began to get low. But if the determination and stamina of the colonists were something to marvel at, that of the indigenous people who were there before them was mind-boggling. In Río Grande, where we took a day off, I found out all about it.

The lady in the tourist information office obviously hadn't had any other visitors all morning. She beckoned us inside with enthusiasm, answered all our questions at length and weighed us down with enough leaflets to start campfires for the next two months. Later, as we sat sleepily digesting pizza in a cosy restaurant, I pulled a couple of the brochures from my backpack. I gave one to Bojo and spread the other on the table, translating it slowly with a finger under each word. What it told me was this.

At the arrival of the first European explorers, who sailed in from the Atlantic in their galleons, there were various indigenous peoples living in Tierra del Fuego. The Yámana (or Yaghan) paddled the length of the Beagle Channel and down to Cape Horn in their bark canoes, fishing, collecting shellfish and birds' eggs, hunting sea lions and penguins and whales. Despite the harsh weather they wore virtually no clothing, choosing to grease their skin with seal blubber instead as protection from the perpetually wet conditions. To avoid freezing to death they relied on fire, carried with them on a bed of sand in the bottom of their boats. Their larger campfires, lit on the shore for warmth and signalling, were the first signs of human habitation apparent to the Europeans. They are what gave the land its current title.

Biologist Charles Darwin's initial impressions of the Fuegians, as described in *Voyage of the Beagle*, were typical of the first explorers and colonists to visit these shores.

'These poor wretches were stunted in their growth,' he wrote. '. . . their skins filthy and greasy, their hair entangled, their voices discordant, and their gestures violent. Viewing such men, one can hardly make one's self believe that they are fellow-creatures, and inhabitants of the same world.'

Darwin's attitude was shortly to be echoed by the works of the Christian missionaries who arrived, with the zeal of the righteous, in the mid-nineteenth century. Viewing the Fuegians as somehow subhuman, they came to 'save' them with clothes, religion and farming. But while their colonial opinions were condescending, at least their intentions were good. The farmers of northern Tierra del Fuego, on the other hand, were tracking the indigenes down and shooting them. Driven to protect their flocks from the sheep-rustling Ona people, who had been forced off their traditional hunting grounds by the white men's fences, the farmers offered a reward for each dead native. The missionaries, landed with a far more pressing case of salvation than they had bargained for, found themselves providing not just education, but exile.

However, not even those with true compassion for the Fuegians could save them from their plight; the missions eventually proved to be equally as fatal as bullets. Imprisoned in what were essentially concentration camps, dislocated from their traditional wanderings and weakened by change of diet and lack of freedom, the indigenes were sitting ducks for imported infectious disease. Less than 100 years after the first mission was opened, the last closed its doors. The races they had intended to 'save' were all but extinct from epidemics.

On the way in to Río Grande we had cycled past one of these old institutions. It was not abandoned – it functions now as an agrotechnical school and houses a museum – but the weather-beaten buildings had seemed somehow forlorn in the barren landscape. We had not felt enticed to stop, but I still had a strong mental image of the place, hunkered down next to the sea, like a monument to failure.

We cycled south with a different perspective. As we set up camp behind barns and under bridges, sheltering from the wind and drawing close to the campfire in the icy night air, I thought about the original inhabitants of the land. So many thousands of years here, surviving the extremes of the erratic weather by huddling around their own fires, yet so swiftly made extinct by the interference of foreigners. I shivered and put some more wood on the flames. We warmed our hands and scorched our shins, and Bojo chased away the shadows with his magic guitar.

I was becoming a willing disciple to the cult of the campfire. My clothes and skin were ingrained with ash.

'I have never before,' said Bojo, 'met a woman with hands as filthy as mine.'

I took it as a compliment.

One evening I confessed that what with his musical abilities, his fondness for his dog back home and his ragged shirt and baggy pants, I couldn't help but think of him as Mr Bo-jangles from the classic song covered by Bob Dylan. He laughed and strummed a chord before revealing the true origins of his name.

It was not because his parents were hippies, as I had thought, but because his mother was a Filipina. In the Philippines, everyone has a nickname.

His real name, he confessed, was Marvin.

As we drew closer to Ushuaia the austere plains of the north gave way to the forested hills of the south and the magical wilderness I had dreamed of finally presented itself. We passed through an inferno of autumnal beech forest. The colours roared like flames. Surrounded by mountains, capped by a ceiling of thick cloud and pelted with remorseless rain, the valleys seemed untouched by man. The road, too, appeared to finally leave the modern world behind. Potholed and puddle-strewn, punctuated by the debris of landslides, it snaked precipitously towards a distant mountain pass, wreathed ominously in cloud.

Bojo was a long way ahead. Looking across a ravine to where the road turned back on itself I caught a glimpse of him, partly obscured by the swirling mist, standing on his pedals with his head down. Battling stoically into the driving rain, with his plastic-bag poncho flapping like an elfin cloak, he was Frodo Baggins on a bike, on the final push to Mount Doom.

And then, sodden and shivering, in serious need of a hot cup of tea, we crossed the final pass and broke through to the coast. Before us were the welcoming lights of ships at anchor on the Beagle Channel, and we knew that we had arrived.

I'm not entirely convinced that any place on a spherical planet deserves to be known as The End of the World, but Ushuaia, in a clever marketing ploy, has nevertheless claimed that title for itself. For us, it was definitely the end of something. Bojo had a job to return home to, I had a journey to continue, and we had to say goodbye.

There is nothing like travel to accelerate a relationship. The stresses and joys of a trip into unfamiliar territory cannot fail to highlight one's strengths and weaknesses, and, more crucially, those of one's travelling partner. The unfamiliar, the unexpected and the uncontrollable of lands unknown have ended marriages, begun romances, and forged lifelong friendships. After only two weeks of sharing food and fires, histories and horror stories, I felt like I had known Bojo all my life. We had barely left each other's side, and it was getting to the point where we needed a surgeon to separate us.

We deliberated for a week. We camped in the National Park, saw sea lions and whales on the Beagle Channel, lingered in cafés, visited bakeries and joined the revelling backpackers for debauched nights in the hostel. But Bojo had sold his bike, and Vagabunda was feeling neglected.

It was time to move on.

Northern Argentina and Bolivia, where metres-high cacti stud the deserts and llamas roam the altiplano.

10

To the North

We flew back to Buenos Aires. After weeks of travelling at bicycle speed, it felt somehow obscene to go such a huge distance in such a short time, and coming out of the domestic terminal was a rude awakening. The hot air of the city flowed around us like scummy bath water and the traffic roared. Horns blared, shonky exhausts spewed black fumes and we looked at each other in alarm. We had left tranquillity and arrived to madness.

Neither of us wanted a long goodbye. We hugged at the bus stop amidst the pollution and the noise as a bus lurched to a stop beside us. Bojo leapt on.

'*¡Que siga el viaje!*' he yelled as the bus pulled away – may the journey continue!

I slung a leg over my top tube and threw myself into the maelstrom.

This time in the city, I wasn't planning to stay. Keeping to the glass-strewn edges of the potholed road, I headed for the bus terminal to book a ticket to Mendoza. It was only a short way, but far enough to remind me that cycling in the capital is wholly inadvisable. I marvelled at the incomprehensible carelessness of the drivers as they charged nose-to-tail at reckless speeds, changed lanes without warning and screeched reluctantly to a halt at traffic lights. The noise was deafening and the heat was stifling. It was just as I remembered.

Before I left England, people had told me I would love Buenos Aires. 'The theatres! The bars! The tango!' they said. 'It's like a little piece of Europe, but with a Latin American flavour.' It was true. The people were beautiful, the streets fascinating and the possibilities for diversion endless. I had lingered for more than a month, more than happy to allow my male friends to show me around the best pizza and beer establishments.

I had stayed with Javier; not the guy whose appearance had initiated my romantic dash across the Atlantic, but a good friend I had worked with on the rickshaws in London. His parents, Leandro and Yoli, welcomed me into their home and treated me like a daughter, feeding me vast meals, teaching me the rituals of *mate* and playing me the best tango tunes. Javier acted as my tireless translator and city guide, and his older sister Karina helped me with my Spanish homework. It was a complete cultural immersion and although it took me the next five months to become fluent enough to properly thank them for it, I was infinitely grateful.

They showed me photos of their family holidays around Argentina and told me where to go and what to see. They also advised me not to make the trip alone on my bike. Although I was sceptical, and subsequently ignored the warnings, I understood what led them to expect the worst. Buenos Aires may be full of culture, cafés and consumer goods but, like any metropolis, it has its unbearably sad face of poverty and crime as well. And things just weren't the same, Javier told me, since the cataclysmic economic crash of 2001.

Before that, he said, for the ten years that the Argentine peso had been interchangeable with the United States dollar, things had been great. Initially helping to stabilise the economy, the one-to-one exchange rate had led the people to feel comfortable in the present and confident about the future. They saved their money in dollars, knowing that even if the good times didn't last for ever, they would have something to fall back on. By the late nineties, however, things were crumbling. Higher prices of goods had made local products uncompetitive on the international market. Industries suffered and the massive layoffs that resulted raised unemployment to over twenty per cent. Soon, over half of the population was living below the poverty line. The people were struggling to eat, and the national debt was enormous.

In a desperate attempt to scrape together enough to pay the whopping sum, the government halted pension payments and froze bank accounts, effectively banning people from accessing their own money. Understandably, the people were furious. Fuelled by indignation, and hunger, they protested by looting shops and supermarkets across the country. When the government responded to the anarchy by giving the police greater powers of arrest, they just made the public angrier.

On the evening of 19 December 2001, a crowd gathered spontaneously in downtown Buenos Aires. They were not activists. They were ordinary people: working- and middle-class citizens forced into action by the perceived ineptness of their government. They took to the streets clanging pot lids and beating casserole dishes.

'You should have seen it,' said Javier. 'Tens of thousands of people, a *sea* of people, marching and chanting and making this unbelievable noise. We all wanted the President out. It turned into a three-day riot. The banks were burnt. People looted the shops. It was total madness.' He shook his head, remembering. 'The police used bullets and tear-gas on innocent people. Nearly thirty were killed.'

'Did the protest do any good?'

'Well, sort of. The President resigned. He left from the roof of government house by helicopter while the crowds were still outside. Then we went through four more presidents in two weeks until we got stuck with the current one, Duhalde.

'He was just as bad though. The first thing he did was to devalue the peso. Pretty soon it was worth less than half what it was before. And when the banks finally let people take money out again, it was only in pesos. All their dollars were gone. Imagine it: saving and saving and saving all your life. Then one day going to the bank and finding that most of it has disappeared. It happened to my Dad.' He looked across at his father and said something in Spanish. An expression of disgust crossed Leandro's face, and he thumped the table with a fist.

'*¡Ladrones!*' he cried. '*¡Qué barbaridad!*' I wasn't sure what the words meant, but I understood him perfectly.

'We were lucky,' Javier continued. 'We got it all back. But there are still a lot of people who haven't.'

That was obvious enough. Every day on my way to Spanish class I saw the metal barriers covering the banks and the armed guards in the doorways. Outside in the street, *los ahorristas* – the savers – protested by hammering on the metal with lengths of pipe, posting manifestos and spraying insults in red paint. The formidable steel doors of the Bank of Boston were covered in slogans. 'Thief!' they accused. 'Give us back the money', and with determination to see justice done, 'We will never give up'.

This was just one symptom of a general mood of discontent. In downtown Buenos Aires the anger towards the government was constantly palpable, although it was the picketers who expressed it the best. *Piqueteros* are out-of-work members of community groups that have formed to feed the hungry and to agitate for change. They protest by blocking roads, bringing the city traffic to a halt for hours on end and braving police bullets to demand food and welfare payments. As I stood with my face next to someone else's sweaty armpit, breathing diesel fumes on an overcrowded, overheated bus that had been stuck for an hour at a roadblock, I realised what an effective method they had of making their plight known to the greater populace.

It was not the outspoken protesters who really brought the desperate state of the nation to my attention, however, but the continuous quiet presence of the *cartoneros*. I saw them at work on every street in the city, at every hour of the day, rummaging in rubbish bags for waste to recycle. When the devaluation of the peso made cardboard (*carton*), paper, plastic and glass too expensive to import, recycling became a key feature of production. With no other work available, some of those who had lost their jobs in the crash took up the task of collecting these items from the streets. I read a bit about them in the newspaper. One estimate suggested there are as many as 40,000 *cartoneros* in greater Buenos Aires, each one eking out a living of around ten pesos (NZ$5) per day by selling what they find. Although officially unemployed, with no form of security, benefits or insurance, this underclass is so massive that the government has been forced to take notice of their appalling working conditions and legalise their activities. A programme of tetanus and diphtheria vaccination has been implemented; a campaign launched to encourage citizens to separate recyclable waste from food scraps and sharp objects; and a six-day-per-week train service provided between the poorer suburbs and the wealthier ones (where rubbish bags are more likely to yield saleable items).

We were waiting at the station one evening when this train pulled up. I went to get on, but Javier held me back by the arm.

'This one's not for us,' he said. I took a step back, and looked in through the glassless window. There were no seats in the carriages. Instead, they were stuffed with wonky-wheeled bicycles and battered trailers. Leaning against the walls, hanging on to shopping trolleys and jiggling overheated toddlers, the workers were grim-faced. Their clothes were threadbare. I watched the train pull slowly out of the station, and tried to imagine the long, sad night of toil that stretched ahead of them.

Even for those who still had their jobs, life was not easy. Although my return to Buenos Aires was brief, and most of it was spent in the bus station, the atmosphere of struggle was nevertheless apparent.

With the ticket to Mendoza clutched in my hand, I stood and watched the two baggage handlers. Their vests stretched tightly across broad backs, and with arms as thick as thighs they threw the bags about like feeble wrestling opponents. They looked angry. They glared at my bike, and at me, and snarled. They hauled and heaved and punched the bags into place, grunting and swearing and working together with fierce efficiency. Then they turned abruptly, grabbed Vagabunda, jammed her brutally into the remaining space and slammed the door on her.

'The tip, the tip, *chica*. Don't forget the tip.'

As if I would. They grabbed the cash and wiped dripping brows on forearms. As they left, one of them glanced back at me with contempt and spat on the ground.

Virtually the first thing I saw in Mendoza, after the long head-befuddling overnight bus trip, was an elaborate piece contemporary art. It was an installation work, cleverly usin both levels of Plaza Independencia and the roof of the subterranean modern art gallery. It consisted of a massive, upside-down articulated truck, and the large crowd that had gathered was contemplating it appreciatively. The cab was dangling from the roof of the gallery, twisted and smashed and resting hard up against a tree on the ground level. Broken glass was scattered around and the police tape and actors in uniforms made it look really authentic. It was a cryptic statement, and I wandered through the crowd to admire it from various angles.

'It's amazing no one was killed,' said someone behind me. 'Unbelievable.'

'Incredible,' said another. 'I guess it was lucky the tree was there, or it might have been worse.'

I blinked and suddenly saw the scene for what it was.

At the top of the steps to the upper level of the plaza, the clues described what had happened. Black tyre skid marks led across the flagstones to the grass, where the trail continued in the form of two long muddy scars. At the edge of the square, where the truck had crashed in off the road, metal bollards were snapped clean off at pavement level. A couple of metres away one of them was driven into the grass up to its base, like a chess piece in a sandpit. Across the road and past the busy intersection was the big uphill where, I later read, the truck had lost its brakes.

Back at the scene, lifting equipment had arrived and the police were moving people out of the way. I could see now that it had all happened by accident, but the truck looked so good lying there on its back that it somehow seemed a shame to take it away.

I had no desire to stay longer than necessary in Mendoza; my brief revisit to Buenos Aires had reminded me that cities were not where I wanted to be. I loaded Vagabunda with tea and biscuits and cycled south on Route Forty, looking for the turnoff to the west that would take me into the hills.

A truck pulled up beside me at an intersection and the driver leant from his window.

'Be careful ahead,' he told me. 'It's a dangerous stretch of road. Go fast.' It wasn't until someone else told me the same thing that I realised he wasn't referring to the traffic.

I pulled in to a service station to buy a map and the four attendants cheered. One of them, egged on by his mates, came over to chat. He wanted to know if I was scared cycling on my own. Well, no. Should I be?

'Si, si. ¡Ojo, chica, ojo¡' he said, and with one index finger he touched his cheek just under his eye. It was a gesture I knew well. Ojo means eye, and said in this context it means 'Look out!' It was something people said to me a lot.

He followed it up with an explanation. 'There are bad people living around here and the next part of the road is dangerous. Go fast, and don't stop for anyone, okay?' I looked him in the eyes; he was serious.

'Thanks for the advice.' I shook his hand solemnly and waved to his mates with a lump in my throat. Whatever would my parents say if I didn't make it back? I had an obligation to stay alive.

I hit the road with such a burst of adrenalin that any potential evildoers must have seen no more than a blur shooting past. I covered the next ten kilometres with record speed and before I knew it was taking a sweeping right-hand corner, charging onto a highway off-ramp and hurtling across a bridge into the countryside with a sigh of relief. I had foiled the thieves and their dastardly deeds.

The landscape differed wildly to that of the south. It was rocky and dusty, prickly with cacti and crisscrossed with dried-up streambeds. Ahead, the Andes rose up like a wall, deeply blue. Beside the Mendoza River, camped in the sand, I built a fire and stoked it up to blistering; in the shadow of the mountains, the cold drew in quickly. I set the billy to boil on a branch above the flames and imagined my position on a map of the world. The fact that my friends and family were so very, very far away no longer made me melancholy. Instead, I felt the excitement of independence and the thrill of solitude. I couldn't wait to see what lay ahead.

My intention was to follow the main trunk line west for a detour to see Aconcagua, the highest mountain outside of the Himalayas at 6959 metres. Just on the other side of the *cordillera* lay Santiago, Chile's capital city, and the road I was following was the most direct way there from Buenos Aires. Replacing the long-defunct railway, it followed the Mendoza River valley into the foothills, rising gently as it went, before plunging through a tunnel to the other side of the Andes. It was a relatively painless way to climb, but treacherous. The traffic consisted almost entirely of lorries carrying loads between the two countries and there was no hard shoulder. When two trucks passed each other on the narrow strip of tarmac, there was no room left for a bicycle.

For the truckies, overtaking one another seemed to be some sort of hobby. I heard a lorry approaching from behind and gripped the handlebars tightly to counter the rush of air as it passed. The road ahead was empty.

'He's got plenty of room,' I thought as the engine got louder. 'He'll pull out and give me space.' But a horrific blast of the horn sent me swerving off the tarmac, and two trucks raced past side by side, mere centimetres apart. Shakily, with my wheels embedded in the sand, I waited for my heart to slow and watched them fight it out. It was a long time before one of them relented. Countless times throughout the day the same thing happened. They were impatient to the point of insanity, and it was not conducive to a daydreaming bike ride.

I couldn't complain though. My ailing knee had miraculously recovered, the sun was hot and for the first time in weeks it was possible to cycle without four layers of clothing. I wore a sleeveless shirt and watched my freckles pop up beneath a glistening layer of sweat. My appetite, which had diminished during the sedentary stay in Ushuaia, came back with a vengeance and by the time I reached Uspallata I was ready to eat the entire contents of the service station grocery shop. I shared some *facturas* with the inevitable stray dog – there's always one wherever there's food – shoved some more into my panniers and set my sights on the hills.

The valley became progressively more beautiful. The peaks towered on both sides, the river began to look a long way below and the occasional iron rail bridge that spanned it provided a profound sense of scale. I was puffing up a short steep section when two cars stopped a couple of hundred metres ahead of me. A bunch of people got out and stretched, looked around at the scenery and started to take photos. Drawing closer, it became obvious that one of them had a video camera, and that she was pointing it at me. As I was red in the face, dripping sweat and having a hard time making it up the hill, I was not particularly keen on being captured for ever on someone's home video. Especially as they hadn't asked me first. I put my head down and pushed hard on the pedals, trying to accelerate out of shot.

'Where are you from?' called the lady on the other side of the lens. I looked daggers at her and wiped my snotty nose on my hand.

'Germany,' I scowled.

Puente del Inca, which I located a hot-and-bothered half-hour later, was worth climbing to altitude for. Past the cluster of ramshackle tourist shops, over the disused rail tracks, a bizarre sight awaited. On the other side of a deep ravine, built into the bank high above the rushing river, a small brick ruin was melting slowly into its surroundings. It was streaked with sulphuric yellow, smoothed by years of water-borne mineral deposits and blistered with cankerous growths. The natural rock bridge that spanned the river towards it was similarly carbuncled, and steaming, as though covered by a layer of bubbling cheese.

I went to decipher an information board and discovered that the building was once a spa. It was built to make use of the thermal waters that flow from the ground all around it, but a flood destroyed the accompanying resort in 1965 and the complex fell into disuse. The waters continued to flow, however, and they were still hot. I locked my bike, crossed the bridge and went to explore the ruin.

Pulsing from holes in the ground and cracks in the walls, the water had long since overflowed the man-made channels and tubs. It dripped from the ceilings and flooded the floors. I sloshed through with my shoes off, left my clothes in a small dry spot and climbed into a steaming tub in my underwear. The water was soft and aerated, and the rising vapour fizzed in my nose like the bubbles from champagne. I floated in the blissful heat and let the medicinal waters work their wonders on my overused legs.

The therapeutic properties of these thermal springs have long been known. Legend says that long, long ago, a ruling Inca came here to heal his son, who was gravely ill with a strange sickness. The prince, who was the only heir to the throne, was deeply loved by his people, who foresaw that he would be a wise and just ruler. They prayed to Inti the sun god and Mama Quilla the moon goddess that he be cured, made sacrifices in his honour, and summoned the best medicine men of the realm to treat him. But the prince remained ill, and a wise man said that the only remedy would be the healing waters of a certain thermal spring, which lay a long way to the south. So the king, accompanied by a caravan of people and llamas carrying supplies, set out with his son from Cuzco – the centre of the Incan Empire.

They travelled for months, crossing the many landscapes and climates of the continent before arriving among the highest peaks of the Andes. There they saw the steaming spring, welling from the ground on the other side of a deep gorge. But the river below was torrential, seemingly impassable, and they despaired that the mission would fail because of this one final barrier. No matter how long they looked, they could not find a way to cross the divide.

Then they witnessed an astonishing event. The sky grew dark, the earth trembled, and from the high peaks that surrounded them fell huge chunks of rock and ice. Tumbling into the ravine, the debris jammed together to form a solid bridge, allowing the king to carry his son across the river to the thermal waters. The prince was finally cured and the rock formation became known as Puente del Inca – Bridge of the Inca.

I soaked in the hot water until I fairly fizzed with health, and climbed out light-headed and decidedly cleaner.

The final climb of the day was especially arduous. The road was steeper than ever and the air was thinner, making me more than usually breathless. I turned off the main road onto a gravel track. Ahead of me, icy blue against the pale evening sky and patchy with late-summer snow, was the gentle curve of Aconcagua. She seemed so close, and so invitingly climbable. I listened for the roar of avalanche and shivered. The shadows were growing and the temperature was dropping; I needed to set up camp before the sun disappeared over the rim of the mountains.

With the tent pitched and the tea brewing I sat in my sleeping bag and watched the light fade. The peaks, huddling around me on three sides, turned gradually to silhouettes. I imagined being here with my brother, imagined his grin and his crazy yellow hair and his faraway look as he searched the mountains for possible ascent routes. I wished, as I had so often done before, that we could share an adventure together. I wished that he could see how alike we had finally ended up.

But they had always drawn him, the high places. The mountains had called him and he had gone.

11

Dames of the Desert

The valley looked different on the way back down. Perhaps it was because the sweat was no longer running into my eyes. With cap on backwards and joints relaxed I freewheeled, leaning smoothly into the sweeping corners and passing a bunch of road workers at terminal velocity. They whistled and called out.

'¡Hola, Preciosa!'

I smiled but didn't stop. I was having too much fun.

From Uspallata I followed a little-used route north into the desert. Brittle, stumpy bushes dotted the plains, the road was loose and dusty, and under the glaring sun it slashed through the landscape like a white line on a green chalkboard. The occasional vehicle appeared far in the distance like a mirage, quivering and dancing in the heat as it drove towards me. One such blob on the horizon took so long to turn into a recognisable shape that I eventually realised it wasn't moving at all. Half an hour after first spotting it I drew alongside. The little van was propped up on a jack and a wheel was off.

'Everything all right?' I asked rather moronically of the two ladies who were motionless in the front seat. They smiled and nodded. One of them gripped the steering wheel as though she was still driving.

'Do you need some help?' They shook their heads.

'No thanks. Someone went to fix our tyre for us already. We're just waiting.'

'Well, do you want some water? It's a bit hot.'

'No, no. We're fine. Thank you.' They smiled again and returned their gaze to the horizon, staring through the windscreen with the hopeful expectancy of nuns anticipating immaculate conception. Behind me, the road was empty for kilometres. The sun beat down on the van roof. Flies buzzed. The women sweated, and awaited the coming of their saviour with saintly patience.

It was just as well that they refused the offer of water as mine was running out. Expecting to cover the hundred kilometres to the next town with relative ease in one day, I had neglected to sufficiently fill my bottles. The road was soft, the wind was against me and I was going a lot slower than anticipated. By mid-afternoon there was still no sign of humanity ahead and around me the parched plains offered no respite.

Then, in the middle of nowhere, as though placed by a beneficent deity, a magnificent sight appeared. In the sun-baked monotone of the desert the lurid colours of a pile of plastic bottles seemed strangely beautiful. Green, red, yellow and orange, the two-litre soft drink containers, all full of water, lay jumbled up at the foot of a small wooden shrine. I dropped my bike and went to investigate.

The water had been left for the Difunta Correa, a sort of folk-hero-cum-modern-day saint. The legend of her death – maybe fact, maybe fiction – is powerful enough to inspire offerings in roadside memorials all over the country. The story goes that when her husband, who was a soldier in the civil war of the 1840s, was sent to a neighbouring province, Deolinda Correa decided to follow him. Carrying their newly born baby and some provisions to sustain her, she set off on foot into the arid San Juan landscape. Alas, under the cruel desert sun it was not long before she ran out of water, and thirst and exhaustion overtook her. A very mortal demise, but one that was lent an air of miracle by one significant fact. When her body was found, her infant son was still alive and suckling at her breast.

In the spot where she is supposed to have died, a little village has grown to accommodate the hundreds of thousands of believers who flock there each year to pay their respects, offer thanks and request miracles. They leave gifts, money, flowers and candles. And, always, they leave a bottle of water.

I didn't think the Difunta would mind if I took just one of the many litres people had left for her at this particular shrine. It was hot and stale, but it would save me from following her fate.

Some kilometres further on, while staring hopelessly at the map as though it might actually tell me my location, I had some unexpected company. It came from a bend in the road, in the form of a rather large truck, and pulled up beside me in a cloud of white dust. The driver's name was written in large letters on the windscreen: Claudio Schummacher. He jumped out.

'Oh,' he said, surprised. 'You're a girl.' I laughed, and held out my hand.

'I am, you're right.' He squeezed my fingers with a huge paw and grinned.

'I passed you a little while ago, and got to thinking that you might want a lift. So I came back. *Do* you want a lift?'

'Well, no. But it's a very kind offer.'

'Do you want a *mate*, maybe?'

'Absolutely.'

So he turned his truck around, parked it neatly behind my

bike, and opened the passenger door. I climbed in. In between the seats, a battered kettle perched on a gas stove. He filled it with water from a bottle, lit the flame and handed me a bar of nougat.

'You'd never catch an Argentine girl doing what you're doing,' he said. 'Aren't you a bit scared?'

'Of what? Of men in trucks, in lonely places?' Claudio laughed, and his belly wobbled.

'Of getting stuck in the desert. There are some very long stretches without bicycle shops.'

'Well, I can fix most things myself, and the empty spaces are the best bits, don't you think?' He nodded, grinning hugely, and told me about his work and the joy of constant motion. At times he missed his five kids, but not the ex-wife, and being on the road was where he belonged. He pointed behind him to his little cabin.

'I'm self-sufficient. I have my bed, my *mate*, some wine for tonight. What more can a man need?' Pouring hot water into the *yerba*, he sucked thoughtfully on the straw. 'Who else gets to see these lonely parts of Argentina except for you and me?' He poured more water and handed me the brew, and we looked out at the desert turning golden in the low light of late afternoon. The Andes were purple with shadow. I slurped the sweet tea with appreciation and handed the cup back with a thank you.

'If I didn't like bikes so much,' I said, 'I'd probably be a truck driver.' He giggled.

'What's a girl like you doing without a boyfriend?'

'Ach, they just slow me down.'

I jumped out of the cab. The shadows were growing and I wanted to set up camp. Claudio started the engine and leant from the window, shaking his head with his lip between his teeth. He looked me in the eyes.

'You're terrible!' he said appreciatively, and drove off towards the distant horizon.

My skin was turning brown after only a few days in the sun, but my face was taking a hammering. There was no shade, and no matter how much sunblock I applied, or how low I pulled my cap, my lower lip was frying. The intensity of the heat was also giving me a headache, and the blood was roaring in my ears. Past the sleepy town of Barreal was the fertile Calingasta valley. Below the road, the river looked cool and inviting, and I puffed on, wobbly with exhaustion, looking for a place to swim.

At the intersection of two roads, where a group of people milled outside a petrol station, my knees gave way. I lay in the road with Vagabunda on top of me, wondering whether I could ever get up again and, if so, how I would regain my dignity once standing. With the utmost air of cool, as though flinging oneself on the road at intersections was *the* way to stop these days, I untangled my legs from the frame, got calmly to my feet and hefted the dead weight of my bike upright with a show of strength. Unfortunately, in my state of wooziness, I exerted a little more force than was strictly necessary, causing my steed to continue her trajectory through the perpendicular and crash resoundingly onto her other side.

It was even more uncomfortable lying on top of the bike than being underneath, but staying there until night fell with my head buried between my panniers seemed nevertheless like an attractive course of action. As that would only have drawn more attention than I had already managed to do, however, I clambered to my feet, rubbed my grazed knees and slunk away to lick my wounds.

On the bank of the San Juan River I finally collapsed. There were vicious prickles sticking into the softer parts of me and sand was getting in my ears but it didn't seem to matter. My eyes were closed, the insides of the lids swirled red and blood pumped in my temples as though my head might explode. Water. I needed water. I eased my scorching body into the shocking cold of the river, sending clouds of steam rising, and a long sigh of relief escaped from my parched lips. I floated until my limbs were numb and crawled out into the shade of the tall grasses.

My hidey-hole was secluded from the road, and once I had cut away all the prickles, laid out the camping mat and cranked the stove up, it felt like home. There was no need for the tent. I drank half a river's worth of tea, ate a vast dinner and wriggled into my sleeping bag. The sky grew dark and the stars appeared; on the bumpy mattress of the Andes the constellation of Orion lay pensively on his side. I listened to the river and watched the moon come up, bright as a bullet hole in the dark of a barn.

Cycling eastwards through the San Juan valley, everything seemed in harmony. The landscape was grand, the weather perfect, I was fit and strong and absolutely without self-doubt. It was a rare and profound feeling and it spurred me on at a cracking pace along the potholed tarmac. The narrow strip of road wound precipitously upwards, cut from a sheer rock face far above the river. Every few kilometres lay the rubble of old landslides, and giant-sized bites from the edge of the asphalt told of erosion from below. The most precarious section, some sixty kilometres or so, was one-way only: westbound until three o'clock in the afternoon and eastbound until dawn. It was a good system, the only problem being that starting from one end several hours after lunch, and having various hills to climb thereafter, it was a rather large task for a heavily loaded cyclist before tea-time. I made it two-thirds of the way along before stopping at some abandoned concrete houses.

The area had been victim to a mudslide, and a couple of the buildings were buried up to knee height. I couldn't tell how recently it had happened, but what looked like hard, sun-baked earth turned out to be no more than a thin crust over sticky clay that threatened to suck me down when I stood still. It was a wide tide that had flowed and settled over a large area and the road was a bulldozed track through piles of flood-borne wreckage.

One of the little houses had escaped the worst of the deluge. It was a bit dusty, but liveable, and someone had used it recently as a picnic spot. There were a couple of fruit-crate chairs, a table made from a roadwork 'hazard' sign, and half a forty-gallon drum served as a fireplace. It was quite homely, a vagabond's dream in fact, but the warm evening air was too good to miss. I swept the wide back doorstep with a conveniently provided broom, unrolled my groundsheet and dragged the fireplace next to it. Then I braved the gloop to collect a heap of wood and lit a hearty blaze. The eucalyptus was so dry that it burned at an incredible rate; the branches disappeared into the flames as though into a wood-chipper. The night filled with the wonderful smells of smoke and gum, and as water heated for tea I sang,

'Once there was a cyclist, camped by a muddy house,
Under the shade of the tall Andes,
And she sang as she sat and she waited till the billy boiled,
Who'll come and bike Argentina with me?'

The flow of traffic was against me on the final stretch out of the valley the next morning, but as there was no more than one vehicle every half an hour it didn't seem to matter. The road flattened out into wide plains of vineyards, the two-way road resumed, and in the little town of Zonda a hurtling pack of bicycles whirred towards me at top speed. It was a Saturday-morning road race and the sight of so many legs and wheels whizzing around under such a sunny sky was uplifting. There were wiry young whippets on too-big racers; grey-haired oldies with all the stretchy lycra gear but none of the puff; lean mean racing machines with thighs like hairy hams; and ponderously pedalling podgies. But in that huge crowd of rattling, whirring and humming bicycles, among the hundred or more competitors, there was not one single female. It was suddenly obvious why people kept stopping me to ask questions.

In the city of San Juan, I spent two days eating. That wasn't the original plan, but as I arrived on Saturday and left on Monday morning, there was sod-all else to do. Apart from a few restaurants and the cinema, virtually everything was shut for the weekend. I treated myself to a cheap hotel room, seeing that all the campgrounds were fifteen kilometres out of town, and set about making the bathroom filthy. Then I went out to buy food.

The only place open during the siesta was the petrol station, where seemingly all of the town's youth could be found. The snack bar was so jam-packed with Saturday-afternoon revellers that people were spilling out onto the station forecourt. Lined up under the plate-glass window a fleet of brightly coloured hot rods was parked, polished to perfection and resplendent in the sun, and inside the shop the babble of excited voices was almost louder than the raucously blasting pop music. Plastic tables were covered in Quilmes bottles and overflowing ashtrays, the till rang incessantly with endless purchases and the smoke was so thick that I wondered if one of the petrol storage tanks was on fire. The atmosphere was as highly charged as a rock concert. The sexual promise was palpable. The girls were batting long eyelashes and hiding coyly behind curtains of shiny black hair, while the boys leered pointedly at denim-wrapped buttocks and tried to look manly by sticking their chests out. It is no accident that in Spanish one does not talk of 'wooing' a woman, but of 'conquering' her.

It was a cultural microcosm and although I had only come in for some juice and a packet of biscuits, I browsed the shelves for ages, surreptitiously studying the fascinating pre-coital behaviour from behind displays of crisps and stacks of *yerba mate*. Not that there was really any need to be furtive about it. They were so busy flirting that I could probably have wandered among them with my pants on my head singing 'Waltzing Matilda' at the top of my voice without attracting any attention. I lurked until the smoke began to make my eyes water, paid for my juice, picked up my bike and left, taking care not to scratch any of those gleaming symbols of machismo as I went.

Back at the hotel, I wondered what to do with myself. At first I was bored, having finished my last book a couple of days before, but once I opened my panniers and surveyed the dusty, dirty, travel-worn contents, I realised there would be easily enough to keep me occupied for an afternoon. My clothes needed washing, the stove had to be dismantled and scoured clean of soot, my shorts had holes that needed darning and my dictionary, shedding leaves like a tree in autumn, required an urgent duct-tape repair job. When all that was done I cut my fingernails, deforested my legs to the thigh, washed a sandpit-ful of grit from my hair and spent a happy half-hour in front of the mirror, peeling bits of sunburnt skin from my shoulders. There were also maps to study, my diary to write, brakes to tighten and a chain to oil, and I began to wonder how I had gone for so long oblivious to the necessity of these housekeeping chores.

With everything spick and span, Sunday progressed in a more relaxed manner. My contented stupor – in which I lay on the bed and stared at the ceiling, feeding biscuits into my mouth one after the other like Homer Simpson with a packet of forbidden doughnuts – was punctuated only by a brief but energetic walk to possibly the only vegetarian restaurant in the whole of Argentina and various forays to the en-suite bathroom to light the petrol stove for cups of tea.

Fully recharged with food and sleep, I bowled north out of San Juan with the assistance of a lively tailwind. To my surprise, the sky was cloudy; what with the scorching heat of the previous few days and the parched nature of the land, I had been under the impression that if it ever actually rained in this region then it was only in brief, cataclysmic, annual deluges. The light drizzle that began to fall soon changed my preconceptions, and before long I was wearing all my warmest clothes and climbing to a pass with my head in the clouds. It grew incredibly cold. My breath was steamy and my hands and feet were numb.

I considered warming up at the Talacasto hot springs, where a tiny cluster of concrete bathhouses crouched in the landscape, but the thought of getting undressed was too painful. My water bottles needed filling though, to see me across the next uninhabited hundred kilometres, and I pulled into the yard of the small establishment to look for a tap. A well bundled-up bloke came out to greet me, rubbing his hands and stamping his feet and cheerfully relating the fact that not one single drop of water thereabouts was drinkable.

'But you can have some of ours,' he offered, going inside to fetch it. When he returned, weighed down by a full plastic container, it was in the company of his wife and his son. They were equally as stout as he, almost spherical in their many layers of clothing, and they stood silent and wide-eyed in the doorway as he filled my bottles. I got the feeling they didn't see too many bicycles around their way.

'So where does this water come from?' I asked.

'From San Juan,' he replied pleasantly.

I felt guilty. San Juan was now sixty kilometres away. I offered to pay but he wouldn't hear of it and he waved me on my way with a smile. Although only a handful of people would pass by his business all day, he seemed amazingly resigned to not taking a single peso from me.

Standing on the pedals, battling the extra weight of the water, I climbed back onto the road. It led steeply upwards to a cliff above the springs, and from my vantage point I could see the three of them standing motionless in the yard, staring up at me with all the wonder of UFO spotters. I threw them a grateful wave and disappeared around the corner.

It was freezing. The traffic-free road continued upwards into an oppressive fog, and snow hung wetly from the bushes. Although hauling myself heavenwards required all of my effort, it was impossible to warm up. I needed refuelling, but it was too cold to stop without a fire. Reaching an abandoned and disintegrating shack, I engaged in a brief session of star jumps and running on the spot before collecting a pile of fallen roofing material. Then, unable to think of anything apart from the immediate need to be warm, I forced my freezing fingers to work, fumbling with matches and scraps of toilet paper until the damp twigs caught. Encouraged to life by the careful fanning of my tin plate, the little blaze gave out the first tentative waves of heat. I huddled closer, feeding sticks into the flames until the fire gained momentum, took off my shoes to warm my icy toes, dried my gloves, boiled water and ate a high-energy lunch. It took an hour for the blood to return to my fingers but eventually, with singed eyelashes and charred socks, I was sufficiently revitalised to continue. Fire is a grand invention.

After two more days of rain and fog – through which I pedalled, padded out with innumerable layers of clothing, like a rotund snowman – I dropped back out of the clouds. The road led me back to the heat of the plains, into the sea of sand and scrub known as *puna*.

The north seemed to be almost as uninhabited as Patagonia. In the weeks to come I would cycle for hours without seeing a person, a house or even a car. I liked it. The solitary spaces between towns – kilometre after kilometre of silent, sun-baked landscape – were never boring. I relished being utterly in the middle of nowhere, self-sufficient and unreachable, unmolested by city noise, pollution, mobile phones, or the garish sight of fast food joints. Sitting in the shade of a bush to eat lunch, sheltering from the midday heat, I would close my eyes and listen. It might be possible to hear the rattle of dry branches in the breeze, but more often than not the only thing audible would be the buzzing of flies. For hundreds of kilometres, I never even heard an aeroplane.

The best thing about being alone in so much space was that I could camp anywhere. There was no need to set goals, no need to reach a certain spot by night time. I simply kept going until the desire for a cup of tea was stronger than the desire to cycle, rolled my bike off the road into the desert and made myself at home. This was good because, in past experience, the time between deciding to stop and actually finding a campsite could be the most trying of the day. On occasions, when fatigue had overtaken me before a decent tent spot had appeared, I had been reduced to a pathetic, quivering scrap of desperation, disposed to irrational flashes of hate for the whole concept of cycle-touring and driven almost to the point of giving it up altogether. Therefore, being able to stop wherever and whenever I chose saved me a great deal of mental and physical anguish.

Taking a tip from an elderly cyclist I had met in Mendoza, I often slept in dry riverbeds where there were fewer spiky plants to puncture tyres. Fallen wood was bone-dry and plentiful, and building a fire each night became something that I looked forward to almost as much as the cup of tea that followed.

The only planning required was making sure that there was sufficient water on board. I could carry twelve litres if necessary – enough for three days – but because of its weight there was no question of taking more than I absolutely had to. Washing was a luxury that occurred only when I stayed in a town, and pretty soon my skin and clothes were smeared with ash and covered with the yellow earth of the desert. But it didn't bother me. In fact, I quite enjoyed it.

I bowled into San José de Jachal like a ball of dusty tumble-weed. It was three days and nearly 300 kilometres since my last shower and, although I had long since become immune to my own smelliness, there was no doubt that parts of me were pretty whiffy. However, my immediate thoughts were not of grubbiness but of grub; my stomach was rumbling.

I cycled around the central plaza in hopeful anticipation, looking for a place to buy a meal and possibly a beer, but everything was closed. All that remained in my panniers were some squashed crackers, some apricot jam and an unpleasantly warm bottle of mayonnaise. I sighed deeply, sat myself on the steps of the plaza and dreamt of home cooking while eating my unappetising rations.

I was in the middle of an elaborate tomato-soup-and-crusty-bread-followed-by-apple-pie-and-custard fantasy, when I was brought rudely back to reality by the noise of splashing water and the prickling of drops on my skin. I looked up to see an old bloke with a hand over his mouth and a horrified look on his face.

'Oops. Didn't see you there!' he said apologetically. The

bucket in his hand dripped fat drops onto the concrete. 'I was just cleaning out the *kiosco*.' I looked over to the little booth that had seemed to be closed.

'Don't worry,' I said, 'I needed a shower anyway. You don't sell beer do you?' He shook his head.

'I don't, I'm sorry.' He looked at me quizzically. 'Are you all on your own?'

'No, of course not.' I smiled. 'I'm with my bicycle.'

'Aah.' He nodded thoughtfully. 'Wait there.' He rushed off into the *kiosco* and returned with a handful of boiled sweets and lollipops, and a couple of bread rolls. 'For energy,' he said solemnly, as he put them into my hands.

At five-thirty in the evening the shops reopened. I was the first one through the doors of the tiny supermarket, cruising the aisles like a hunter and falling on my prey with cries of triumph. I staggered to the fruit and vegetable counter under the weight of my basket and got chatting to the man who weighed my bananas. Intent on conversation, it was something of a shock to catch a glimpse of myself reflected in the glass cabinet behind him. I was filthy. My hair was wild and there was chain oil smeared across my cheek. I apologised.

'Well, at least your face is cleaner than your hands,' he said, passing me the bananas. He was right. They were covered in grease and the nails were edged with black. It was true that I had been conserving water, but the extent of my muckiness did seem a bit unnecessary. I bit my lip and looked at him sheepishly. He just smiled.

But if my appearance and odour were more than unsavoury, they didn't stop the pump attendant at the petrol station from taking an interest. I was filling up my water bag at the tap when he came sauntering across to chat. He was about my age but far more fashionable and his funky haircut looked out of place in this little backwater. In keeping with his unconventional appearance, he had a unique approach to conversation.

'Do you like rap music?' he asked, as an icebreaker. I thought about it.

'Umm, it depends. Why, do you?'

'Yeah, and hip hop, and house music. I like going to raves. D'you like dancing?'

I didn't have to think about that.

'I *love* dancing.' Suddenly, the thought of clean clothes and cocktails and a night on the town crowded my desert-dazzled brain. I imagined myself whirled around by a succession of dark-eyed Latino boys. We looked at each other and grinned. 'I *love* dancing,' I said again.

An angry banging on the plate-glass window made me spill water all over my shoes. A young woman was glaring out from inside the shop and gesturing to my music-loving friend that he should get back to work. I looked at him in surprise.

'Your boss?'

'My wife.' He put a finger to his temple and twisted it. 'Insane, in the brain,' he said in English. His workmates were laughing at him as he went back to the petrol pumps.

'She's a bit jealous,' one of them shouted across to me. 'You'd better go before she sets the fire-hose on you.'

I really didn't see how such head-to-toe filth could be any provocation for marital disharmony, but I caught the eye of the pump attendant on the way out and he winked at me saucily.

12

Desolate Roads and Adobe Abodes

There seemed to be no rhyme or reason to the condition of the roads. While some remained unpaved despite being well frequented by local vehicles, others were as wide and flawless as runways but virtually devoid of traffic. I clattered down the potholed track from a small range of hills, turned a corner and found myself on a pristine stretch of empty asphalt, perfectly straight for as far as the eye could see.

I wanted to enjoy the emptiness of the desert. I set a steady pedalling rhythm and tried to allow my mind to roam, but with so few features in the vast landscape it was impossible to ignore the kilometre posts. No matter how hard I tried to avoid it, my eyes flicked automatically towards each one, straining to define them through the heat haze and counting them off as they slid past to starboard. Unable to free my mind from this constant cycle of calculation, I even began to count the revolutions of my pedals between posts. Each kilometre stretched out to interminable proportions and my tyres were like liquorice pinwheels sticking to the long black tongue of the road. It was for this very reason that I didn't have a cycle computer or wear a watch. I didn't trust myself to use them wisely and I knew that the compulsive ticking off of minutes and metres would eventually drive me mad.

It was a relief to cross the provincial border between San Juan and La Rioja and find myself back in unmarked territory. The asphalt was even smoother on this side, and the road flatter. I increased the pace and settled into a meditative state where time and distance had no importance.

The petrol station at Guandacol rose up from the horizon like an oasis. Although the silence of the desert had left me with little appetite for buildings or conversation, it really was time to have a shower. I pulled up in the gravel of the forecourt, propped my bike against a pump and stepped into the cool of the shop.

The young owner of the establishment was mopping the already spotless floor.

'*¡Buenas tardes!*' he greeted me with enthusiasm, brought me a glass for my beer and went to switch the hot-water heater on. Outside on the step, I sat in the shade and closed my eyes for the first heavenly draught of Quilmes. It was worth every one of the last hundred kilometres that had brought me to it.

The man with the mop came to chat. He had recently bought the business, he told me, and was taking a while to get used to the rhythm of it; talking with his customers helped to pass the time.

'What do think of Argentina?' he asked.

'I love it. It's perfect for cycling. I've never cycled on such traffic-free roads.'

He leant on his mop and stared out into the blinding sunlight. The horizon pulsed in the heat and the asphalt shimmered. Silence.

A brief frown wrinkled his brow.

'You're right,' he said after a pause, 'there's hardly any traffic.'

After four days without washing, a simple shower takes on a whole new meaning. Sploshing about in the steamy torrent of hot water I slathered soap and squirted shampoo, slipping and sliding in the growing tide of scum. My skin slowly revealed its true colour, with some persuasion from a scrubbing brush, and I did my best to remove the black from beneath my nails. The water swishing around my ankles, in which toiletries and clothes floated like flood-borne flotsam, was deep red-brown.

Pink and tingling, I emerged reborn into the afternoon sun. A light breeze had picked up, the shadows were growing and the single Quilmes was acting like a tranquilliser on my overworked legs. I thanked the station owner earnestly, unable to convey the true extent of my appreciation, and cycled off to the dry bed of the Guandacol River to get dirty all over again.

The landscape was becoming more and more surreal. Sheer red cliffs loomed to the east and the parched earth around me was deeply cracked. In the riverbeds, delicate crusts of sun-baked clay curled at the corners and lifted like scabs.

At a roadside shrine, where the Difunta Correa and Jesus appeared to be on an equal footing, I spent a happy half-hour watching an army of ants systematically deconstructing a bunch of chrysanthemums. The flotilla of little yellow sails moved unfalteringly past my feet, fluttering in the breeze and heading purposefully across an ocean of sand. Hurrying in the other direction, unburdened by cargo, a line of tiny workers returned to the shrine for more. Curious, I followed the bobbing petals for several hundred metres, noting the width and smoothness of the path worn by endless activity. It was as well defined as a bicycle tyre print, trodden flat by millions of toiling feet and completely cleared of obstacles. I surveyed the endless comings and goings until such tireless diligence made me feel lazy. Then I jumped up, left the Difunta a horseshoe I had found, and rode.

I made it to Villa Union just in time to empty the shelves of the local shop before it closed for siesta. Settling myself on the grass of the plaza I perused my purchases: some bread, a jar of peach jam, a packet of biscuits and four tomatoes. I rubbed my hands together and chuckled with glee. The state of excitement brought about by such small pleasures was indicative of my state of mind. It was not that I was bored by the empty spaces between towns, far from it, but the stillness and solitude led me to view the delights of the urban world with the wonder of a child at Christmas. By far the best item in my basket that day, the one that kept me spluttering with ill-suppressed mirth as I ate my sandwiches, was a roll of toilet paper whose brand name was 'Happening!'

As I said, the desert had rather affected my mind.

The previously bustling town plaza was virtually empty by the time I finished eating. The only people who hadn't gone home for lunch were three small and grubby boys. They were playing with a dog on the grass, running around in circles, beating each other up, laughing and hollering and hurling themselves to the ground with reckless abandon. They worked the dog up into such a state of excitement that when the boys finally collapsed, exhausted, he simply couldn't stop. Quivering and panting, slobbering with pleasure, he rubbed himself feverishly against the upturned backside of the smallest of the lads. The other two squealed with delight. They egged the dog on, clapping and cheering and imitating his movements until he appeared about to achieve the relief he was striving for. But just as he gained top speed, jerking and trembling like a wind-up-toy, one of the boys grabbed a fallen branch and whacked him a merciless blow up the rear end. He yelped, heartbrokenly, and ran across the road with his tail between his legs.

And with that disturbing image replaying itself in my mind, I left Villa Union to the locals and cycled out of town.

In a steep valley of ochre cliffs and tiny villages, I fought the temptation to squat an abandoned house. Like most in the rural north it was made from sturdy mud bricks and thatch, a cheap and resourceful building strategy that has one unfortunate drawback.

The innumerable crevices of adobe houses provide shelter for a bug that feeds on the blood of mammals. The bite from the vinchuca, usually sustained at night when it comes out of hiding, is not, in itself, dangerous. But the parasite that lives in the bug's faeces, and which enters the human bloodstream through the mouth or any small wound in the skin, can cause a long-term degenerative illness known as Chagas' disease. Once in the body, the parasite is with the victim for life, and the chronic stage of the disease can appear up to forty years later. Manifesting most commonly as swelling of the heart, oesophagus or bowel, it can cause heart attacks, choking, severe constipation and chronic fatigue. Buildings can be improved, by plastering mud walls and replacing thatched roofs with metal, but for the poor this is often not an option. The further north I went the more advertising I saw in each town to warn the locals of the dangers. Chagas' is the curse of rural South America.

I took a curious look inside the tumbledown building. In the dry heat of the desert it was slowly desiccating in the sun, literally turning to dust bit by bit. The fallen bricks would have made a brilliant fireplace, and the roofing material excellent fuel, but I left everything where it was and laid out my sleeping bag in the sand instead. It was warm enough to camp without the tent, and I quite liked having a cactus for a neighbour.

The night grew to impenetrable blackness. I lit a fire. I was happily feeding branches into the flames, cocooned in a cosy ring of dancing light, when a sudden sound from the shadows nearly caused me to have a spontaneous happening in my knickers. It sounded like the cough of a fifty-a-day smoker about to bring his lungs up. I held my breath and waited to hear it again; was it an axe murderer, waiting in the bushes for the right moment to pounce? Or a bandit, hoping to steal my bicycle while I slept?

It was neither. Another throaty cough was followed by a stamping of hoofed feet, a swift inhalation of breath, and a long and sonorous moan. From across the valley came an answering call, and two donkeys commenced a lengthy and discordant dialogue.

The following afternoon, in the town of Chilecito, I installed myself in a cheap hotel and painted the bathroom red with desert dust. Then I set out in search of a decent lunch. I was sick of sandwiches. Sick of biscuits and bananas and badly cooked pasta. I wanted to eat something delectable, delicious, divine; something that was worthy of the effort that had gone into growing such an acute appetite. For a vegetarian in a beef-loving country, however, this was no easy task.

Apart from a few regional specialities, and with the exception of upmarket tourist restaurants, the eateries of Argentina almost all sell the same dishes. Whether it's topped with fried eggs, surrounded by chips, slapped between hearty slabs of bread or simply eaten alone, meat is the unquestionable centrepiece of any full-sized meal. The tradition of the *asado* has elevated the simple grilling of steak to such an art that the array of cuts on the indoor barbecue can be quite mind-bending. For the faint of heart, or delicate of stomach, all that remain are pizza, uninspired salads of wilted lettuce and tomatoes, stodgy spaghetti with tomato sauce and, on the odd lucky occasion, *empanadas* with cheese or corn. The only place where I could be certain that vegetables would be on the menu were buffet restaurants known as *tenedor libre* – literally 'free fork'. There, the selection at the salad bar was often as extensive as that on the grill, but as I could never exercise the restraint required to stop eating before feeling physically sick, these places had to be avoided.

Usually, after taking an optimistic glance at the menu to ensure that nothing new or exciting escaped my attention, I would order a sandwich *without meat*. This would have the effect of making the waiter look at me as though I had two heads, both of them ugly, and more often than not the meal would arrive with a layer of ham in it.

I wandered around Chilecito's Plaza Sarmiento, squeaky clean and ravenous. It was the middle of the afternoon, on a Sunday, and the restaurants were closed. The only place that looked like it might sell food was jammed with men, drinking and smoking and watching football on television. I caught the waiter's attention, and he came to take my order at an outside table. There was no food, he said, not at this hour. A sandwich, maybe, chips even, but nothing more. I sighed.

A sandwich then, and a beer.

There seemed to be a hell of a lot of traffic in Chilecito. From my position on the edge of the plaza I considered the constant procession of clapped-out cars and scratched-up scooters and wondered where everyone was going. For a town small enough to walk across in ten minutes, it was absurdly busy.

It wasn't until the rusty white hatchback had passed by for the third time, and its trendy young driver had blown me the third kiss, that I realised the traffic wasn't actually going anywhere. It was going round and round the plaza, yes, but reaching a destination was obviously not the point of the exercise. The chosen form of entertainment, it appeared, was to dress up, pack as many friends as possible into the car and drive around town checking out the opposite sex. As the heat was truly sweltering, it must have been something of a challenge to keep looking cool, but everyone seemed to be having fun nevertheless. Round and round they went; round the plaza, round the town and round the bend, in my view. To waste such glorious weather packed shoulder to shoulder, overheating in a hot metal box, seemed entirely ridiculous. Then again, as I chose to spend *my* time alone and dirty in places without water, and to cycle thousands of kilometres just for the fun of it, my opinion was probably not to be trusted.

After two nights of lying awake listening to the revving of engines, the rattling of mufflers and the screeching of brakes as boy racers used the road outside my window as a drag strip, it was high time to return to the peace of the *puna*. More sun, more silence, more solitude to lose myself in. There were no markers to tell me how far I had gone, and few features in the landscape to indicate that I was making progress. It was great.

Only a handful of vehicles passed the entire day. Considering the straightness and emptiness of the road, all of them travelled at a surprisingly sedate pace. I put it down to the calming effect of the desert. If it worked on them like it worked on me – like a sedative for the mind – they would soon lose any ambition to reach their destination, possibly even forgetting where it was they were going.

I felt like I could stay there for ever. All I needed was to find somewhere with a water source, within a day's cycle of a town, and I could set up home. Build a permanent fireplace. Build a sun shelter. Cook bread. Watch ants. Lie and look at the stars each night. I sat under a thorn tree to eat lunch, and thought about it.

The wider the horizons around me, the less my own personal horizons seemed to matter. All worries about the future had long since disappeared, as had any doubt that cycling around alone was an acceptable way to conduct my life. My existence had shrunk to the private pleasure of the immediate: *this* was my life now, this moment, right here, right now. All that mattered was drinking enough water, exercising, feeding myself and getting enough sleep. Pared back to the basics, life seemed so simple.

Unfortunately, my new-found self-awareness didn't extend to knowing when I had eaten enough lunch. Within a few minutes back on the road I was having serious regrets about the extra banana. The weight of everything in my stomach, combined with the heat of the sun, caused a sort of instant fatigue that caused me to creak to a halt, topple off the bike and fall profoundly asleep in the shade of a bush. For half an hour of complete unconsciousness I lay spread-eagled on the soft shoulder like the victim of a drive-by shooting. Had anyone passed by and decided to steal Vagabunda, I would never have known until it was too late.

In the little town of Belén, in the province of Catamarca, I stopped to send an email to my long-suffering parents. They had been really very good about letting me disappear into the depths of an unfamiliar continent. Knowing as they did that asking, or demanding, that I reconsider such a rash move would do nothing to deter my enthusiasm, they had barely uttered a word of protest. This had been quite a relief. It was so much nicer to embark on a journey with their blessing than to know they were sitting at home cursing me for being so stubborn and wilful. It wasn't that I was a rebellious daughter, far from it, but they had raised me to make my own decisions and have confidence in myself, and although they may have had their doubts about this particular adventure they also wouldn't have wanted me to back down and stay at home just because they were worried about me. I loved them for that, and for such resigned acceptance the least they deserved was an occasional sign that I was still alive.

So there I was in the internet café, hitting the keys furiously in my gee-I-wish-I'd-learnt-to-touch-type two-fingered manner, when an entirely unexpected noise roused my attention. I looked out of the window with surprise. It was raining.

Let me get this straight. It wasn't just raining in a light, pitter-patter, make-the-daisies-grow sort of way. Oh no. It was absolutely biffing it down in the manner of an angry hurricane trying to annihilate a small Pacific island. Unbelievable volumes of water hammered onto the tarmac, gutters overflowed and the streets around the plaza turned rapidly into lakes. I thought about the riverbed I had camped in the previous night, tent-less and oblivious to the potential floods gathering in the sky above me. It was only a matter of timing that had allowed me to escape being sluiced away to the Atlantic.

I lingered at the computer as long as possible, peering hopefully out at the sky and wondering if the deluge would stop as suddenly as it had begun. But the clouds were thickening, the temperature was dropping and it looked as though the weather was settling in for the afternoon. What to do? Maybe I had been a bit spoilt by the constant heat and sun, but the thought of getting cold and wet just didn't appeal to me at all. I went and checked in to a hostel.

It had looked quite cosy from the outside. The husband-and-wife team who welcomed me in had been very nice – generously letting me wheel my muddy bike across the polished white tiles of the reception area – and they cut me a good deal on the price of the room. But it was, without a doubt, the coldest building I had ever had the misfortune to stay in. The walls were made from concrete breeze-blocks, there was a brisk wind whooshing in from the large gap at the bottom of the door and the solitary blanket on the bed was about the size and thickness of a tea towel. I tried to warm up under the shower, but the timidly dribbling water was tepid and the air in the bathroom icy; I got out colder than when I went in. The only thing that might warm me up, I thought, was a hot drink. I pulled some clothes on, cranked up my petrol stove on the tile floor of the shower and huddled over it while the water boiled.

There was a knock on the outside door of my room. Tentatively, I opened it a fraction, wondering if the proprietors had heard the stove and were about to tell me off. But the landlady, presumably aware of how fridge-like the rooms were, had just come to offer me a cup of coffee.

'Oh. Well, that's very kind,' I said, 'but I'm fine actually.' The roar of the stove was clearly audible.

'But you must be freezing! A little coffee, to warm you up? I can bring it over.' She looked past me into the room with a quizzical look on her face.

'No, no,' I said loudly, to cover up the sound of the rattling billy lid, 'I don't drink coffee, and it's really very warm in here. Thanks, bye!' I shut the door on her and ran to save the kettle before it boiled over.

Oh dear. I climbed into my sleeping bag with all my clothes on, slurped scalding hot tea and wondered at my hitherto unknown capacity for rudeness. It would have been nice to go and have coffee with them, maybe chat a little, but instead I had managed to portray myself as some weirdo recluse who didn't appreciate Argentine hospitality. Then again, maybe I *was* a weirdo recluse. The real reason I didn't want anyone to know what was going on in the bathroom was not because it was dangerous, but because it seemed to be such an intimate sort of activity. In the same way that it is embarrassing to be caught squeezing spots or sniffing socks, I couldn't bear to be discovered using the toilet as my kitchen.

Later that evening, wandering around in the rain looking for somewhere to have a hot dinner, I saw a couple of girls trying to crash-start an enormous flatbed truck. The weedy teenager, with arms and legs as frail as toothpicks, was pushing with all of her not very considerable might, while in the driver's seat her older sister was fiddling with the gears and shouting encouragement. I crossed the road to offer some help.

Victoria, the younger, laughed like a loon when I took up position beside her, and increasing fits of giggles soon reduced her pushing capacity to rather less than nil. My efforts were not much better. After we had tried several times without success, she ran across to the nearest café and fetched her big brother Matias. He sauntered over casually, put one massive shoulder against the tailgate and leaned into the task like a forward in a scrum. The truck rolled, coughed, shuddered and roared into life. Matias smiled nonchalantly and went back to his beer.

Úrsula revved the accelerator and leaned out of the driver's window.

'Do you want to come to our place for dinner?' she asked. I grinned.

'Absolutely!' I climbed into the front bench-seat with Victoria and we hung on tightly as the truck lurched away from the curb, surged forward into the traffic and swung wildly out of the plaza with a bow-wave of floodwater rising grandly on each side of the bonnet.

A pack of mangy dogs greeted us when we arrived at the house, bounding about in the puddles and slobbering liberally. They licked our hands with long tongues, whipped our legs with wagging tails and shoved snouts up crotches with enthusiastic affection. Úrsula shooed us inside and closed the door on them.

'Come and see the house,' said Victoria, taking me by the hand. 'It's not really so . . . beautiful, but we have some nice things.' She showed me the macramé lampshades that her mother had made, and the twisted branches that her father had varnished. On the concrete walls were family photos, and she explained who all the people were. That very day, she told me, was the tenth anniversary of the death of her mother. Back in the kitchen, Úrsula was preparing a stew. Refusing all offers of help, she moved about the room with perfect efficiency, holding an effortless conversation at the same time. I guessed, from her air of practice, that she had been filling her mother's shoes for the last decade.

Victoria sat me next to her at the table and showed me more photos. They were mostly of her in various stages of childhood; as the youngest, she was obviously the family favourite. She certainly had a winning way about her. At thirteen she was still a skinny kid, but her big brown eyes and curly hair promised great things for the future, and her perpetual giggle was infectious. She giggled at my bad pronunciation and she giggled when I tickled her for giggling at me. In fact, the only time she stopped giggling was when she screwed her face up in serious concentration and tried to tell me the time in English.

Matias came home with his younger brother Elías, Úrsula served up the stew and we ate while Argentina lost resoundingly to Brazil at football on television. The boys looked downcast. They managed to cheer themselves up, however, by turning their attention my way. They teased me relentlessly, as though I was one of their sisters, and it was probably a good thing that I was often lost in their rapid-fire language. The four of them had an easy relationship, joking and laughing and seemingly a complete unit despite the absence of parents. It was nice to watch, and to be a part of, and in some way it reminded me of my own unconventional home-life. My brother and I were teenagers when my father remarried; not only did we gain a Cambodian stepmother but two new sisters as well. It had taken a while to get used to, but in the end the mixing of cultures had made me far more adaptable, tolerant and open-minded. I loved them all, my old relations and my new ones, and the few times we had all gathered around a table together had been really special. I was proud to have such a unique family, and I always found it fascinating to experience other unusual domestic situations.

There was the sound of a vehicle outside. The dogs barked. Victoria turned to me with big eyes.

'Papa's coming,' she said solemnly. Boots scrunched on gravel and the door opened. Elías got up from the head of the table, shook his father by the hand, then sat back down in a different seat. Mr Díaz sat down in the empty chair and nodded at me.

'We found her in the town,' said Úrsula, putting a plate of food in front of him. 'She helped us to start the truck.' Another nod. He put his eyes down and concentrated on the stew. I followed the example of the others and turned back to the television.

He didn't stay long. Pushing his chair back when he had finished, he bid us all a gruff goodnight and drove off. Victoria started giggling again.

'He's a real womaniser,' she said. 'The ladies just love him.'

13

Mind Your Language

It was midnight when Matias finally dropped me back to the hostel. The reception area was cold and silent, and the landlady was sitting alone in a chair. She didn't smile when I walked in.

'*Buenas noches,*' I said. 'Were you waiting for me?'

'Well, yes, actually.' She stood up with a long-suffering sigh, as though I was a teenager home late from a party.

'Oops. Sorry. I suppose you hate it when people come in at this time.'

She frowned.

'Yes, it's really difficult, you know? Waiting, waiting, waiting. Being here all day in case people come. Being here in case they go. I don't like it, but what can I do?' She shook her head, despairingly.

'Oh,' I said, somewhat taken aback, 'it must be awful.'

'It is. Especially after living in the capital. We used to run a business there and we were always busy. We were doing very well, too, but now . . .' She sighed again, and sat back down. I perched on the arm of the sofa.

'So what made you move away from Buenos Aires?'

'Well, times got hard, you know? The economic crash . . .'

'I see. But don't you like living somewhere a bit smaller and quieter?'

'Not at all. We've only been here two months and already I'm bored. I don't like the local people either. Argentines are so lazy.'

'Really? It seems to me that people work very hard in this country. They *have* to work hard.'

'Well, yes, the white people do, of course. But I'm talking about the Indians. Lazy, lazy, lazy, they are. Always have been, always will be.'

My jaw dropped. It was nearly 500 years since the Spanish first began to impose their social judgments on the indigenous people, but it seemed that old-style racial prejudice was still alive and well. I fixed her with a hard stare and wondered if it was worth debating the issue. Your native brothers, I wanted to point out, lived here for millennia before the arrival of the *conquistadores*. Their survival in these harsh lands doesn't exactly point to an inherent laziness. Furthermore, being shot at, rounded up and enslaved, having their land stolen, given government food rations to put an end to traditional hunting methods and generally being treated as less than human wasn't exactly likely to provide a subjugated race with the means and motivation to thrive in the alien social system forced upon them.

But I didn't say anything. Not only was I speechless with indignation, my Spanish was nowhere near good enough for such a challenging monologue. And anyway, I wasn't going to right the injustices of the world by arguing with a bigoted hostel owner from Belén.

I left her to stew in her own bitterness, and took myself to bed.

For the first few hours of the following freezing morning I stayed under the covers, sipping hot tea, reading a trashy book and shivering. The weather hadn't improved overnight, and my thin streak of stoicism – the one that occasionally allowed me to venture out into inclement weather – was nowhere to be found. I decided to stay another day.

By noon I had sunk into a funk of solitude and boredom. The book, which I had found lurking under the bed, was proving to be rather dull. The only exciting thing about it, in fact, was the moment when a large and furry dead moth fell suddenly from between pages thirty-two and thirty-three and hit me in the face. That got my heart racing for a few moments, and the discovery of several more specimens a few pages further on kept me in a mild state of anticipation, but it wasn't really enough to constitute a thrilling morning. At half past twelve I had had enough. I slammed the book shut – causing a sudden dusty shower of desiccated insect – clambered from my sleeping bag, pulled on my wet shoes and rain jacket and dragged myself out into the downpour to look for somewhere to eat.

The only restaurant that was open suffered from a severe lack of heating. A white neon strip-light did nothing to enhance the frigid atmosphere, and the flickering television in the corner added no hint of cosiness. Apart from the waitress, who was wiping red crusts from the tomato sauce bottles with a dirty cloth, and her two young sons, tucking into platefuls of steak and pallid potatoes, I was the only customer. I left my jacket on, sat down at a rickety Formica table and shivered while reading the menu.

'Is there anything nice to do in Belén?' I asked the waitress when she came to take my order. She frowned.

'Um. No. I don't think so.' She thought about it for a minute. 'We have a statue of the Virgin. On a hill. There's a good view from there on a sunny day.'

We looked out of the window at the pelting rain.

'Anything else?'

'Err . . . let me see.' She put her head on one side. 'Nope. Nothing I can think of.' She shrugged. 'Do you want the special? It's beef.'

I ordered a beer, in the hope that alcohol might help me to forget the cold, fuelled myself with forkfuls of tasteless pasta and listlessly watched local television. It was appallingly bad. There was a soap opera showing – one of those where the quality of the acting is inversely proportional to the height of the drama – and I watched with rising fascination as the characters struggled to display the emotions appropriate to each scene. At the climax of the episode, when the doctor solemnly informed the family that their wife/sister/daughter was afflicted with terminal cancer and had less than a month to live, I saw the art of acting drop to unprecedented lows. Lower lips wobbled, eyebrows quivered and nostrils flared like those of racehorses in distress. Their shoulders shook in unison as they sobbed theatrically and I watched to the end, mesmerised by the comical expressions, the jerky camerawork and the wobbling walls of the set. It was so bad it was almost good.

The rain was still falling in merciless volumes after lunch but the beer leant me a sort of woozy optimism. I ignored the rivulets of freezing water that trickled down my collar and took an investigatory turn of the plaza: there might be a bookshop or a craft shop or a place to buy cake. Sloshing through the puddles with perverse delight, at times up to the ankles in scummy floodwater, I peered hopefully into each shop window. Everywhere was closed. It was only after gazing for several minutes at the window display of a shoe repair shop, trying to drum up enthusiasm for bootlaces and tins of polish, that I finally conceded defeat. There were no people in the streets and no traffic. The cloud had descended to just above roof level.

I went back to the hostel and got back into bed.

Seen through the prison-style iron bars of my concrete cell, to which I clung with the grim desperation of a long-term inmate, the tiny patch of weak blue sky raised my spirits like a flag of freedom. The rain had eased off to a drizzle during the night and the cloud seemed to be dissipating. It was all the inspiration I needed to make a break for it.

The road out of Belén led directly into the *puna*. The surface was of rocks and washboard but the patch of blue was growing steadily in the east and I cycled towards it with little concern for the obstacles. With lungs filling to capacity at each breath and legs spinning at a frantic rhythm, I put all my effort into shaking off the lassitude of the previous day, setting my pace as though pursued by a crack team of convict-hunting prison dogs.

Sometime in the late afternoon, after several hours of non-stop pedalling, I skidded to a sudden halt. There by the side of the road, lying in the dirt, was a bicycle. Behind it, resting against a tree and drinking from a leather water bag, was a man. He smiled broadly. His round face and dark skin clearly indicated indigenous origins.

'*Hola*,' I said.

'*Hola*.' He scrambled to his feet, shook my hand and offered me the bag to drink from. I took a slug. It was wine.

As we had progressed from complete strangers to drinking buddies in a matter of seconds, it seemed natural to me that we should address each other as equals. This very quickly proved to be a mistake. In Spanish, there are two distinct grammatical forms to choose from. The first is the one you might use to speak to, for instance, your teachers, your boss, a stranger in the street or the policeman who has just pulled you over for speeding. The second form is the one with which you speak to your family and friends. Somewhat confusingly, however, there don't appear to be any hard-and-fast rules about when and with whom it is necessary to use which grammatical form, or when you can drop the barriers and move from formal to informal language. This seems to vary from country to country and even, as I was about to discover, from province to province. Due to the fact that the people of cosmopolitan Buenos Aires had, without exception, spoken to me informally, as had the tourist-savvy Patagonians, I had become used to using only the friendlier style of grammar. The other form, the more polite one, I had happily dismissed as unnecessary for now: why learn two ways to say things when I could just use one?

Pablo, the man with the bicycle, was not from Buenos Aires. He was from remote Belén where, at the age of forty-something, he still lived with his mother. He wasn't married. He was shy, reserved and very polite. I was soon in a linguistic pickle.

We cycled on together, speaking of bicycles, and I tried to get my head around the situation. Here I was, a woman at least ten years his junior, talking to him as though he was my best mate while he, with grave reserve, treated me like a visiting dignitary. It was ridiculous, but it seemed that neither of us was going to bend. There was no point for me to start being formal so far into the conversation, and he obviously had no intention of changing his tone. Maybe he spoke to his mother like that too.

We stopped every few kilometres for a swig from the wine skin – the effects of which helped me to forget my confusion a little – and to admire each other's bikes. His was an inexpensive, one-geared affair, but he had personalised it with a paint job, home-made carriers and various dangling ornaments including a set of rosary beads. Attached to the seat tube, strapped into a leather sheath, he carried a full-length *facón*, the traditional knife of the gaucho. His rear carrier was loaded with baggage but he wasn't touring. He was on his way to the next town in the hope of a job.

'It's not so easy to get work these days,' he told me, 'no matter what skills you have. I can do pretty much anything: building, painting, mechanics, etc, but I have to travel all over the province for it. I like the bicycle, so it's not really a problem for me, but it's a bit tough on the youngsters. Once they finish school there's not a lot for them to do.'

'Where do you stay when you're not in Belén? Do you get accommodation where you work?'

'No, not usually. I can stay with friends in some towns, like I'll do tonight, but I camp out if I have to.' He waved an arm at the horizon. 'We're not exactly short on space out here.'

The sun was low as we reached Andalgalá, and the mountain range that rose up before us glowed golden. We stopped to say goodbye at the town plaza and Pablo, like the gentleman that he was, offered me the last of the wine. I didn't like to offend; I drained the bag dry.

Maybe it was because the overnight rain had wet all the wood, making it impossible to light a morning fire; maybe it was that the newly opened packet of coffee turned out to be barley substitute (a taste comparable only to freshly boiled tar); or perhaps it was just that I got out on the wrong side of my sleeping bag. But whatever the reason for the bad mood I began the day with, no matter what caused the lack of cycling enthusiasm that followed, there was no justification for what I did next.

I hitched a ride on a truck.

In my defence, let it be known that it wasn't actually my idea. It wasn't as though I was standing by the roadside with my thumb out, or lying in the dust waiting for someone to take pity on me. Nothing of the sort. Let the jury know that I was, in fact, doing my valiant best to overcome my evil temper while *simultaneously* dealing with the acute inclination of the sadistically potholed road. I even – and this, surely, will testify to my character – refused two separate offers of assistance from passing truckers. By the time the battered Ford pickup lurched to a halt beside me, however, I was ready to listen to what its occupants had to say.

'Do you want a lift?' the driver asked.

'Um. No. I'm okay, thanks,' I replied without conviction.

'Are you sure? Do you know what the road's like up ahead?'

'Um. No. Not really.' On the map it was an innocent red squiggle.

'Well, it's awful. It gets steeper than this, and it goes on for ever. It'll be dark before you reach the top.'

Oh God. I wasn't in the mood for a whole day of climbing.

'Do you have room for me?'

'Of course!'

The driver, who was squashed into the cab beside two gargantuan women, jumped out to help me lift Vagabunda onto the flatbed of the truck. I climbed up there too. The ladies gave me a thumbs-up from the front, the driver engaged first gear, and we pulled away up the hill with a succession of ominous rattles from the engine and a cloud of black smoke. And that, Your Honour, is how I ended up cheating. I plead guilty.

We twisted and turned up a set of pendulous switchbacks, each turn taking us to a more precarious position on the cliff face. As we faltered at each corner, stalling and restarting, rolling back and heaving forward again, I gazed into the abyss beneath us. Then, as each perilous moment passed, I looked up to where the switchbacks continued towards the heavens, like something from the madcap imagination of Dr Seuss.

I tried to envisage the state of my temper had I cycled the whole way. Around a quarter of the way up I would have been thinking, irritable and impatient, 'I *must* be nearly at the top now.' At a third of the way, tired and tearful, I might have had a little tantrum and stamped my feet in frustration. And around halfway I would surely have sat by the side of the road and bawled, renounced cycle-touring for ever and maybe pushed my bike off the cliff. As it was, I sat serenely and admired the view while congratulating myself on having made the right decision; for once I had let my common sense triumph over my stubbornness.

An hour or so later we stopped at the top to unload my bike and the women handed around sweet coffee and crackers. The driver, whose enormous belly was a classic example of a lifetime on the meat, chips and white bread diet, munched steadily and considered me with a critical eye. Then he looked at his two spherical companions, put his head thoughtfully on one side and turned back to me.

'Could do with a couple of bicycles for these two, no?' He grinned devilishly.

The ladies giggled, unconcerned, and wobbled their massive thighs. Then the three of them squeezed back into the cab, spreading to fill all available space like well-risen bread rolls in a tin, and drove away across the hilltop in a cloud of yellow dust.

I camped the night at the foot of another switchback mountain pass. The next morning, with fresh legs, it seemed only half as long and tiresome as the previous one, and quite soon I crested the hill and crossed the provincial border. After the desert palette of San Juan, La Rioja and Catamarca, the verdant rainforest of Tucumán was a surprise for the eyes. Below me, seen through a gap in the drifting wet mist, a deep green valley was cut by a silver slash of river. Descending, the sound of rushing water grew steadily louder, as did the whirring and chirring of a million hidden insects. The humid air grew thick as soup. The road was steep and I dropped swiftly, ricocheting like a pinball between the rocks and ruts all the way to the valley floor. The river roared, as though in welcome, and I followed it due east onto a fertile plain of grasses tall as people and trees with leaves like umbrellas.

I was planning to invest in a decent meal in the next town that appeared. A shower, some clean clothes and a hearty plateful of grub seemed like tangible heaven. But such simple pleasures were to prove elusive. I was thwarted by the football.

In Concepción, at four o'clock on a Sunday afternoon, it seemed that the entire male population was watching the live game. At the pavement tables of every bar and café on the plaza, men sat huddled over beers. They leaned forward avidly, all eyes on the televisions that had been rigged up especially for the occasion, and not one of them spoke as they watched play. I circled the square just once, looking for a possible place to eat, but there was not a spare chair to be seen. Even if I managed to find a seat and attract the attention of a waiter – a feat in itself due to the fact that most of them were standing with their arms crossed watching the game – I didn't think I could handle sitting among all that testosterone. My stomach would have to wait.

On the corner, I stopped to talk to a man selling team flags.

'*Banderita*?' he offered, holding up a choice of colours.

'No thanks. I just want to know who's playing.'

He looked at me for one disbelieving second before bursting into laughter.

'But *chica*, how can you not know? It's a *superclásico* between River and Boca.' He shook the flags, to illustrate. 'It's a very important game.'

Of course. I should have guessed. River Plate and Boca Juniors – both from Buenos Aires – are the two most loved and respected *fútbol* teams in Argentina. When they play against each other the entire country gets involved. Fans worship their chosen side with religious commitment, and a *superclásico* produces a sort of national mania. I had witnessed this during my time in the capital and had seen, scrawled on a graveyard wall in the middle of the pampa, a piece of graffiti that summed it up perfectly:

Boca mi vida,	Boca my life,
Boca mi pasión,	Boca my passion,
Locura de mi corazón . . .	Madness of my heart . . .

I was several blocks away and almost out of town when the next goal was scored but even then I nearly fell off my bike in fright. The cheer that erupted, the collective enthusiasm of hundreds of voices, was a tsunami of sound.

River won the match. In Monteros, where I arrived at dusk with my stomach grumbling audibly, the streets were full of fans. Their attention was no longer on the television, their spirits were buoyed by victory, and there was no avoiding their whistles and stares.

'*¡Hola gringa!*'

'*¡Chau bonita!*'

I pulled my cap low, and disappeared into the first cheap hotel that appeared.

Looking out of my third-floor window, I considered the crowds below. It was football madness outside, and although my stomach cried out for a decent hot meal there was no way I was wandering around out there alone. There was nothing left in my panniers to cook either. Damn it. Maybe this was my punishment for taking that lift in the pickup. Frustrated, I braved it as far as the *kiosco* across the road, bought three packets of crisps, a box of biscuits and a litre of apple juice, returned to the room, lay on the bed and scoffed the lot while staring at the damp patch on the ceiling.

If I had thought the climb into Tucumán was arduous, I certainly wasn't counting on the climb back out. It was the map's fault, again. The red line that stood for the hill to come was no different to the red lines I had been following across the dead-flat pampa. There was shading, of a sort, to indicate hills, but it was so badly done that it misled more than informed. No matter how closely I analysed the map, it gave me no idea what was in store for me.

The tarmac road out of Monteros led into the heart of another river valley. Ferns drooped with moisture, insects buzzed and clicked, and little streams gushed down the hillside. It started to rain. The road began to climb. I put my hood up, my head down and all my concentration into ignoring the discomfort.

A whole day later, after a somewhat squelchy overnight stop in a bog by the roadside, I was still climbing. A thick white cloud surrounded me, obscuring any view of the route ahead, and the rain was heavier than ever. My 'waterproof' gloves were soaked through and the plastic bags inside my shoes (a cunning improvisation designed to keep my socks dry) had long since filled up with water. Shivering, I thought longingly of the dry heat that awaited me on the other side of the mountains.

The tooting of a car horn pulled me back to reality. Beside me, stuffed with grinning faces, a little white car had slowed to my pace. It hovered there for a few seconds, its occupants waving madly, before pulling ahead and skidding to a halt on the wet tarmac. A sprightly old man bounded from the driver's seat and jogged towards me.

'*¿Andás solita?*' he asked, as I drew up beside him. He sandwiched my hand between both of his and shook it energetically. 'How brave! Has any son of a bitch given you any problems?'

I laughed.

'No, not yet.' My bones creaked as he squeezed my hand harder.

'Good, good, that's great! What a wonderful way to travel!' He pumped my arm vigorously and nodded towards the kids in the car. 'My grandchildren wanted me to stop to wish you luck. So, good luck!' He turned, sprinted back to the car and flung himself behind the wheel. And with no more than a screech of tyres and a few muffled cheers from the backseat, my mini fan club was gone.

The *buena onda* they left behind kept me going all the way to Tafí del Valle. There, wet and hungry, in grave need of fuel, I stopped at the first restaurant. To my delight, it had hot food *and* an open fire. I shed several layers of wet clothing, took off my shoes, got as close to the flames as possible without actually climbing into the grate and ordered a pot of coffee.

That, in retrospect, was a fairly bad idea.

Anyone who hasn't been born and raised at altitude will experience some breathlessness in the thinner air above 3000 metres. Add a little exercise, which demands more oxygen for your muscles, and breathing can become even more difficult. Most people will eventually acclimatise, and altitude sickness is rare for those gaining height slowly (by bicycle or on foot, for example), but it doesn't take a genius to work out that raising your heart rate with caffeine is best avoided until you're sure of the capabilities of your body.

Tafí del Valle perches on a plateau at 2100 metres, and above the town the road continues steeply for another twenty kilometres to a pass of 3046 metres. That would be, if I actually managed to reach it, the highest pass I had ever crossed by bicycle. Until now my claim to fame was 1991-metre Col de Larche, where I had traversed the Alps from France into Italy a couple of years earlier. Breaking my own record was a challenge to be savoured. Stuffed full of food and awash with coffee, I slung myself back into the saddle and attacked the acute climb out of town.

It became obvious that things weren't going so well when the corn I had eaten for lunch tried to make a surprise reappearance. Furthermore, my pulse was racing, my legs were shaking and my vision was blurry. I didn't feel a lot like cycling. But the wet fog was still thick around me and above the tree line there was no protection from the wind; I had to keep going, or freeze.

Visibility had shrunk to about five metres and the cloud was blindingly white. Each slow revolution of the pedals took me further towards the sky, and in my light-headed state it seemed remarkably like cycling into heaven. Unfortunately, I felt more like I was on my way in the other direction. Blood pounded in my ears, my limbs trembled like those of an alcoholic in withdrawal, and every few hundred metres I was forced to stop for a session of heavy breathing. The climb was apparently endless.

But then, finally, I hauled myself above the clouds. Up on top of the weather it was a beautiful day, and the warmth of the sun was like the breath of God. I stopped at the pass, with several deep sighs of immense relief, and looked behind me. Enclosed by curving mountain ridges, full of floating fog, the valley below was like a giant mixing bowl of fluffy meringue.

14

Cyclists, Singers and Celebrations

Sleeping at altitude can be a chilly experience. It was cosy enough when I first went to bed, wearing three layers of clothing inside my four-season sleeping bag, but the coldest hours before dawn were another matter. I woke shivering. My joints ached and my nose – the only part of me exposed to the air – was completely numb. It was impossible to sleep. I fidgeted drowsily and willed the sun to rise.

If my tent hadn't been parked next to a stream, I would have had to forgo the morning cup of tea; at 7 a.m. there were two litres of solid ice in my water bag. A shower of icy dandruff flaked off the tent fly and fell into my hair as I clambered out into the frigid atmosphere, and my recently rinsed socks and knickers hung stiff as wood from the guy ropes. I stumbled down to the water, trying to kick some feeling into my toes, and filled the billy. At the edges of the flow, intricate ice formations had grown overnight, like fungus.

While I thawed out with a hot brew, the sun's early rays fought back the morning chill outside. The frost on the flysheet evaporated in seconds, the grass turned from white to wet and my socks drooped, dripped and steamed. Reluctant to move on before the cold had been well and truly vanquished, I used the time to cook a hot breakfast. I mixed up some flour and water, greased a pan and fried rounds of dough on the camp stove. Slathered with butter and apricot jam, washed down with tea and eaten in bed to the tune of the stream, it was bread to be remembered.

For more than thirty kilometres I freewheeled down the mountainside, swinging around sweeping corners and reaching top gear with ease. The view was surreal. Directly ahead, like the turreted façade of a fortified castle, the Andes formed an impenetrable barricade. At their feet sprawled a wide, dry valley of stunted scrub and *cardón* cacti, the typical spiky subjects of wild-west cartoons. I stopped to take a few photos of these thorny giants, and to snigger in an infantile manner at their comically phallic shapes, before completing the high-speed ride to the desert floor. Energised and euphoric, flooded with endorphins, I felt the kilometres flash past beneath my whirring wheels.

It seemed to take no time at all to reach the ruins of Quilmes, an archaeological site with yet another story of oppression to tell. I left Vagabunda in the car park and wandered the rocky paths of the settlement, once home to an indigenous community who put up a notoriously brave fight against the Spanish conquerors.

The Quilmes had lived in the valley for centuries. They grew crops and farmed llamas and built cosy stone houses in the lap of a small mountain, which curved protective arms around them on either side. At the first sign of any trouble the whole population could retreat to the safety of the heights, making it a prime location for self-defence. Using bows and arrows, the Quilmes fought the colonists with fearlessness and ferocity, managing to resist the invasion for over 100 years.

Divine intervention, the Spanish believed, was the only explanation for the momentary lack of defence that allowed the settlement to finally be overcome. In 1667, with their guard down as they gathered the harvest, the Quilmes unwittingly gave their aggressors an opportunity to take control. The sudden attack sent the whole village fleeing to their hilltop fortifications, in too much of a rush to take the newly gathered food supplies with them, and the invaders could barely believe their luck. Rather than face the terrible wrath of the indigenes at ground level, all they had to do now was sit tight and starve them out.

Left with no option, the Quilmes finally surrendered. Trading their freedom in exchange for their survival, more than 200 hungry families came down from that mountain, although many lives were later lost on the 1500-kilometre march to Buenos Aires. There, depleted and dispirited, the community dwindled, surviving barely a century in their new neighbourhood. Nowadays, for most Argentines, the word Quilmes brings to mind only one thing: the cool taste of the nation's most popular beer, brewed in the suburb where little but the name remains of this once proud race.

Back in the car park, I was just about to leave when a busload of *porteños* arrived. They filed off the coach like excited school kids, jostling and chattering, pointing cameras and fingers, and trotted off without delay in two different directions, the men heading with purpose towards the beer fridge at the cafeteria while the women made a beeline for the toilets. That was before one of the ladies spotted me. Within seconds, I was surrounded.

'Are you from Germany?' one of them asked.

'No. I'm from New Zealand.'

'Really? You *look* German. Can we have a photo with you and your bike?'

They fiddled with cameras, fussed with hairdos and posed one by one with their arms around me. They didn't seem to notice that I hadn't had a shower in three days.

'*¡Qué preciosa!*' they cried, '*¡Qué linda!*' The shutters snipped, snapped and clicked.

Their enthusiasm was inspiring, but I wondered if they would later remember exactly why they had a photo of themselves embracing a dirt-sullied desert urchin.

'Do you recall why we took this picture dear? The one of me with the filthy hobo?'

'Well, honey, I'm not exactly sure. But isn't it that nice German girl with her bicycle?'

I'm not sure what I ate for dinner that so disagreed with me, but the variety of gurgling noises, bubbly feelings and intermittent cramps that subsequently assailed my lower regions made getting to sleep an almost insurmountable challenge. I could have done with a hot-water bottle and a soothing lullaby, but what I got instead was a late-night cacophony of donkeys – there must have been five or six of them exercising their vocal chords nearby. I listened with my eyes closed. Depending on the speed and pitch of their braying, each one conjured a different mental picture. The breadth of their repertoire was astounding. While one reminded me of a rusty swing rocking gently in the breeze, another made a noise like a block of wood being sawn in half at top tempo. Then there was a series of short, high-pitched blasts reminiscent of the whistle of a steam train, followed by the creaking and groaning of a steel-frame bed being put to the test by a bout of vigorous lovemaking. There was also someone grunting continuously (but quite contentedly it seemed) directly outside the tent. I lay awake in a semi-delirious state, trying to decipher which noises were coming from without and which from within, until a particularly violent attack of nausea caused me to get up in a rush and offer my dinner to the desert. After that, and a prolonged session of blowing the chunks out of my nose, I was finally able to fall into an exhausted but fretful sleep.

In order to recuperate, not to mention recoup some measure of cleanliness, I headed the following morning for the oasis of Cafayate. The dry, hot climate of the surrounding region makes for perfect grape-growing territory, and for kilometres I passed expansive vineyards worked by sun-browned locals. Closer to town, I joined a pack of them making their leisurely way home for lunch on rattletrap bicycles, passing a bottle of wine between them as they went. We saluted each other with the trilling of bike bells.

After installing my tent in a corner of the campground I began, as was my custom, to make extensive use of the luxuries of civilisation. I showered for an hour, lunched for two, and lay on the grass of Cafayate's central plaza for more than three to enjoy the slow-paced ambience of a tourist town in the off-season. There were school kids to watch, newspapers to read, postcards to be written and ice-creams to be eaten. In the end though, I just fell asleep.

The cold woke me. With the sun out of sight behind the *cordillera*, the temperature was dropping fast. It seemed like a perfectly good excuse for an early night. Back at the campsite, on my way to the toilet block for after-dark ablutions, I met a man in a van. He was sitting in the open back door of his vehicle, playing a melancholy song on an acoustic guitar.

'*Buenas noches,*' he said. 'Where are you from?'

'New Zealand.'

'Ah,' he nodded wisely. 'Fucking Kiwi.' A mischievous grin spread across his face, and his eyes twinkled. I nearly wet myself laughing.

'How did you know that we're called Kiwis?' I asked.

'Had a Kiwi friend once.' He strummed a chord. 'Fucking Kiwis . . .'

It looked like we were going to be great friends.

His name was Roberto, otherwise known as Ytch, and he was a middle-aged, full-blooded Mapuche.

'Sit down,' he said, 'I'm going to sing you something.'

I sat down. He sang me something. And from the first bar of the first song I was in love with Argentine folk music. The rhythm was toe-tapping, the melody stick-in-your-head catchy, and the strength of voice with which it was delivered sent a shiver up my spine. Ytch had talent and charisma to burn. Each time he finished one song I begged him for another. Each time he obliged. In the end, he sang me an entire concert.

'I'll play more for you tomorrow,' he said, when we finally called it a night.

'But I'm leaving in the morning.'

'Where are you headed for? Salta? I'll give you a lift.'

'Well, thanks, but I'm on my bicycle.'

'That's okay. We'll put the bike in the van.'

It took a fair amount of polite refusals before he eventually conceded defeat.

'Well, all right. If you won't come with me, I'll wait for you along the way. There are some great places I want to show you.'

I didn't doubt it. I had already heard great things about the landscape ahead.

The cumulative pleasure of being well fed, well washed and well rested allowed me to leave Cafayate with my spirits soaring. Even so, my enthusiastic expectations were more than exceeded by the remarkable day that followed.

The first unusual thing that happened was encountering a

French couple on matching bikes. I caught them up and cycled alongside on the traffic-free road. Cathy and Raphael, who spoke perfect English, were the first cycle-tourists I had seen since saying goodbye to Bojo a month before. Since then I had been enjoying my solitude, but being suddenly in the company of other like-minded individuals caused me a certain amount of excitement. There was something very satisfying about sharing my experiences with people who were doing the same thing. Swapping information, telling anecdotes, discussing bikes and kit: it was conversation that only a cyclist could love, but every cycle-tourist I had met had enjoyed it just as much as I had.

So there we were, three people on six wheels making our unhurried way north, when the nasal honking of a car horn broke the flow of our conversation. A little white van passed us on the wrong side of the road, fishtailed slightly, and pulled to a stop at the next corner. It was Ytch. He stood on the roadside to wait for us, a bottle in his outstretched hand.

'Something for the legs,' he offered, as we drew alongside. I looked at the viscous liquid with suspicion.

'Is that wine?'

'Of a sort. Try it.'

It was only 10 a.m. Had we been floating about on a boat on the Atlantic, rather than adrift in a sea of sand, the sun would have still been a long way below the yardarm. There was, however, neither ship nor sail in sight. I took the bottle, and tried a tentative sip. Its contents were sweet and thick, honey-like, and left a long trail of heat as they slipped southward. I licked my lips in appreciation, passed the bottle on and made some introductions.

'Right,' said Ytch. 'Now that we all know each other, I invite you to a concert in the *quebrada*. See you soon!' He waggled the bottle at us as he drove off. 'More later . . .'

La Quebrada de Cafayate – the Canyon of Cafayate – is a long valley of dazzling colours, bizarre landforms and ever-changing lighting effects. Salvador Dalí, had he ever visited, would have felt right at home. The climate is mostly dry, but slow erosion by a salty river has exposed rainbow-like sedimentary layers to view. For sixty-odd winding kilometres the road passes crenulated cliffs, teetering towers and humpback hillocks, striped and stippled with stones like decorated sandcastles. Offset against the lapis blue of the desert sky, the palette is a feast for the eyes: toffee brown, custard yellow, creamy caramel and raspberry red are layered between the muted greens, blues and purples of sugared almonds. My mouth never stopped watering in this Willy Wonka world of endless delight.

The wind, made gale force by the tunnel effect of the valley, slowed our cycling pace to snail-like, but it hardly mattered with so much to see. And Ytch's van, parked by a roadside stall, was persuasion enough to stop and make the most of our surroundings. He introduced us to his friends, who lived in a tiny building next to the road and made pottery to sell to tourists, and they fed us with *mate* and home-made bread. We lounged on the ground listening to the promised concert, along with a couple of dusty dogs and a baby llama who, regarding us shyly from beneath long eyelashes, was the epitome of pretty. She hovered on the margins as Ytch sang, watching us warily and turning away as coyly as royalty when we smiled at her.

It was tempting to stay there all afternoon, but eventually we said goodbye to the artisans to continue our exploration of the *quebrada*. We made slow progress. We stopped to stare and we stopped for photos and we stopped each time Ytch pulled up to offer us more wine. At one stage it seemed I would be stuck in the same spot until nightfall when a busload of Argentine tourists waylaid me for questioning. With two home-video cameras recording my every badly pronounced word and the paparazzi four-people-deep on all sides, I could do nothing but answer their demands and wait for rescue by Cathy and Raphael.

After a last round of *chacarera* rhythms from Ytch's guitar, played in the resonant throat of a natural rock amphitheatre, he bid us goodbye. Handing me his phone number, scribbled on a scrap of paper, he made me promise to call him when we reached Salta. I promised.

We camped next to a little house beside the river. The family who lived inside didn't seem at all surprised to see us.

'We have a lot of cyclists through here,' said Luis, the father of the tribe. 'Everyone takes longer than they expect to get through the *quebrada*, and a lot of them end up camping with us.' He showed us a folder, full of postcards of gratitude from all over the world.

He told us how he and his wife had travelled when they were younger, hitchhiking all around Latin America with three tiny children in tow, raising the money to keep going by making and selling jewellery as they went. Finally, they had come to rest on the patch of riverbank that they had been squatting for the last seventeen years. They had built their adobe house themselves and brought up all of their seven children there. The oldest three had now left home.

'Is it easy to squat in Argentina?' I asked Luis. 'Did you have any hassles with the authorities?'

'The thing is,' he told me, 'there's so much space that no one really bothers to move you on. If you can find a place that nobody wants for anything, with a decent water supply, you can pretty much call it your own. And once you're established, the council is obliged to provide you with certain basic necessities. Of course, it took them years and years to do that for us. They come and fill our tank with fresh water now, but most of our kids grew up with just the salty water from the river to drink.'

The local authority had also given them a solar panel, for electricity, but I noticed they only had the light on in one room at a time. While Mum fired up the wood stove to make bread and the kids gathered around the bare bulb above the kitchen table to do homework, their father went to spin wool in the darkness of the workroom.

They made their money now as they had when they were travelling: making and selling their crafts to passing tourists. In the morning, they showed us the earth kilns where chunky terracotta plates, bowls, mugs and casserole dishes were fired. The tableware, like the house, was made from the rich red clay of the riverbank.

With such a large family in such a modest house, and with such a vagarious means of earning a living, I imagined that life could be a constant struggle for this little band of self-proclaimed hippies. But their unity as a family, their beautifully tended cacti garden and the tenacity and optimism that kept them there seemed to indicate that, whatever the hardships, they had found their little slice of paradise.

I was about to turn another year older. For this reason, I was keen to get to the city for a proper knees-up. Maria José, a back-packing friend from the youth hostel in Ushuaia, was waiting in Salta to take me out for dinner. However, there are times when speed cannot be dictated by desire, and although I was as keen as a puppy on a leash, Cathy was feeling less than fit. With a thumping headache and steadily diminishing energy, she ground to a halt at La Viña.

By now we had left the arid climate of the *quebrada*, and back in green territory it was cold and rainy. Looking around town for a possible place to camp, we wound up at the local sports field where a muddy muddle of teenage boys played *fútbol* with intense concentration. Long limbs lunged for the ball, faces were set with grim determination and it was apparent that each imagined himself as the next Diego Maradona. They were wetter and dirtier than we were by far, but nevertheless their kindly coach took pity on us and offered the use of the clubhouse for the night. We took possession of the key and made ourselves at home. While Raphael and I cooked up a pasta storm and braved the rain to buy wine, Cathy smothered herself in covers to convalesce.

Having spent most of the previous month more or less alone in the middle of nowhere, it was really a brilliant stroke of luck to wake to my twenty-ninth birthday in the company of friends. At 8 a.m. I was snuggled in my sleeping bag with my eyes still closed, listening to the pattering of rain on the tin roof, when a muted whispering from the other side of the room alerted me to furtive goings-on. Then there was a suppressed giggle, the flare of a match, and two voices bursting into a resounding rendition of 'Happy Birthday' in French. I blew out the candle and opened my present. There was a home-made card, with dried Patagonian flowers on the front and multilingual blessings inside, and two family-sized blocks of chocolate. I felt as rich as a king, as pleased as Punch and, shortly after, as sick as a dog after demolishing a quarter of a kilo of dairy-milk before breakfast.

That evening, after reaching Salta, installing ourselves in a hotel and washing off the grime of days, we went out for dinner. I got in touch with Maria José and Ytch, and Cathy and Raphael met up with a Swiss couple they knew who were also headed north on bicycles. In a restaurant on Salta's central plaza the seven of us ate pizza and drank copious quantities of local beer. And after dinner, to both my delight and embarrassment, they sang me a high-volume, lager-powered version of 'Happy

Birthday' in all the languages they knew: Spanish, English, Swiss-German and French. I blushed bright red and wondered at the good fortune that had placed me among them.

And so began an entire week of sloth.

Salta, by a cyclist's standards, is the perfect place to recharge. Not only is the city centre compact and hill-less (providing the perfect shuffling-ground for recovering legs), the bakeries and restaurants overflow with irresistible edibles. While other tourists might be inspired to wax lyrical about the city's beautiful colonial architecture, the awesome view from the top of the nearby cable car or the charm of the poncho-clad folk-musicians, from my perspective it was all about the grub. Whether it was meals out with Maria José and the cyclists, ice-creams with Ytch or bags of *facturas* eaten in the park, the days were marked by the hourly ingestion of calories and the steady thickening of my waistline.

I did get some culture, in the form of sing-along sessions with Ytch. He kept the words to all his folk songs in the glove box of his van, and when he drew out his guitar with a flourish, I knew that was my cue to open the folder of lyrics and try my best to keep up. Despite my best and persistent efforts, however, my failure to enunciate the rapidly read lines, not to mention my complete inability to stay in tune, turned our duets into little more than a farce. But Ytch didn't seem to mind. He mimicked my pronunciation, called me 'Fucking Kiwi', and took me to Salta's most famous nightspot to watch the professionals play. There, at Casa del Molino, I forgot my ineptitude as one performer after another coaxed unforgettably captivating melodies from the strings of their guitars.

I was staying in a *casa de familia* – literally a 'family house' – a common form of lodging where local people rent out rooms in their own homes. It was run by a mother and daughter, each as dumpy and conservative as the other, and between them, as we sat together at the breakfast table, they attempted to dissuade me from continuing my journey. With a theatrical assortment of gasps and sighs they shook their heads and raised their eyes to heaven.

'You're going north? But it's getting so cold now!' They looked at each other and nodded in agreement. 'You can't possibly sleep in a tent. You'll freeze! And the altitude is terrible; it's very bad for the heart.'

'Well, I think I'll be okay.'

'Oh, but you must be so careful,' said Mother. 'There are some very bad people about . . .' She waved a hand around the kitchen, as though thieves and murderers lurked behind the furniture.

'Yes,' said her daughter, 'Argentina is really dangerous. You'll need a lot, a LOT of caution.' She started at me earnestly, as if memorising my features in case she was ever called upon to identify my remains at the morgue.

But I wasn't worried. I knew by now to take pessimism with a pinch of salt, and the only words that revolved in my head as I finally left the city were the flattering lyrics of a song that Ytch had composed just for me.

15

From One Extreme
to the Other

My body was noticeably rounder after seven days of indolence, but my legs felt like new. They were more than up to the challenge of powering my increased circumference up the hill and through the pass to San Salvador de Jujuy. Invigorated by movement, inspired by renewed solitude, I arrived in town with a glow of good cheer.

The hotel I checked into was named, invitingly, Residencial Río de Janeiro. Alas, the ambience inside was far from tropical – rather more polar, in fact – and the forty-watt bulbs in reception did nothing to dispel the gloom of the overcast afternoon outside. The girl behind the desk, bundled up in a thick black duffle coat, must have been hired specifically for her personality because it matched perfectly with the frigid atmosphere. She showed me to my room with obvious resentment and brought me a cruel ration of toilet paper, folded on top of a towel the size of a facecloth.

'Checkout time is ten o'clock sharp,' she told me. 'Any later and you pay another day.'

I shut the door on her and looked around. The jaundice-yellow walls bloomed with damp patches and the grey plaster of the ceiling was cracked and flaking. I had no intention of staying any longer than strictly necessary.

It was dead on 10 a.m. when the duffle coat made her next appearance. I opened the door smartly to her strident knocking.

'Staying?' she asked.

'No. I'm just leaving.' My stuff was almost packed.

She looked pointedly at her watch and heaved an exasperated sigh. And in case it wasn't already clear that my time was well and truly up, she pushed past into the room, flung the windows open and began to rip the sheets from the bed. I picked up my bags and left her to it.

Climbing northward through the province of Jujuy is the colourful Quebrada de Humahuaca. Cut through by the salty Río Grande, the valley rises gently in elevation until it joins the altiplano, the wide high-altitude plateau that stretches into Bolivia and beyond. Dotted with archaeological remains that point to 10,000 years of habitation, the *quebrada* is a 155-kilometre-long national treasure. Used as a caravan road by the Incas and a trade route by the early colonials, it has served as a link between South American cultures, societies and economies for centuries.

Now, with my back to the semi-sophistication of Salta, it seemed that the valley was carrying me steadily towards the native heart of the continent. As one of the last corners of the country where native Quechua is still spoken, and where the locals wear traditional dress, the Quebrada de Humahuaca has far more in common with Peru and Bolivia than it does with the rest of Argentina. So much so, in fact, that small reminders of the western world seemed to me somehow incongruous. A little old lady, dressed in the knee-length pleated skirt, woollen cardigan and wide-brimmed felt hat typical of the area, tramped solidly along the riverbank in a pair of unbecoming white running sneakers; and a toiling farmer, tilling his field with a horse-drawn plough, left neat furrows beneath the enormous Mercedes Benz billboard that sprouted from the land.

In Humahuaca, the main township of the valley, I stayed a day to adjust to the altitude. The road ahead was going to climb steadily higher, but at 3000 metres I was already feeling a distinct lack of strength. My pulse, at rest, was racing at eighty beats per minute – some twenty beats faster than normal – and the thinner air caused an unshakeable lassitude. Frequently, during the previous two days, I had lain by the side of the road, stared into space and wondered if I would ever regain the enthusiasm for anything other than breathing.

And I didn't just need to acclimatise to the elevation; the change of culture took some getting used to as well. Just a couple of hundred kilometres away from the anonymity of a city such as Salta, it was a surprise to become suddenly conspicuous. Despite my raggedy clothes and battered shoes, my presence there was evidence of relative western wealth. In a poor town that lives mainly from tourism, I was a prime target for everyone who had something to sell.

But apart from the trinket-vendors, who clung tenaciously to my sleeves in the plaza, Humahuaca was a pleasant place. The adobe houses were painted in bright colours, the cobblestone streets were narrow and charming and the vegetable market sold the hugest avocados for ridiculously cheap prices. Even the youth hostel, where I stayed for the ultra-bargain fee of five pesos per night (NZ$2.50), had a certain picturesque appeal to it. Next to the rockery in the garden, at a table made from the holey wood of the *cardón* cactus, I sat in the sun, drank *coca* tea and waited with anticipation for its beneficial effects.

The small, dark green leaves of the *coca* plant, the very same that cocaine is derived from, have been valued by the people of the Andes for thousands of years. Used in religious rituals and social ceremonies, valued for their medicinal properties, exchanged in place of money and functioning as tokens of wealth and power, they have long been an integral part of the Andean social fabric.

Most importantly for the people of the altiplano, *coca* is used to reduce high-altitude stress. Regular chewing of the leaves can stimulate the respiratory system, improve circulation and assist the body in using oxygen more efficiently. Also considered to help withstand the cold, improve strength and stamina and suppress hunger, *coca* is often chewed while working, and the increased mental alertness that it brings, as well as the elimination of fatigue and a slight sensation of euphoria, leads some workers to stop for *coca* breaks as people of the West stop for pick-me-up cups of coffee. This mild narcotic appears to have no negative side effects (apart from green teeth and lopsided expressions) and despite being strongly habitual in a social sense is not addictive.

Although the true health benefits are only seen with frequent use, the instant mental stimulation can be enjoyed as follows. Take a few leaves and place them on one side of your mouth between the teeth. Moisten, and chew gently, squeezing out the bitter juice and compressing the wad until there is space for more. Move the masticated ball to the space between your cheek and gum and add a pinch of *bica* – bicarbonate of soda – to maximise the effects. Then add another wad of leaves and keep chewing until your mouth goes numb, your brain wakes up and your cheek, ballooning like a bubble, can hold no more. It's an acquired taste, and one that I found much too bitter, but it can be taken instead in tea form. That, however, with its much less potent effect, is undoubtedly the sissy way to do it.

Onwards and upwards, battling with altitude-induced lethargy, I followed the road towards Bolivia. My surroundings were

Technicolor-vivid in the thin atmosphere, and the air was cruelly cold. Despite the brightness of the sun, the river was edged with crusts of ice even at midday. Out of the canyon and onto the altiplano, the landscape opened up around me. The peaks and ridges of the Andes – which had been a perpetual presence on my left-hand side since leaving Mendoza some six weeks ago – gave way to a rolling, sun-bleached plateau. It stretched ahead for as far as I could see.

In tiny settlements, mud houses crouched beneath whining power lines and the wind channelled dustily down unpaved streets. Each village had its own defunct train station: woe-begone places of rusted rails, cracked platforms and broken signals where skinny dogs lay between the tracks and birds roosted in the eves of the station houses.

The wind blew from the north-west, at a force almost comparable to that of Patagonia, and I camped in a ditch for shelter. Eating dinner, I noted that neither a day of acclimatisation nor quantities of *coca* tea had made the slightest bit of difference to my physical capabilities. I had given in to fatigue around four o'clock in the afternoon, and even the simple task of chewing pasta brought on a severe bout of deep breathing.

Huddling in my sleeping bag at the door of the tent, using the last of the light to write in my diary, I was suddenly struck by the sensation of being watched. I looked up. A couple of metres away, perfectly still and regarding me with a regal expression, was a splendid, chocolate-coloured llama. The wind buffeted his dreadlocked coat, his ears twitched, and his long lashes blinked thoughtfully over large brown eyes. We stared at each other, and I imagined that we shared a profound moment of cross-species understanding. That was until he tossed his head with a snort of disdain, turned his back on me and stamped off with his nose, and his tail, in the air.

The llama may have been scornful of such a lowly tent-dweller, but he wasn't my only visitor for the evening. The two men who pulled up in a battered old truck a few minutes later seemed more inclined to make friends. They came to greet me with handshakes and curiosity.

'Why are you camping out here where it's so cold?' they asked. 'There's a village a few kilometres further on.'

'Yes, I know. I prefer camping, that's all.' They looked at me in amazement.

'Really?'

'Yes, really.' They shook their heads in disbelief.

'But it'll be freezing tonight.'

'Yes.'

'And you're all alone.'

'Yes.'

The wind snatched at their shirts and they wrapped their arms around their chests. They stared at the horizon for a bit, towards the source of the wind, and they stared at me and my tent. Then they climbed into their truck and left. I could see them laughing as they went; the gringa, they had obviously concluded, was absolutely *loca*.

I arrived the following afternoon at La Quiaca, the border town where I planned to leave the country. On the outskirts a sign pointed south: '5121 kilometres to Ushuaia,' it read. I thought about that for a while. All those bus trips I had taken. All that money spent and hassles-with-baggage-handlers suffered. And for what? I had been to one end of the country, and now here I was at the opposite extreme. If I added up the kilometres cycled on the various legs of my journey, it was more or less equal to the number on the sign in front of me. If only I had known just how friendly the country would turn out to be, I could have started here in La Quiaca and cycled in one long unbroken line all the way to the far south.

But it was too late for regrets. This was just about as far north as it was possible to go in Argentina, and Bolivia was but a stone's throw away. Once again, it was time to meet the unknown.

After a shivery overnight rest in a frigid cell at Hotel Frontera (I could swear the tent would have been warmer), I joined the flow of heavily laden pedestrians to the border crossing. There, where the Villazón River marked the country boundary, I stopped to watch the crowds bustling back and forth across the narrow bridge.

Traditionally dressed Quechua people lugged enormous loads wrapped in brightly coloured shawls. Babies, shopping, beer crates, furniture; it seemed that nothing was too big or too awkward to sling on their backs. The more they carried, the closer their noses were to the ground, but I noticed that even the heaviest weights didn't seem to slow them down. They trundled along with the hip-rolling gait of long-distance walkers.

No one appeared to be showing documents, but I did things the official way and got my passport stamped with a visitor's visa. Then I wheeled my bike over the bridge into a world of vivid colours, blaring pop music and delicious smells. Street vendors sold oranges, *empanadas*, freshly squeezed juices, hot peanuts and greasy soups from steaming saucepans. Women with long black plaits and bowler hats called out the prices of bananas and frostbitten tomatoes.

The streets were full, and although dozens of fascinating things jostled for my attention I tried to keep a wary eye out for dodgy characters. Other travellers had told me to be careful here; on this side of the river, apparently, thieves and scoundrels waited on every corner. Whether this was true or not I couldn't tell, but there was certainly an entrepreneurial feeling in the air.

I had barely set foot in the country before a ragged individual approached.

'How much for the bicycle?' he asked.

'It's not for sale.'

'So how much do you want?' He stroked the saddle with covetous fingers.

'Nothing. It's not for sale.'

'But how much did it cost you?'

'I don't remember. It's very old, and a bit broken. It's not worth anything now.'

'Ah. I see.' He nodded. 'Well, if you change your mind . . .'

It seemed unwise after that to leave Vagabunda alone and vulnerable in the street, but there was no option: I had to change money. I was shackling my worldly goods with a hefty D-lock when a small voice came from somewhere near my left elbow.

'I'll look after the bike, *señora.*'

A boy of about eight was standing beside me. He was thin and dirty, with big eyes. I shook my head at him. Not only had I decided to distrust everybody for the moment, I couldn't condone child labour.

'No, thank you. It's okay.'

'*Señora,*' he insisted. '*I* will look after the *bike.*' And with arms firmly crossed and legs set stoutly apart he stared unblinkingly at my possessions, like a miniature superhero with a force-field gaze.

When I returned, with a wallet full of bolivianos, he was still in exactly the same position. I released him from his task with a handful of coins and some *facturas* fresh from the bakery and asked him which side of the border he was from. He smiled at me for the first time, mischievously.

'All sides, *señora.*' We laughed together. He was street wisdom personified.

As a major link between countries, the route north from Villazón should have been full of buses carrying travellers and trucks carrying freight. Instead, there was no traffic at all. For fifty kilometres, across the washboard and around the potholes, I pondered the emptiness until a wiry man on a bike stopped to put me in the picture. There were blockades on the road ahead, he told me. There had been no vehicle movement for a week, and it looked like the situation might continue for days more. But not to worry. They had let him through on his bicycle, and he felt sure they would let me through on mine.

The first sign of the *bloqueo* was a long line of motionless trucks. At the head of the queue, where a row of rocks and a flimsy pile of thorn bushes formed the blockade itself, a group of bored-looking truck drivers sat by the side of the road, chewing *coca* and snoozing in the sun. They invited me to join them.

The protesters – a small group of locals huddled around a fire a few metres away – didn't look powerful enough to stop a speeding tricycle, let alone a convoy of ten-tonne trucks, but there was no point arguing with them, the drivers said. This was just one part of a much wider protest. In the town of Tupiza, another forty kilometres on, hundreds of demonstrators were pressuring the government into negotiations.

'Negotiations about what, exactly?'

'Oh, a few local issues,' one of the drivers replied. 'The people want the roads to be improved, for a start.'

'That sounds reasonable. The roads are terrible.' He nodded in agreement.

'The protests are always for good reasons.'

'So, are you angry at being stuck here? Or do you support them?'

'Well, we're losing money and time, but they have the right

to ask for the things they need. A lot of these villages don't even have electricity.'

His patience was impressive, but I didn't think I could match it.

'Do bicycles count as traffic?' I asked, 'Or will they let me through?'

'Not without a boyfriend,' quipped the oldest and fattest truckie. 'But if you let me come on your bicycle with you I'll make sure of it.'

I went to talk with the protesters. They let me pass.

A few kilometres further on, near the small village of Suipacha, another crowd blocked the road. Some basket-laden local women, on their way to feed the protesters, arrived at the same time as I did and invited me to eat. We sat at the edge of the throng, near a campfire that burned in the middle of the road, ate pastries and noted a heated argument that was going on nearby.

'Don't worry about them,' said one old lady as she smoothed her voluminous skirts. 'They're just drunk, and a bit bored. We've been here for days waiting for the authorities to come and talk to us.'

'Were you out here during the nights as well?'

'Of course.'

'But you don't have any shelter. And the nights are freezing.'

She smiled proudly and drew a woollen blanket tighter around her shoulders.

'It's true,' she said. 'We're brave.' And she handed me another *empanada*.

A group of curious faces had gathered around us in the few minutes since our arrival. In the tedium of waiting, the white woman with the funny Spanish was as good a diversion as any. Teenage girls hid crooked teeth and shy smiles behind hands, young boys stared openly and men examined my bicycle, nodding appreciatively and murmuring approval. One of them wheeled his own rusty one-speed over for my appraisal.

A man of about my age stood with his hands in his pockets and watched me eat.

'Are you married?' he asked. I shook my head. The *empanada* lady chuckled.

'It's colder at nights for the bachelors,' she said to me, and looked up at him cheekily. 'Are you looking for a spinster to keep you warm?'

The crowd roared with laughter and the young man shrugged.

'Is there room in your tent for two?' he asked.

Dusk was falling as I left the *bloqueo* and people were preparing for the long cold hours ahead. Women tended fires and boiled kettles above the flames, and children wrapped themselves in blankets. The men kept themselves warm with tumblers of spirits. On the way out of the village, written in blue paint on the whitewashed wall of an adobe house, was this:

> SUIPACHA
> CLAIMS JUSTICE
> ENOUGH OF PROMISES THAT NEVER ARRIVE
> OUR NECESSITIES – WATER AND LIGHT

It was dated 1998.

After a night in the *puna*, I headed for Tupiza. It was just an hour away by bicycle – some twenty kilometres – but a far more arduous task for those who were walking there from the blockade. There were dozens of people on foot, striding along at an unfaltering pace on the bumpy road and carrying surprisingly little considering their all-night vigil in the freezing cold.

In Tupiza a twelve-year-old boy with deft salesman's skills hauled me in off the street. It was a Wednesday morning and as he showed me to my room in the hostel he explained that he should have been in class. But the teachers were on strike, he said; they were holding out for better wages and the schools had been closed for five weeks. On the town plaza, all the shops were shut. One or two appeared to be opening their doors furtively to select customers but roaming bands of protesters kept the shop owners on their toes. By stopping trade, and thereby making life uncomfortable for everybody, the demonstrators were slowly gathering the support of the whole community. It was all done in the best of humour and I had a chance to see it properly in action the next morning while shopping at the vegetable market.

I was in the midst of deciding how many avocados I could squash into my panniers when the protesters arrived. A wave of shouted warnings washed my way and the girl who was running the stall grabbed the avocados from my hands.

'Go!' she said urgently, turning me around and propelling me out of the market and into the street. I stood in the sunshine, blinking, and peered back in to watch her hastily pulling a cover over the vegetables. Her neighbours did the same, grinning and giggling and trying to act nonchalant as the protesters strolled by. Some fifty or more people passed, joking good-naturedly with the traders as they made sure the market was well and truly closed.

The last one was barely out of sight around the corner when a voice broke into my thoughts. It was the stallholder who had ejected me so abruptly.

'Hey! Do you want to buy these avocados, or not?'

The largest demonstration yet was on the way north out of Tupiza. I wheeled Vagabunda through the mob and asked for the road to Uyuni.

'You're not going there by bicycle?' said a man, with a frown. 'Do you know about the big uphill ahead?'

'Er, not really. But I'm sort of used to hills.'

He looked at me solemnly and shook his head.

'This one's different,' he said. 'It's very, *very* big.'

'Really?'

'Really.'

I shrugged. After months of listening to people's warnings, I knew better than to accept any 'helpful' information as fact. Altitudes, distances and road conditions as described by the locals were invariably misleading. Anyway, I had no option but to continue. The roadblock ensured that the *only* way to Uyuni at this time was under my own power.

I forked left, onto the sandy road west, to meet whatever challenge lay ahead.

16

I'll Take the High Road

My bike seemed extraordinarily heavy. Supposing, at first, that it had to do with an excess of avocados, I considered lessening the load by eating a few, but the thought of food made me nauseous and a quivering in my limbs soon told me that the luggage wasn't to blame. Weak and light-headed, I got off the bike and pushed, stopping every few minutes to catch my breath and curse. Altitude, once again, was playing havoc with my energy levels.

I climbed all day. The valley below grew ever more distant but the road ahead continued, apparently infinitely, in a series of sadistically steep switchbacks. Each time I arrived at what appeared to be the top of the hill I would round the corner to see, with a profound sense of disbelief, several more kilometres of rocky, sandy road stretching away towards the heavens. The guy in Tupiza had been right; the hill was very, *very* big.

The pass was still nowhere in sight when I stopped to camp. It wasn't yet growing dark, but my feeble state was worsening and gaining more altitude seemed like a bad idea. There were no sheltered spots to pitch the tent, the ground was too rocky for pegs and with a growing sense of panic as the wind sucked the heat from my body I struggled with guy ropes, tying each with fumbling fingers to an insubstantial rock or bush. My limbs quivered, my stomach churned and an immense desire to sleep washed over me. I crawled into the badly secured tent, hoping that at least my body weight would stop it from being whipped away during the night, and lay shivering in my sleeping bag.

Then I got up again and projectile-vomited onto a nearby shrub.

I slept a feverish sleep – in which I hauled myself, bloody-fingered, up endless cliff faces – and woke with relief at the rising of the sun. At rest in the tent, in the calm of the morning, the difficulties of the day before seemed indistinct, imaginary and as unlikely as my nightmares. But the sight of the hill above me, as I loaded Vagabunda, caused a knot of anxiety in my stomach.

The exhaustion returned almost as soon as I left the campsite. My stomach was still rejecting the idea of food, and with no fuel in the tank my strength was completely drained. Shaking with effort, keeping the bicycle upright seemed like a task for a gladiator. The rest stops, at first every few hundred metres or so, became progressively more frequent until in desperation I flopped across my handlebars, hung my head and burst into tears. I couldn't remember ever feeling more wretched, helpless or alone.

It was then that I heard footsteps. I wiped my tears and looked up. Coming down the hill, stout leather shoes kicking up dust, was a young Quechua man. He stopped a respectful distance away and nodded in greeting. I asked him where he was going.

'Tupiza,' he answered. His sun-beaten face was resolute.

'What, today?' Tupiza was about sixty kilometres away.

'Yes. Today. To support the *bloqueo*.'

'I see.' It had taken me a day and a half to come that far – uphill, admittedly – but this guy was going to walk there in an afternoon. Suddenly my self-pity seemed pathetic. I wished him luck and headed for the pass with renewed determination.

Maybe the lack of oxygen was making me hallucinate, but the road seemed to have a personality. We fought each other mercilessly. Picking myself up after a rest stop, I cursed out loud and kicked a few stones to assert my authority. Before long the road kicked back, throwing me off balance with an unexpected sand trap. Then the wind joined in with a sudden blow from the side, followed by a demoralising barrage from in front, and my brave resolve evaporated. In anger, I flung both my bike and myself into the roadside dust and bawled.

Staring at the sky through a blur of tears, I summoned my brother for inspiration. What would he have done if he were here? Would he have pushed on patiently, stoic and uncomplaining? Would he have swallowed his frustration and endured in silence?

I thought not.

One thing we had shared as children was a talent for tantrum. Venting our emotions, volcano-like, had been a feature of our childhood relationship and although we eventually learnt not to focus the rage on each other, the ability to explode was something that neither of us completely lost. Anger, it seemed, was our natural reaction to exhaustion, and the thought of him there with me, swearing and spitting and stubbing his toes on rocks, was incredibly comforting. Picking up my bike, I mustered the determination to carry me the final kilometres to the top of the mountain.

At the pass, a small pyramid of stones pointed to the sky. This, I recognised, was an *apachita*, an informal monument built and maintained by those who travel the road. Located at the highest points of the landscape, vulnerable to the destructive force of the wind, *apachitas* retain their form by the addition of one stone by each passer-by. Archaeologists contest the original purpose of these constructions, but the common belief today is that every rock is a symbolic offering to Pachamama – Mother Earth – who is worshipped in Andean cultures as the source of earthly life. Some indigenous travellers, on arrival at the top of a mountain, also spit out chewed *coca* leaves and spill alcohol as a sign of respect.

At 4500 metres (nearly 750 metres higher than Aoraki/ Mount Cook, New Zealand's highest mountain) it did seem like a fitting place for reflection. I climbed up the bank to add a smooth pebble to the pile – fitting it into a niche so that the wind couldn't dislodge it – and prayed, to whoever might be listening, to reach Uyuni unscathed.

Sometimes cycling, sometimes walking, I inched across the desolate, tree-less landscape. My appetite had returned but my limbs were still shaky and as I wound my way laboriously from one summit to the next, plummeted into dry river canyons and crawled torturously back out, the journey began to seem like a nightmare from which I would never wake up. This time, I admitted to myself, it might have been wiser to listen to the locals than to venture blindly into this vast, empty place for which I was so laughably unprepared.

Not even my map was of any use. Colourfulness and simplicity were its key features, like a bus map, and the road to Uyuni was an innocuous straight line, drawn boldly in reassuring red. On paper, the route looked well established and well frequented. In no way whatsoever did it bear any relation to reality. It was sheer foolhardiness to expect this cartographical disaster to guide me through such inhospitable terrain, but even so I scrutinised it every kilometre or so as though it might suddenly reveal some hidden information – as though I might actually be able to divine where the hell I was and how far I had to go.

And it wasn't just a proper map that I lacked; a guidebook would also have been useful. And a cycle computer. Off-road tyres. Maybe even a Global Positioning System.

Or a Jeep. A Jeep would have been perfect.

It was late afternoon when the flatbed truck passed by. There was just enough room on the back for a bicycle, but I missed my chance to ask for a lift. The driver, making up for time lost at the roadblock, had the accelerator to the floor. Various expletives escaped my lips as the vehicle disappeared around the corner, and an irrational fury welled up inside me. What sort of a heartless bastard *was* he? What was he *thinking*, leaving a poor defenceless woman alone in this wilderness without even slowing down to see if she needed anything? I threw Vagabunda to the ground and kicked her tyres. Then I threw a couple of rocks off the cliff, swore at the top of my voice and lay down in the middle of the road.

When my heart rate had returned to normal, and my tears dried to salty crusts in the corners of my eyes, I sat up and thought about it more reasonably. Why, in this bleak and isolated place, would anybody stop if they didn't have to? Why should anyone feel obliged to look after *my* welfare? I stood up, brushing the dust off of my shorts, and heard my brother's voice. *You climbed up*, he said. *You know how to get down.*

It was just as well that this little epiphany came when it did, or I would probably have given in to temptation and flagged down the next vehicle that came along. The road was busier now; every hour or so a four-wheel drive passed by, full to bursting with people and piled high with luggage. I resolved, firmly, not to ask anyone for assistance, but it was comforting to know that if I broke a leg or ran out of water there wouldn't be long to wait before help arrived.

On the third afternoon after leaving Tupiza, having covered a mere hundred kilometres, I limped at last into semi-civilisation. In any other circumstances, the ugly collection of ramshackle slums that form the mining town of Atocha would be unlikely to inspire delight, but the fact that I was now more or less halfway to Uyuni, and finally able to pinpoint my position on the map, caused me a sense of relief so great that I fell in love with the place immediately. Even having to drag my bike towards town via a wide and muddy riverbed – due to the inexplicable disappearance of the road – didn't dampen my enthusiasm, nor did the malodorous piles of rubbish or the signs requesting the locals to refrain from urinating or defecating in the streets.

I followed the train tracks (what? I could have caught the train here?) to Atocha's central plaza and chose the most colourfully painted hotel. A podgy little lady, made rounder by the several layers of petticoats under her heavily pleated skirt, welcomed me in a motherly fashion and looked aghast that I should be travelling all alone. She caught her bottom lip between her teeth and shook her head in dismay, as though I'd just told her I only had a week to live.

'Poor little thing,' she said.

She showed me to a concrete room, in which the only furniture was a rusty iron bed and an ornate hat stand, and let me wheel Vagabunda inside for company.

'Do you know anything about the protests in Tupiza?' I asked her.

'Of course, I've been watching it all on television.'

'So, did the people get what they wanted?'

'Well,' she said, 'there've been plenty of promises from the government, but that doesn't mean anything. They never do what they say they're going to do.'

'Does this sort of thing happen often then?'

'All the time. Right now there are *bloqueos* all over the country, for various reasons. A couple of days ago in the north-east three people were shot dead when the police tried to clear the road.'

'But there was no violence in Tupiza?'

'No. The protesters stopped the blockade when the government said they would meet their demands. But I can guarantee that nothing changes.'

There was a toilet in my hotel – a luxury, for Atocha – but nowhere to wash, so I gathered a towel and my soap bag and walked around the corner to the local shower house. It was a squalid place, with a vicious dog on a chain who threw himself at me with undisguised fury. Straining against the leash, baring his fangs and barking at a deafening volume, he made it quite plain that he would have my throat out if I went any nearer.

'Don't worry about him,' shouted the shower attendant above the din. 'He's a softy really.'

It was so cold that I went to bed at eight o'clock. After an unappetising meal at a local restaurant – greasy soup and rice followed by black coffee – there was nothing else to do after dark. My bedroom was no warmer than outside but there were blankets to cover my sleeping bag, and what with the added advantage of lying a couple of feet above the ground I had an almost cosy night. But at dawn, braving the cold for an early-morning wee, I melted a hole in the five centimetres of ice that had formed in the toilet bowl.

For breakfast, I shuffled across the train tracks to a row of dilapidated shops. No more than tiny wooden shacks roofed with corrugated iron, they each contained an old lady selling sweets and soft drinks or oranges and bread. In one, an ancient wizened *señora* prepared cups of instant coffee, while outside her companion fried golden rounds of dough in a vat of boiling oil. I ducked my head under the low doorway and squeezed onto the bench behind the table. Sun poured in through the window, steam from the kettle swirled in the beams and the atmosphere was warmer than anywhere I had been in days. I slurped coffee, ate deliciously greasy bread, watched Spanish versions of Beatles songs on a black and white television and wished to stay there for ever. The thought of a further three days battling with the road made me feel distinctly queasy.

It was with great reluctance that I dragged myself back outside. It was still unbearably cold, but early-morning solar action was beginning to have an effect. Chunks of ice big enough to kill slid from the roofs of the shanties and hit the ground with explosive force. I stepped around the debris, blew clouds in the air and took a walk down to the river where, placing a foot on a low concrete wall, I leant on one knee and gazed out across the mud. Then I looked down.

Next to my shoe, black and shrivelled like the body of a dead mouse, was a human turd. Frozen. There was another one a bit further along the wall, and after that a whole row of them. I took my foot down and turned around. Stretching back towards the town, all the way up to the house advertising the use of a 'hygienic toilet' for twenty centavos, the ground was studded with faeces. Each small pile was a polite distance from its neighbours, but I still couldn't understand how it was possible to have walked all the way through such a dumping ground without a) noticing it was there, and b) stepping on anything undesirable. I checked the bottom of my shoes, just to be sure – they were miraculously free of excrement.

Gingerly, I picked my way back through the minefield. It was only once I was safely out of danger, mopping a sweat-prickled brow with the back of my hand, that I noticed a young girl hovering shyly on the fringes. She was waiting for the gringa to stop sightseeing in the latrine before she could answer the morning call of nature.

I tried to summon some optimism as I wheeled Vagabunda across the sun-filled plaza and through the backstreets to the edge of town. Several people had assured me that the remaining leg to Uyuni was nowhere near as bad as that from Tupiza, and I really, *really* wanted to believe them. Alas, my hope was short-lived.

Where Atocha ended, where the last of the shanties huddled in a mire of black mud and discarded plastic bottles, the road disappeared again.

'Which way is it to Uyuni?' I asked a man in a blue balaclava. He pointed upriver.

'Just follow the road.'

I looked incredulously at the kilometres of wet sand stretching ahead and wondered if I had heard him right. My definition of 'road' may have widened a bit in the last few days, but this was getting ridiculous. Just then, an overloaded Jeep whizzed past, spraying us with toxic water and leaving me in no doubt. In Bolivia, if you can four-wheel-drive it, consider it a highway.

For twenty kilometres or so I followed the soft and not entirely dry riverbed, pushing almost all the way as my wheels sunk up to the rims in soggy mud. When something resembling a road finally reappeared, snaking a way through the dunes and climbing upwards out of the valley, it was of sand so thick that I felt like burying my head in it, ostrich-like: anything to make reality disappear for a while. But I knew I shouldn't complain. My limbs still functioned, there was food and water in my panniers, I wasn't ill or injured or dying. In between the tantrums, I tried to be thankful for the chance to push my own limits of patience and endurance. I hadn't come to South America just to enjoy the sunshine, after all. I had expected to find challenges that would test my mental and physical strength, and that was exactly what I had got.

Back on the plains, the pace remained snail-like. The road was firmer, more or less rideable except for the occasional sand dune, but the roaring headwind kept me from making any swift progress. By late afternoon, when my exhausted muscles were crying out for rest, I felt no closer to my destination. Frustrated, I placed the tent in the lee of an adobe ruin and tried to ignore the ribbon of road ahead.

What with the cold wind, the harsh sun and the dryness of the air, my skin was taking a battering. Perpetually exposed to the elements, my shins had become tough and scaly, almost reptilian, and my hands looked like they were ageing three times faster than the rest of me. I even discovered, during my in-tent examination, that calluses had formed on the insides of my thighs where they rubbed against my bicycle seat. I longed for a hot shower, a scrubbing brush and a vat of moisturiser.

On the fifth day since leaving Tupiza, with my destination still nowhere in sight, I was suddenly struck by the notion that I was on the wrong road. According to the map, the route should have been leading me north-west towards Uyuni. My compass, however, clearly indicated that I was travelling south. Had I missed an important turnoff? It was possible. There were very few other roads, but even fewer signposts. In fact, I hadn't seen one for the last 150 kilometres. Bloody hell. I would have to go back to the nearest village and ask someone. To continue travelling southwards with limited water supplies was asking for trouble; that way lay Chile and the Atacama Desert, the driest place in the world. I turned around and retraced my tracks, plainly visible in the thick sand.

After a couple of kilometres, by a brilliant stroke of luck, I met some roadworkers who hadn't been there earlier. They wore yellow plastic raincoats, despite the harsh glare of the sun, and wielded thick-bristled brooms. They had no other tools.

'What are you doing?' I asked. They leant on their brooms and grinned.

'We're cleaning the sand off the road,' they said.

I tried hard not to laugh. No doubt the futility of their occupation hadn't escaped them, but it didn't seem polite to mention it. Instead, I asked directions. I had, they assured me, been going the right way, and they crowded around my map with fascination. Fingers pointed to familiar place-names and traced the paths of local roads. I tried to explain that as a navigational guide it was less than useless – although perhaps okay as a fire-starter or toilet-paper substitute – but they weren't listening. They were captivated, as I had been when I bought it, by the spider's web of brightly coloured lines.

'So, do you know how far it is to Uyuni from here?' I asked.

'*Si, señorita*. Seven, more or less.'

'Seven kilometres?' That didn't sound right.

'No, no. Seven *hours*, by bicycle.'

Their own two-wheeled contraptions lay on the roadside. They obviously knew what they were talking about.

It was too cold for mirages, but distant peaks began to float on the horizon like islands. The crisp line between land and sky disappeared, and a shimmering whiteness took its place. It looked like a nothing, but I knew it was a something. It was the Salar de Uyuni.

This massive salt flat, dry and hard during winter like a giant white scab, was my very reason for coming this way. Other travellers had insisted that it was not to be missed, and my friend Mariano told me that he had once cycled across it. For the last few days, while struggling in the sand, I had been picturing the perfectly solid, perfectly flat surface with a pathological craving. It was the sort of longing I had only before experienced while dieting and thinking about chocolate cake. And now I had the *salar* in sight. It didn't matter that there were still fifty or more kilometres of sand and washboard separating me from the object of my desire, or that I would have to spend another freezing night in the tent before getting anywhere near it. It shone like the Promised Land, and the difficulties of the road were suddenly insignificant.

Erecting the tent by the roadside, in the calm of the evening, I looked around at the vast and silent altiplano. It was overwhelmingly beautiful: the delicate colours, the immensity of the sky, the utter stillness and solitude. Herds of llamas roamed the horizon, the sky was cloudless, painted subtly in dusky pastels, and I had the 360-degree panorama all to myself. How could I, for the last five days, have been so wrapped up in my emotions that all this had passed by me virtually unnoticed? No matter that my skin was wind-crisped, my lips sun-blistered and my whole body aching and filthy; my suffering was self-inflicted and transient. And every moment of pain was worth it just to be there.

17

Mad Dogs and Englishmen

The first thing I did in Uyuni was to look for something to eat. Stalls lined the main street and vendors beckoned me to try all manner of hot and cold snacks. I bought some fried potato patties, doused them in spicy sauce and sat on the curb to eat surrounded by a ragtag bunch of hopeful dogs. I didn't care that they slobbered on my shoes, or that the chilli burnt my damaged lips; the relief of arrival made it an unforgettably delicious meal. During the following three days I sampled almost every type of street food. I visited the juice squeezer, the ice-cream maker and the bread fryer in perpetual rotation, as well as getting familiar with the girl at the cake stand. After the rigours of the road it seemed perfectly justifiable to stuff myself silly, and any extra padding would act as insulation when I started camping out again.

Uyuni was good to my stomach, but in other ways it unsettled me. Unlike the small towns I had passed through, where people were openly friendly and helpful, here the inhabitants only smiled at me while trying to sell me a tour to the *salar*. The place was jam-packed with gringos, and the residents were hell-bent on making the most of the tourist dollars. Not that I blamed them for that; on the contrary, I admired them for maximising the business potential of their astounding local attractions. It was just that, after such an extraordinary first week in Bolivia, the forced friendliness and fawning attitudes of the business owners were a bit disillusioning.

And that wasn't the only thing I found disconcerting. Many of the restaurants were far too expensive for the average Bolivian, with a basic meal costing five or six times what it might in the marketplace. Catering to western tastes, these places were always full of travellers, but although this meant cash to the local economy it also meant complete segregation from the citizens. Maybe I was being naïve to expect things to be any different, but it seemed sad that economic factors should create such a distinct divide between the visitors and those we had come to visit.

The route towards the *salar* was being upgraded. Before improvements could begin, however, the existing road had been ploughed up into a soft and unrideable strip of loose clay and rocks. It was prime tantrum territory and after a couple of hours moving at less than snail's pace the scrunch of salt beneath my tyres could not have been more welcome. I cycled onto the *salar* and let out a whoop of joy. After so many days off-tarmac, rolling on the concrete-hard surface was like suddenly being motorised. Unleashing the stifled power of my legs, I accelerated into top gear and let go of all my frustration.

The Salar de Uyuni is both the highest and largest salt flat in the world. At 3653 metres above sea level, measuring 12,106 square kilometres, it is estimated to hold around ten billion tons of salt – the deposits of a massive saline lake that dried up millennia ago. The whiteness is all-consuming. I had heard about people going blind by crossing the salt without sunglasses, and the potential for extreme sunburn is high. I covered my face with a balaclava, to stop UV damage, and put on my gloves against the cold. Despite the brilliance of the reflected light, the air temperature was frigid.

The salt forms naturally in large hexagonal patches that fit together in flawless tessellations, separated from one another by delicate raised edges of crumbling crystals. Through these, like smudged pencil lines on starched linen, the wide grey tracks of tour vehicles are unsightly and indelible, and studded with the detritus of thoughtless sightseers. I followed one of these trails towards the centre of the *salar*. Without a reliable map to take compass readings from, it was definitely safest to stick to the beaten path.

Around me stretched perfect emptiness. It was unlike anywhere else: as cold, sterile and lifeless as a morgue yet as awe-inspiring as an ocean. The size of it, the brightness of it, the sheer *whiteness* of it made it somehow inconceivable. Was that really salt flashing past beneath my wheels? Or was it ice? Here I was, in the tropics, as close as I might ever get to Antarctica. The light played tricks with my eyes. On the horizon hovered indistinct blobs, stretching and joining like wax in a lava lamp, morphing slowly into distant volcanoes. I strained to see the tiny island for which I was headed, some eighty kilometres onto the *salar*, but promising black dots turned time and again into Jeeps, speeding towards me en route for land. Kilometre after effortless kilometre I rolled onwards, mesmerised by the engulfing luminosity and the subtle transformations on the far shore.

The reflective quality of the salt means that it absorbs no heat from the sun. Even at midday it was cool to the touch, and at night, with only a thin foam camping mat to sleep on, the warmth would be sucked from me in no time. The flimsy shelter of the tent would never be more necessary. I was unprepared, as usual, and had forgotten to bring a rock to bash the tent pegs in with. Fortunately, there was an overabundance of tools in my panniers, carried for more than 5000 kilometres mostly unused. Going against everything my father had ever taught me about using the right tool for the job, I employed a Phillips screwdriver as a chisel and an adjustable spanner as a mallet, and did considerable damage to both while making peg-sized holes in the salt. I didn't care; it was preferable to sleeping without shelter.

The sun, dipping slowly towards the horizon, threw my shadow for kilometres. The salt turned pink, then blue, and the bruise of night grew in the eastern sky. All was silent. I drank tea and watched the colours shift, watched the stars punch through the darkness one by one and the Southern Cross appear to hang directly above my tent. The temperature plummeted, I burrowed deep into my sleeping bag and shivered until dawn. Then, with aching joints, I forced myself out into the raw air, made an embarrassingly vivid yellow stain on pristine salt and star-jumped my way back to warmth.

In such a vast desert, where almost everyone travels in identical and anonymous pods of motorised glass and steel, it seemed unlikely that I would bump into anyone I knew. The possibility had never even crossed my mind, in fact. So when the shapeless dots on the horizon transformed into people on bicycles, and when those people drew near enough to address me by name, it has to be said that it came as quite a surprise. Especially as I had no idea who they were.

'Don't you remember?' they spluttered. 'Salta . . .? The pizza . . .?' They removed the scarves that obscured their faces and briefly lifted their mirrored sunglasses. Of course I remembered. Without their disguises they were Miriam and Philippe, the Swiss couple who had shared my birthday dinner.

They introduced me to Hugh and Gwen – from Wales and France, respectively – and we compared Bolivian horror stories. All of us had travelled the road from Tupiza, within days of each other it seemed, but both couples had ended up catching public transport: Miriam and Philippe because of illness, and Hugh and Gwen because of their tandem (it went like the clappers when mounted, they explained, but was virtually impossible to push while loaded). It made me wonder. Would I too have ended up on the bus if I hadn't been alone? My stubbornness had kept me going, but it might not have been enough to inspire a jaded travelling partner. And if anyone had pushed me to continue when I wanted to lie down and cry, I would no doubt have hitched a lift purely out of spite. Bolivia by bicycle seemed like a particularly trying test for a romantic relationship, but both of these intrepid couples appeared to be weathering it well. The six-wheeled foursome was heading back to Uyuni, from where they would travel north. I wished them luck and struck out alone for Incahuasi Island.

Rolling in from the frozen sea, washing up on the deserted shore, I felt like a solitary shipwreck survivor. Marooned on the beach, with just my sandwiches for company, the only thing missing was the motion of the ocean and the sound of waves. I had no idea if it was prohibited to camp on the island, but the only other option was to stay in the hotel around the promontory. It was like a Disney theme park over there, with Jeeps disgorging travellers by the hour and cutesy buildings made of salt bricks and thatch, and the solitude of the eastern bay seemed preferable by far. I settled in for a lazy afternoon.

It was a tiny island – small enough to circumnavigate in ten minutes – but it supported an astonishing number of cacti. Some of them were huge. And ancient. Growing at a rate of around one centimetre per year, it was possible to estimate their age by their size. The tallest, towering around twelve metres, were approximately 1200 years old. At dusk I walked to the top of the island, weaving a path through the prickly giants. As though it was the very heart of the *salar*, this little outpost of life was joined to each horizon by a network of silvery veins, carrying the last of the day's Jeeps towards the hotel. There must have been dozens of people staying on the island, but I watched the sunset alone.

The return across the salt, eighty identical kilometres, was meditative. It put me in such a serene mood that when I bumped into José, the egotistical Argentine who had travelled with me in the first week of my journey, I actually expressed delight. I hadn't expected to see him again – had hoped *not* to see him, in fact – but this chance meeting was so unlikely that it seemed the universe must have thrown us together for a reason.

'What are *you* doing here?' he asked, incredulous. 'I thought you were going south?'

'I did go south. I thought *you* were going north. You should be in Central America or somewhere.'

'Well, I spent some time at home in Mendoza, you know? I'm pretty famous there now. They treat me like a hero.'

'Really?' I said wryly. 'How interesting. What a shame we're going in different directions, or you could have told me all about it.'

He smiled broadly.

'But we'll have plenty of time! I'm going back to Uyuni too. We'll go together.'

Back in town we dropped our bikes in a cheap hotel and went out for dinner. Talking about our travels over plates of rice and fried eggs, any doubts I might have had about the reliability of my memory were soon gone. He was just as annoying as I had thought, and then some.

'So why didn't you stay for a night on the *salar*,' I asked, 'after you've come all this way to see it?'

'Because I have a train booked for tomorrow morning, to take me back to Villazón.'

'Oh. So you didn't cycle here then?'

'No. This is just a detour and I wanted to save a bit of time.'

'Well, maybe that was a wise choice, you know? The road here from Tupiza is just horrendous. All thick sand and washboard, huge mountain passes, freezing nights and headwind. It took me five and a half days, if you can believe that.'

He smiled at me kindly, and laughed lightly.

'El, you always did have problems cycling in sand. Don't you remember what I told you? It's easy if only you have the right attitude. You should follow my example and try to make friends with nature.'

Saying goodbye to José for the second time was even more wonderful than the first. If we were, in fact, supposed to learn something from our against-all-odds chance encounter I didn't know what the hell it could be. The only thing it had taught me was that my initial impressions were right. He was a patronising pain in the arse.

I left Uyuni a few hours after he did, laden with plenty of good food for the final few days. There were just a couple of hundred kilometres left to my ultimate destination, and no matter what condition the roads were in I was determined to enjoy myself. Even though this notion was seriously challenged by the perpendicular climb out of town, I managed to keep my enthusiasm up long enough to decline the offer of a lift from a passing bus, ignore the disbelieving stares of a band of roadworkers and to crest the hill without once throwing a tantrum.

In the small town of Pulacayo, which clung to a hillside of metallic blue, I stopped to take a photo. A rickety old man was labouring up a path towards me and when he drew level I said,

'I hope you don't mind, *señor*, but you were in my photo.' He looked thrilled. He straightened his hat, patted some dust off his suit jacket and indicated that I should take another. The shutter snapped as he stood solemnly to attention.

'Where are you from?' he asked.

'*Nueva Zelanda.*'

He looked puzzled.

'*¿Holanda?*'

'No. *Nueva Zelanda.*'

'*¿Irlanda?*'

'No. *Nueva Zelanda*. It's near Australia.'

'Aha!' a light went on in his eyes. 'Of course. In Europe!' He leant forward and took my hands in his. 'You're frozen,' he said, and held on to me tightly as though he had been a long time without love. For minutes we stood together in the chill breeze, squinting against the sun and gazing out across the valley. And when my hands were warm he kissed me tenderly on one cheek, as though I was his own daughter.

'Go well,' he said. 'Be safe.'

There was yet another roadblock, and almost all the people I met over the next three days were walking. They carried little and moved swiftly; their rate of travel slower but more efficient than mine. People stopped me to ask about the traffic situation, but I had little information for them. The best I could do was offer water.

Just outside Tica Tica two old ladies bent low beneath enormous bundles of firewood. They were tiny, their faces of carved mahogany, and they looked up at me from under their hat brims with twinkling brown eyes. As native Quechua they spoke no Spanish, but we communicated with gestures and laughter. They pointed to my heavily laden bike and mimed astonishment at how strong my legs must be. I looked at their postures, their inappropriate sandals and the weights they were carrying and felt their admiration to be a little misplaced. I told them so, and they smiled shyly. They crowed with delight when I proffered my drink bottles, and exclaimed amazement at the technology of the pullout nozzles. They guzzled like they hadn't drunk for days and handed the bottles back empty, smacking satisfied lips. Despite their age, their weather-beaten faces projected a youthful joy of existence.

Pushing up yet another formidable incline, weak despite a high-calorie lunch, I wondered if I would ever be strong again. It seemed that every time the road forced me off the bike, every time my feet came in contact with the earth, my energy and enthusiasm flowed out through the soles of my shoes to be sucked up thirstily by the sand. I imagined myself in a television advert for long-lasting batteries; I was the one fitted with the 'other' brand. While my batteries were rapidly wearing out, causing me to move slower and slower, fresh-legged cyclists fitted with the superior brand pedalled past at light-speed. Old men on rattling boneshakers zoomed by as though on fast-forward and octogenarian Quechua ladies overtook me like Olympic medallists. In my imagination, my joints stiffened, my limbs locked and I ground to a halt, doomed to be stuck there for ever, petrified by the freezing nights into a monument to foolishness.

Fortunately, what actually happened was that I crested the hill, climbed back into the saddle and started the long freewheel down the other side. I hadn't gone far when a roadworker barred my way. He was outrageously drunk. He wanted to talk. His companions watched with amusement.

'Brakes,' he slurred.

'Pardon?'

'Brakes! Downhill!' He flung out one arm to indicate the

steep drop, a motion that almost resulted in him rolling down there himself.

'*Si, señor.* I have brakes.'

He frowned, and waggled his shovel doubtfully.

'You'll lose them!' He swayed slightly, and made a valiant effort to focus both eyes on my face.

'Honestly. My brakes are fine. Please don't worry.'

He paused for a second and, in a moment of emotion, grabbed my hand and kissed it. It seemed a bad move. Not only was my glove filthy enough to leave him with terminal health problems, the alcohol on his breath was strong enough to melt the nylon to my skin. I took my hand back as politely as I could and left him to stagger on up the hill, his shovel the only thing propping him upright.

The dogs in Bolivia answer to nobody. Their owners exert no control, and the sight of a lone cyclist inspires the wolf in them. They want blood. I had taken to wearing a whistle around my neck, which was more effective than my voice, but even that couldn't deter the hungriest beasts. And on this particular day it was only the gradient of the downhill that saved me.

They came from nowhere. With fangs bared and saliva flying the hairy mongrels sped towards me like heat-seeking missiles. I didn't even have time to engage the whistle tactic. With head down and legs pumping, I accelerated from sedate to suicidal in seconds, spurred to insanity by their ferocious barking. They nearly caught up with me at the bend, but I gained an advantage when they skidded in gravel. By the time they recovered, Vagabunda was unstoppable.

My limbs were still trembling at the bottom of the hill and it took an encounter with another cyclist to soothe my jangled nerves. Nigel, from England, was on his way from Alaska to Patagonia and he wanted to know if I found it hard work to cycle at altitude on unpaved roads. With no lack of expletives, I assured him that he wasn't the only one suffering. We talked cycle stuff for a while and he described his route through the Americas.

'I've travelled with some interesting people,' he said. 'There were these two young English lads, really nice guys, but they were trying to do the whole thing in six months. Crazy sods. I let them go on ahead.'

'That wouldn't be Will and Chris, would it?' I asked. He looked astonished.

'Er. Yes, as a matter of fact.'

'I thought so. They worked with me on the rickshaws in London.'

The world was beginning to seem like a very small place.

I could happily have talked with Nigel for hours, but the night was beginning to close in and he had a big hill to climb. I warned him about the hounds of doom and hoped he would make it through alive.

18

The City of Silver

Journeys should finish triumphantly. If I could have chosen the perfect end to mine it would have involved a celebratory sprint on flat roads, a swooping downhill with an entourage of local kids on bicycles and a victory lap around a sun-filled plaza. As my destination was the world's highest city, however, the last moments of the voyage were considerably less glamorous. Sweating and swearing, plodding grimly up the final sandy hill, I coerced Vagabunda onwards like a recalcitrant donkey. Passing vehicles showered me with gravel, the faces of passengers without compassion. And when I rounded the corner onto tarmac and saw, cradled neatly in a tilting valley, the city of Potosí, it was still kilometres above me.

From a distance, it was hard to tell that this was once one of the richest cities in the world. It looked grey and grimy and at the tail end of town all I could see in detail were squalid slums. But towering over everything, as a constant reminder of the city's illustrious beginnings, was the magnificent Cerro Rico – Rich Mountain. At more than 4000 metres above sea level, an altitude that turns getting out of bed into an aerobic exercise, this metropolis exists only because of the silver inside the *cerro*. When riches were first discovered in 1544, the initial excitement drew men across the altiplano like iron filings to a magnet, and within three years the boomtown had grown into a city of 14,000 citizens. Some two and a half decades later, on what was once a bleak and empty hillside, Potosí had swelled to become what was then the largest city in the western hemisphere.

It took over an hour to push the final stretch to the centre of town. The gradient was unprecedented and a backstreet short-cut – pointed out to me by a kindly but unthinking local – nearly finished me off. Hauling Vagabunda up the potholed, urine-stinking, nearly vertical alleyway, I expected at any moment to tumble over backwards and cartwheel gracelessly to the bottom, scattering old ladies and small children like ninepins. When the plaza finally appeared, a bit blurry due to the sweat in my eyes, I could do no more than collapse onto a bench and weakly thank whichever deity had ensured my safe arrival.

Only after a restorative lunch of squashed bread rolls and bananas could I contemplate movement again. I didn't have a map of the city and the information office was closed, so bump-ing into Philippe and Miriam was a stroke of luck that saw me checked into a hostel, unpacked, showered and changed in record time. Then all I had to do was follow them to a local res-taurant, say hello to Gwen and Hugh, shake hands with three other cyclists, sit down grinning, and wait for a steaming plate of soup to arrive. It was the happiest moment of the day.

It was also a moment that was repeated again and again over the next indolent week. Any poundage that had been used up on the road was promptly restored to my midriff during long meals of excess food and tall tales at the vegetarian café; sometimes we yarned for so long over breakfast that we ended up staying for lunch as well. In between mealtimes I explored the city, visiting the royal mint (now a museum) and the many elaborately decorated Catholic churches that serve as reminders of Potosí's ostentatious past. At street level, where children as young as six or seven offer to shine your shoes, or work on buses calling out destinations, it was impossible to ignore that the glory days have long gone.

Even more fascinating than the colonial architecture was the central street market, to which I shambled most mornings to photograph stacks of fruit and vegetables, baskets of bread, piles of *empanadas* and mini mountains of spices. Red chilli, yellow chilli, black and white pepper, cumin and *bica*; together they formed a paintbox of colour. For the faithful, dried llama foetuses were on sale as offerings to Pachamama, but best (and worst) of all was the meat section, in which stomach-turning piles of viscera lay just centimetres above the quivering noses of mangy street dogs. There were brains and spines, trotters and intestines and pallid pigs' heads with gaping mouths. Multiple strands of unidentifiable ropy flesh hung in grisly curtains and, like a bad-taste B-movie, blood-splattered butchers chopped through meaty bones with gleaming cleavers. Despite frequent waves of nausea, I was compelled to return time and again with morbid fascination.

Without a doubt, the most notable attraction of Potosí is Cerro Rico and the ongoing mining within. Although most of the silver has now gone, leaving the mountain riddled with holes like a worm-eaten apple, miners still disappear into its depths each day in search of tin, lead, copper and zinc.

The history of this conical red mountain is dirty with the blood of those who lost their lives in the process of extracting the immense wealth that once came out of it. For two hundred and fifty years, before Bolivia's liberation from Spain, all working-age indigenous men within a radius of hundreds of miles were forced to serve time in the Potosí mines. Working conditions underground were so harsh, and miners died at such a fast rate due to accidents and lung diseases, that Cerro

Rico came to be known in Quechua as The Mountain That Eats Men. Nowadays, the only thing forcing men to suffer this hell is the poverty that plagues them and their families. Some of them work in small co-operatives, where any profit is shared out equally, but many more slog away on their own, earning next to nothing. They work long hours in extremely difficult conditions, and a full-time miner has a life expectancy of just ten to fifteen years due to constant exposure to noxious chemicals and gases.

No one really gets rich any more at Rich Mountain, although some local operators take good advantage of gringo dollars by running tours in which visitors don hard-hats and follow their guide underground to see the miners in action. Tourists are encouraged to take presents of dynamite, *coca* leaves or alcohol for the workers, and many people come away from the experience profoundly moved by the sight of men and boys toiling away with hand tools in the oppressive heat and filth. Not surprisingly, this is not an activity that appeals to everyone, and many question the morality of making an 'attraction' out of the wretched existence of desperately poor people. Personally, I found the whole concept unnecessarily voyeuristic, and opted instead to go for a walk up the *cerro* with Hugh and Gwen, with the excuse of gaining the best view of the city.

Following my friends up a rocky red path, past the gaping mouths of mine shafts, I was surprised to see a pair of young girls coming down the hill towards us. They approached shyly and the eldest held out a wooden box full of colourful rocks.

'Do you want to buy some precious stones?' she asked.

We didn't, but we did ask them what they were doing up here, all alone, on a Sunday.

'We live here,' they said, and led us up the path to their house, a tiny, windowless shack built into the scree slope, half buried by the precarious load of rocks above. I didn't know if Potosí was subject to earthquakes, but it looked as if one slight tremor would bring half the mountainside down on top of them. The door creaked open and a boy of about ten came out, wearing gumboots and a plastic miner's helmet with an electric torch. He carried a pickaxe.

'*Hola*,' said Gwen. 'Where are you going dressed like that?'

'I'm going to help my *Papa*,' he said proudly. 'He's down the mine.'

'Even on a Sunday?'

'Yes. He has to work a lot 'cause a rock hurt his leg and now he's a bit slow. So I go and help him. I have to, 'cause I'm a man.' He threw a look at his big sisters, who had gone back to washing clothes in a bucket.

'Don't you have school sometimes?' asked Gwen.

'Yes. I go in the mornings and then go to the mines. But on a Sunday I can work whenever I want.'

'And what do you want to be when you grow up?'

He leant on his pickaxe and rapped a fist on his hard-hat.

'I'm going to be a miner. Like my *Papa*.'

While Gwen and Hugh started back down the mountain, I followed the path upwards and found a place to sit. Far below me, earth-coloured and dusty looking, sprawled the city where my journey had come to an end.

It was all over now. I'd done what I came for. It had been elation and exhaustion, joy and despair, but above all an irrefutable confirmation that I had finally grown up. The memory of my brother had travelled with me, spurring me on, but in the end that had only proved the truth of what he had taught me: I really didn't need anyone else to push me forwards; all the motivation I required was already inside me. I felt strong and capable, and ready for anything. It no longer mattered that I had no grand plan for my life; this *was* life, and I was more alive than ever.

You see? said Dan. *I knew you could do it.*

He had been gone a long time, nine years in fact, but he still felt close to me. I had always admired him for his lifestyle, admired how he shunned 'responsibility' in favour of the sport he loved and reached for his own goals despite the risks. Even when his life was taken from him so suddenly, by the very mountains he loved, it had seemed to me like a final defiant statement. To live, he had always told us, is to accept the inevitability of death. And not even that potential conclusion had stopped him from following his dreams. In the last photos we have of him, the ones taken a couple of evenings before he died, the satisfaction of success is written all over his face. Standing at dusk on the top of Mount Crosscut, the sun burning orange behind him, he looks into the camera with absolute confidence and contentment.

He and Joe, his climbing partner, had taken two days to reach that peak, some 2263 metres above sea level in Fiordland's Darran Mountains, and their safe arrival was testimony to their courage and skill. With crampons and ice axes they had scaled a route known as the Cul de Sac, as vulnerable as ants in a drainpipe but equally as steadfast in purpose as they moved slowly but surely up the long chute of snow and ice. Joe's photos of the climb are both beautiful and terrifying. In one, looking upwards, swirling snow powder partly obscures the figure of my brother as he inches up a near-vertical gradient. The rope, joining him to Joe like an umbilical cord, is a tenuous thread, blown in a fragile arc across the cliff face by the gusting wind. It seems an impossibly difficult task: the ice looks too sheer, the wind too strong, the air too cold and the climbers too tiny. The mountain looks harshly unforgiving.

But it was not the going up that was my brother's undoing. It was the coming back down. After two days climbing and two nights roped to the cliff face in their sleeping bags, Dan and Joe began their descent towards the Gertrude Valley. They were walking across slopes of freshly laid snow, not roped together, and Dan was ahead, out of sight of his partner as he looked for a route down.

It was then that the pocket of snow released itself from the ridge above.

The image of that avalanche, sweeping its inexorable path down the mountainside towards my brother, is imprinted on my mind as vividly as if I had been there. But I can only begin to imagine the sensation of impotent panic that Joe must have experienced as he watched it happen. He called out, but got no answer, and when he finally reached the base of the cliff where the snow debris had come to a stop he could find no signs of life. A search-and-rescue team had no success either, and due to bad weather and the danger of further avalanche the search was postponed until the spring.

We spent seven long months waiting for the thaw to return Dan to us. It was a time of irrational hope and suspended belief, in which all of us secretly expected him to turn up unannounced on the doorstep. He had often come home from climbing trips without warning, delighting us with his sudden appearance, increasingly wild hair and archipelagos of freckles, and it seemed somehow feasible that this time would be no different. But eventually the call came, the one that stripped us of any last shreds of faith, and with the discovery of his body came the second wave of grief.

Nearly a decade later, the intensity of the loss had subsided, but it seemed that Dan's influence on me was as strong as ever. There would always be a brother-sized hole in my life, but I could see quite clearly how the strength of his memory had helped to shape me into the woman I was. I looked up, into the endless blue of the Bolivian sky. My big brother had always told me that I could do anything I set my mind to, and had he been able to see me there on that mountaintop, really believing it, I knew he would have been proud of me.

EPILOGUE

Two Wheels Good, Four Wheels Bad

Leaving Potosí was almost as difficult as getting there, although this time it was not uphill climbs that impeded my progress but bureaucratic befuddlements in the bus station. I had bought my ticket well in advance, asked all the necessary questions regarding my bicycle and turned up on the correct day with an hour to spare. Buses came and buses went, and as the time of departure drew closer I began to wonder where mine was.

'Excuse me. Where's this bus going?' I asked an official-looking man. He stared at me and grunted. I asked the baggage handler instead.

'Excuse me, is this bus going to Villazón?' He nodded. 'Oh good. Can I put my bike on board please?'

'Have you got a ticket?'

'Yes.' I showed him.

'Not that one. A ticket for your bicycle.'

'I didn't know I needed one.'

'Well, you do. Upstairs.' He pointed towards the ticket office on the first floor. 'They'll put your bike on the roof of the bus from there,' he added.

Bloody hell. I looked around for help.

'Do you want to earn some money?' I asked a strong-looking

boy. He nodded, grabbed Vagabunda's back end, and together we staggered up three flights of stairs.

'Fifteen bolivianos for the bike,' said the woman at the office.

'You didn't tell me that the other day,' I said. She shrugged. 'All bikes cost extra.'

'Well, that's okay, but I could have paid for it when I bought my own ticket.' She looked away, uninterested.

'Fifteen bolivianos. And quick – the bus is leaving.'

I fumed and handed over the money as an agitated man rushed up.

'We're waiting to leave!' he said, grabbing Vagabunda from me. 'The bike has to go downstairs.'

'Wait!' I was panicking now. The ticket lady was thrusting a receipt book at me to sign, I was trying to pay the boy who had helped me, and my faithful companion of twelve years was disappearing in the hands of a complete stranger. For all I knew, it could have been an elaborate scam designed to part me from all my worldly goods.

'Wait!' I yelled again. Loudly. Everyone in the ticket hall stared. Suddenly I saw myself from the outside: another confused, short-tempered gringa, too stupid to know how things worked here and arrogant enough to be bossy about it. I blushed vermilion, put my head down and followed the porter to the bus with as much dignity as I could.

It was a sign, I thought to myself as we rumbled out of the station. A little farewell reminder that no matter how much my Spanish had improved, how many things I had seen or how many people I had met, I still had one hell of a lot to learn. I made myself comfortable against the squashy Quechua lady next to me, pulled my jacket over my head and closed my eyes with a smile.

The lesson was obvious.

I would simply have to come back.

Acknowledgements

My infinite gratitude goes to: Galo Dominguez, for starting the whole thing off; Javier Fernandez, for unswerving friendship; Yoli, Leandro and Karina Fernandez, for stocking my energy reserves for the road ahead; Mariano Lorefice, for the advice and inspiration; Majo, Diego, Carlos (Charlie Brown), Antonio and Ulices, Roberto (Ytch), the Díaz family of Belén, the Nini family of La Quebrada de Cafayate, and everyone else who showed me such warmth and generosity along the way; Bojo, Christoph, Cathy and Raphael, Luis, Miriam and Philippe, Gwen and Hugh and assorted other cyclists for sharing kilometres and calories; my friends back home, for reading my interminable emails; Michael Gifkins and Rebecca Lal, for the wit, wisdom and expertise that made this book happen; and last but not least my parents, Julie and Roger, for being brave enough to let me go.